Lecture Notes in Computer Science 3665

Commenced Publication in 1973
Founding and Former Series Editors:
Gerhard Goos, Juris Hartmanis, and Jan van Leeuwen

T0218636

K. Selçuk Candan   Augusto Celentano (Eds.)

Advances in Multimedia Information Systems

11th International Workshop, MIS 2005
Sorrento, Italy, September 19-21, 2005
Proceedings

 Springer

Volume Editors

K. Selçuk Candan
Arizona State University, Ira A. Fulton School of Engineering
Department of Computer Sciences and Engineering, Tempe, AZ 85287, USA
E-mail: candan@asu.edu

Augusto Celentano
Università Ca' Foscari di Venezia, Dipartimento di Informatica
via Torino 155, 30172 Mestre (VE), Italy
E-mail: auce@dsi.unive.it

Library of Congress Control Number: 2005931596

CR Subject Classification (1998): H.5.1, H.4, H.5, I.7, C.2, I.4

ISSN   0302-9743
ISBN-10   3-540-28792-2 Springer Berlin Heidelberg New York
ISBN-13   978-3-540-28792-6 Springer Berlin Heidelberg New York

Springer is a part of Springer Science+Business Media

springeronline.com

© Springer-Verlag Berlin Heidelberg 2005
Printed in Germany

Typesetting: Camera-ready by author, data conversion by Scientific Publishing Services, Chennai, India
Printed on acid-free paper   SPIN: 11551898   06/3142   5 4 3 2 1 0

Preface

This volume collects the proceedings of the 11th International Workshop on Multimedia Information Systems, MIS 2005, which was held during September 19–21, 2005 in the beautiful town of Sorrento, Italy.

The MIS series of workshops started in 1995 with the aim of fostering interdisciplinary discussions and research in all aspects of multimedia information systems, in all their diversity. Since then, in MIS workshops, issues ranging from fundamental multimedia information management research to advanced applications in multimedia systems related fields have been discussed, new systems have been reported, and the lessons learned have provided new insights into this dynamic and exciting area of computer science and engineering.

As the program chairs of the MIS 2005 workshop, we note that while designing an effective multimedia system, two complementary issues have to be taken into account: (a) the need to use appropriate technologies in acquiring, processing, and delivering multimedia data which manifest themselves under very different shapes; and (b) the need for modeling, indexing, querying, retrieving, mining, and visualizing data under different system and device capabilities, for different users. Therefore, besides the development of more traditional content management technologies, there are emerging needs to gather media from sensing devices in the environmental context, for informed processing of media based on the current task and resources, and for making the results available to the user in the most suitable form based on the capabilities and preferences of the user.

For this edition of MIS, we selected 15 high-quality papers, out of 30 submissions, which address different aspects of multimedia information management in context. These papers address topics related to multimedia databases, multimodal interaction, video and audio applications, multimedia performances, and context-aware modeling, communication, and retrieval of different types of data.

The MIS 2005 program also included two invited talks, by Prof. Peter Buneman from the University of Edinburgh and Prof. Letizia Tanca from the Politecnico di Milano, who discussed fundamental issues spanning two diverse data management contexts: large, complex, archival information systems on the one side, and open, dynamic, ubiquitous environments on the other. Prof. Latifur Khan, from the University of Texas at Dallas, presented a half-day tutorial on data annotation for enriched semantic treatment of multimedia data, a prerequisite for informed handling of media in different semantic contexts.

We thank the authors, the speakers, the Program Committee members, the external reviewers, and the local organizers for making this workshop a success.

September 2005   K. Selçuk Candan and Augusto Celentano

Organization

The local organization of MIS 2005 was supported by the University of Napoli "Federico II" and the University of Salerno.

General Chair

Angelo Chianese   University of Napoli "Federico II", Italy

Program Co-chairs

K. Selçuk Candan   Arizona State University, USA
Augusto Celentano   "Ca' Foscari" University, Venezia, Italy

Program Committee

Sibel Adalı	Rensselaer Polytechnic Institute, USA
Laurent Amseleg	IRISA, France
Ramazan S. Aygün	University of Alabama in Huntsville, USA
Edward Chang	UC Santa Barbara, USA
Alberto Del Bimbo	University of Florence, Italy
Ombretta Gaggi	"Ca' Foscari" University, Venezia, Italy
Brigitte Kerhervé	Université du Québec à Montréal, Canada
Wolfgang Klas	University of Vienna, Austria
Robert Laurini	INSA Lyon, France
Raymond Ng	University of British Columbia, Canada
Vincent Oria	NJIT, USA
B. Prabhakaran	UT Dallas, USA
Hanan Samet	University of Maryland, USA
Maria Luisa Sapino	University of Turin, Italy
Raimondo Schettini	University of Milano Bicocca, Italy
Timos Sellis	Natl. Tech. Univ. of Athens, Greece
Cyrus Shahabi	University of Southern California, USA
Hari Sundaram	Arizona State University, USA
M. Tamer Özsu	University of Waterloo, Canada
Belle Tseng	NEC Labs Cupertino, USA
Vassilis Tsotras	University of California at Riverside, USA
Can Türker	Swiss Federal Institute of Technology, Zurich, Switzerland

Özgür Ulusoy	Bilkent University, Turkey
Clement Yu	University of Illinois at Chicago, USA
Philip S. Yu	IBM T.J. Watson Research Center, USA
Aidong Zhang	SUNY Buffalo, USA

Organizing Chair

Antonio Picariello	University of Napoli "Federico II", Italy

Steering Committee

V.S. Subrahmanian	University of Maryland, USA
Satish Tripathi	University of California at Riverside, USA
Dave Hislop	ARO, USA

Reviewers

Ali Akoğlu
Preetha Appan
David Birchfield
Luciano Bononi
Fabian Bustamante
Yi Cui
Marilena De Marsico
Hasan Davulcu
Mehmet Emin Dönderler
Abdulmotaleb El Saddik
Helmut Hlavacs
Daoying Ma

Luca Mainetti
Ankur Mani
Piero Mussio
Anurag Phadke
Yan Qi
Martin Reisslein
Ediz Şaykol
Mehdi Sharifzadeh
Bageshree Shevade
Yao Wang
Kim Jong Wook
Kiyoung Yang

Table of Contents

What Is Interesting About Scientific Databases?

Peter Buneman

University of Edinburgh,
Scotland, UK
opb@inf.ed.ac.uk

Abstract. Much of modern scientific research depends on databases, but do we need anything more than conventional database technology to support scientific data? One of the reasons for the development of the Grid is the sheer size of the datasets involved. This has introduced new problems for distributed data, distributed scientific programming, and the combination of the two. However there are other, equally important issues which demand new database technology. In this talk I want raise some of them.

Annotation of existing data now provides a new form of communication between scientists, but conventional database technology provides little support for attaching annotations. I shall show why new models of both data and query languages are needed.

Closely related to annotation is provenance — knowing where your data has come from. This is now a real problem in bioinformatics with literally hundreds of databases, most of which are derived from others by a process of transformation, correction and annotation.

Preserving past states of a database — archiving — is also important for verifying the basis of scientific research, yet few published scientific databases do a good job of archiving. Past "editions" of the database get lost. I shall describe a system that allows frequent archiving and efficient retrieval with remarkably little space overhead.

Finally, what do scientific databases have to do with multimedia information systems? Ostensibly nothing. However presentation of data has given us some clues about how to approach some of the problems above.

K.S. Candan and A. Celentano (Eds.): MIS 2005, LNCS 3665, p. 1, 2005.

Early Data Tailoring for Ubiquitous Information Access in Highly Dynamic Environments

Letizia Tanca*

Politecnico di Milano,
Piazza Leonardo da Vinci 32, 20132 Milano, Italia
tanca@elet.polimi.it

Abstract. Nowadays content and services are available at different sources and places, thus a user can be seen as an integral part of numerous applications in which he/she interacts with service providers, product sellers, governmental organisations, friends and colleagues.

Information access personalization can be defined as any set of actions that can tailor information to a particular user or set of users. To achieve effective personalization, single users and organizations must rely on all available information, including: user profile, channel peculiarities, users current interests and typical behaviour, source content, source structure, as well as domain knowledge. In addition, efficient and intelligent techniques are needed to effectively use the discovered knowledge to enhance the users' experience.

These techniques must address important challenges emanating from the size and the heterogeneous nature of the data itself, as well as the dynamic nature of user interactions with data sources. These challenges include scalability of the personalization solutions in the process of data integration, and successful integration of techniques from knowledge representation, semantic web, information retrieval and filtering, databases, user modelling and human-computer interaction.

Our approach addresses these issues with particular attention to the process of data tailoring, which consists of the exploitation of knowledge about *the user*, the *adopted channel* and the *environment*, altogether called *context*, to the end of reducing the amount of information imported on the mobile device. Tailoring is needed because of two main reasons: one is the need to keep information manageable, in order for the user not to be confused by too much noise; the second reason is the frequent case that the mobile device be a small one, like a palm computer or a cellular phone, in which condition only the most precious information must be kept on board.

We consider open, networked, peer-based systems, according to paradigms where there is no previous knowledge and relationship among the parties, which may be mobile as well as fixed devices. The interaction among such devices is transient, since it is subject to network and device availability: indeed the nature of these devices and the variety of ambient strongly affect the cooperation methods and techniques. Semantic based caching techniques are exploited to cope with the above mentioned

---

* Joint work with C. Bolchini and F. A. Schreiber

K.S. Candan and A. Celentano (Eds.): MIS 2005, LNCS 3665, pp. 2–3, 2005.

network availability problems, always allowing the single party to retain the appropriate portion of needed data, while other fragments, stored at different peers, can be queried only when a connection is available. The mobile and dynamic context where the devices cooperate determines the fraction of data located on board, which, due to the limited amount of memory available, must be refreshed according to semantic context-based criteria. On the other hand, power aware data access techniques must be employed to manage the problem of limited battery life.

Consider the example of a semantic community formed to enable scientific collaboration in the medicine context; here, different resource structures and meanings are provided by the community peers. Besides selecting and semantically integrating the most appropriate resources provided by the various peers, it is the special goal of such techniques to obey the constraints imposed by the device context. For instance, during a home visit, a doctor in need of information about the symptoms of a rare disease can search, through his/her PDA or cell phone, clinical databases and research reports on the web looking for assistance in his/her diagnosis. Obviously the doctor must not be disoriented by the different formats of the retrieved documents, by the possible lexical discrepancies in their contents and by information which would be useless in the specific environment (tropical diseases symptoms in an Eskimo patient), but the most valuable information must be presented in the most suitable form for the operational context and the available device.

In this work we describe the *methodology* driving the selection of the device-residing portion of data; *analysis dimensions* for the detection of the context provide the different perspectives the mobile device is viewed from, and are used to set out its *ambient*. The identified dimensions and their current values drive the choice of the information to be kept on the mobile device, to be actually selected at run time. In order to formalize and then automatically obtain this view (the device ambient), we model the dimensions as a hierarchical, DAG-shaped, structure which allows us to consider an ontological specification of each considered concept, and to model semantic constraints between different dimensions as well. The dimension DAG contributes to the automatic selection and interpretation of the shared resources to be imported to the device.

Moreover, when interesting concepts are found and selected from the available data sources, it is also useful to collect on the device other concepts which are possibly related to them. However, since devices may have a limited memory, dynamic conflict resolution strategies must be devised, possibly based on various notions of semantic nearness, to decide which data must be retained and which can be discarded.

Translating Images to Keywords: Problems, Applications and Progress

Latifur Khan

Department of Computer Science,
University of Texas at Dallas Richardson,
Texas 75083-0688, USA
lkhan@utdallas.edu

Abstract. The development of technology generates huge amounts of non-textual information, such as images. An efficient image annotation and retrieval system is highly desired. Clustering algorithms make it possible to represent visual features of images with finite symbols. Based on this, many statistical models, which analyze correspondence between visual features and words and discover hidden semantics, have been published. These models improve the annotation and retrieval of large image databases. However, image data usually have a large number of dimensions. Traditional clustering algorithms assign equal weights to these dimensions, and become confounded in the process of dealing with these dimensions.

In this tutorial, first, we will present current state of the art and its shortcomings. We will present some classical models (e.g., translation model (TM), cross-media relevance model etc.). Second, we will present weighted feature selection algorithm as a solution to the existing problem. For a given cluster, we determine relevant features based on histogram analysis and assign greater weight to relevant features as compared to less relevant features. Third, we will exploit spatial correlation to disambiguate visual features, and spatial relationship will be constructed by spatial association rule mining. Fourth, we will present the continuous relevance model and multiple Bernoulli model for avoiding clustering. We will present mechanisms to link visual tokens with keywords based on these models. Fifth, we will present mechanisms to improve accuracy of classical model, TM by exploiting the WordNet knowledge-base. Sixth, we will present a framework to model semantic visual concept in video/images by fusing multiple evidence with the usage of an ontology. Seventh, we will show that weighted feature selection is better than traditional ones (TM) for automatic image annotation and retrieval. Finally, we will discuss open problems and future directions in the domain of image and video.

K.S. Candan and A. Celentano (Eds.): MIS 2005, LNCS 3665, p. 4, 2005.
© Springer-Verlag Berlin Heidelberg 2005

One to Many 3D Face Recognition Enhanced Through *k-d*-Tree Based Spatial Access

Andrea F. Abate, Michele Nappi, Stefano Ricciardi, and Gabriele Sabatino

Dipartimento di Matemarica e Informatica,
Università di Salerno,
84084 Fisciano (Salerno) Italy
{abate, mnappi, sricciardi, gsabatino}@unisa.it

Abstract. Most face based biometric systems and the underlying recognition algorithms are often more suited for verification (one-to-one comparison) instead of identification (one-to-many comparison) purposes. This is even more true in case of large face database, as the computational cost of an accurate comparison between the query and a gallery of many thousands of individuals could be too high for practical applications. In this paper we present a 3D based face recognition method which relies on normal image to represent and compare face geometry. It features fast comparison time and good robustness to a wide range of expressive variations thanks to an expression weighting mask, automatically generated for each enrolled subject. To better address one-to-many recognition applications, the proposed approach is improved via DFT based indexing of face descriptors and *k-d*-tree based spatial access to clusters of similar faces. We include experimental results showing the effectiveness of the presented method in terms of recognition accuracy and the improvements in one-to-many recognition time achieved thanks to indexing and retrieval techniques applied to a large parametric 3D face database.

1 Introduction

Currently, there is a growing demand for biometric systems to be used not only for security related applications, such as access control, but even for commercial and service providing purposes. Biometric systems rely on biometric identifiers [1] to recognize individuals through their distinctive physiological and behavioral characteristics which cannot be easily misplaced, forged or shared, as it happens for traditional token or knowledge-based methods.

Furthermore, biometric systems has the prerogative to allow both positive and negative recognition applications. In a positive recognition application, the system establishes whether the person is who he or she claims to be, to prevent multiple persons from using the same identity. In a negative recognition application, the system establishes whether the person is who he or she denies being, to prevent a single person from using multiple identities.

Among various available biometrics, face is one of the more interesting as it represents one of the most common methods of recognition that humans use in their visual

K.S. Candan and A. Celentano (Eds.): MIS 2005, LNCS 3665, pp. 5–16, 2005.

interactions, operating not intrusively without requiring any physical contact between user and imaging device. A face based biometric system could operate either in verification or identification modality, better known as one-to-one and one-to-many recognition [2]. While a face verification system compares the captured facial characteristics of a known subject to its pre-stored template to authenticate it, a face identification system tries to recognizes an unknown individual by searching the entire template database for a match. Only identification mode allows both positive and negative recognition applications, but it results to be much more computationally expensive than verification mode if the template database is large.

In the past years a lot of studies have been conducted on the face recognition topic, but most of them are focused on maximizing recognition accuracy and robustness, rarely addressing the computing time issues particularly in one-to-many applications.

This is partly due to the complexity of tasks such as 3D face acquisition and feature extraction/matching (e.g. posing and facial expression issues), which in many approaches lead to comparison time unsuited for identification applications. Anyway, as face become a more and more diffused and mature biometric, issues like facial feature classification and indexing should gain more attention from the scientific community similarly to what is happened with other more established biometrics like fingerprints.

In this paper we present a 3D face recognition method based on normal map to represent and compare faces. This approach, features a high recognition precision, a good robustness to expressive variations and a low comparison time, and is further enhanced through DFT based indexing of normal maps and k-d-tree based spatial access to clusters of similar faces to efficiently work on a very large gallery.

This paper is organized as follows. In section 2 related works are presented and the proposed method is introduced. In section 3 the proposed face recognition method is presented in detail. In section 4 the indexing and retrieval techniques adopted to speed up search in large database are discussed. In section 5 experimental results are shown and commented. The paper concludes in section 6 showing directions for future research and conclusions.

2   Related Works

Face recognition has been originally approached as a 2D pattern recognition problem. Several 2D methodologies briefly classifiable as Image Based [3] (analyze face image as an array of grey shaded pixels), Features Based [4] (analyze anthropomorphic face features and geometry), or Combined [5] (extract areas of features and apply image based algorithms on these areas) have been proposed. All this face recognition methods are based on 2D image processing using intensity or color images or video footage but, as showed in Face Recognition Vendor Test 2002 [6], current 2D approaches could not be sufficient to achieve optimal performances when subject pose is not carefully controlled.

The term 3D face recognition refers to a recognition methodology operating on three-dimensional dataset representing face (or head) shape as range data or polygonal mesh. 3D face representations promise to better cope with the large amount of variations present in human face: extra-subject variations (individual appearance) and intra-subject variations (facial expression, pose, lighting and aging). Various extensions of 2D face recognition techniques applied to range images have been proposed, such as those based on eigenface [7] or Hausdorff distance matching [8]. Other works compare faces through a spherical correlation of their Extended Gaussian Image [9], or through Principal Component Analysis (PCA) [10], or even measure the distance between any two 3D facial surfaces by the Iterative Closest Point (ICP) method [11].

We present a 3D face recognition method aimed to identification systems and based on normal map [12], a bidimensional array representing local curvature of a 3D polygonal mesh in terms of RGB color data. This approach features a high recognition precision, a good robustness to a broad range of expression variations and a low comparison time and together with Discrete Fourier Transform based indexing of face descriptors and k-d-tree based access, allows to efficiently work on a very large gallery.

3   Face Recognition System

A normal map is simply an RGB color image providing a bidimensional representation of a 3D surface, in which each normal to each polygon of a given mesh is represented by a RGB color pixel. More precisely, each pixel in a normal map encodes the three scalar components of the normal to a particular polygon in the mesh surface using the three RGB channels usually associated to a color image. To this aim we project the 3D geometry onto 2D space through spherical mapping. The result is a bidimensional representation of original face geometry which retains spatial relationships between facial features. As shown in the flow-chart in Fig. 1., after a face has been enrolled and a surface mesh generated, the preprocessing pipeline provides the corresponding normal map through the 2D projecting and sampling steps. This descriptor is then compressed via Discrete Fourier Transform to extract feature indexes which allow to compare the query to only the subset of faces in the gallery featuring similar indexes, exploiting the k-d-tree arrangement of the gallery.

Finally, the comparison between the normal map extracted from the query and each normal map belonging to the compatible subse t found in the k-d-tree is performed

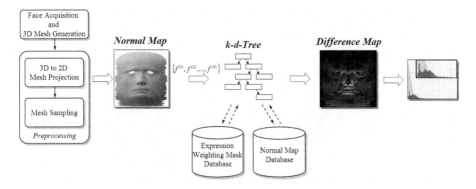

Fig. 1. Face Recognition workflow

computing a new array called the difference map, which is a gray scale image obtained subtracting pixel by pixel the two normal maps, multiplied by a previously built expression weighting mask. The whole procedure is detailed below.

3.1 Face Capture

As the proposed method works on 3D polygonal meshes we firstly need to acquire actual faces and to represent them as polygonal surfaces. Laser or structured light scanning technology could be used to this purpose, capturing range data and then converting them in 3D vertices and polygons. Stereoscopic imaging is another feasible option for 3D face digitizing which relies on 2D images shot by known angles and reconstructs a 3D mesh conform to a set of feature points previously correlated between the different views. Even if any of these technologies could provide valid 3D data for the presented method, we opted for a feature based mesh warping technique [13] because it requires a much simpler equipment more likely to be adopted in a real application (a couple of digital cameras shooting at high shutter speed and strobe lighting from front and side position) and, though the resulting face shape accuracy is inferior compared to real 3D scanning, it proved to be sufficient for recognition.

3.2 Extracting Normal Map from Face Geometry

As the 3D polygonal mesh resulting from the reconstruction process is an approximation of the actual face shape, polygon normals describe local curvature of captured

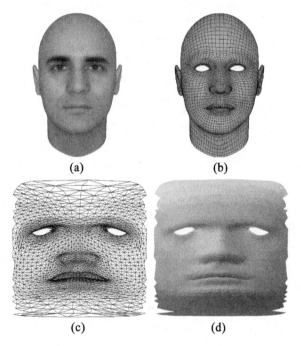

Fig. 2. (a) 3d mesh model, (b) wireframe model, (c) projection in 2D spatial coordinates, (d) normal map

face which could be view as its signature. As shown in Fig. 2, we intend to represent these normals by a color image transferring face's 3D features in a 2D space and, to this aim, we first need to project vertices' coordinates onto a 2D space using a spherical projection (opportunely adapted to mesh size). At this point, we can store normals of mesh M in a bi-dimensional array N to represent face geometry using the previously 2D-projected vertex coordinate and quantizing the length of the three scalar components of each normal. We refer this resulting array as the *Normal Map N* of the mesh M and this is the face descriptor we intend to use for one-to-one face comparison.

3.3 Comparing Normal Maps

To compare the normal map N_A from input subject to another normal map N_B previously stored in the reference database, we compute through:

$$\theta = \arccos\left(r_{N_A} \cdot r_{N_B} + g_{N_A} \cdot g_{N_B} + b_{N_A} \cdot b_{N_B}\right) \tag{1}$$

the angle included between each pairs of normals represented by colors of pixels with corresponding mapping coordinates, and store it in a new *Difference Map D* with components r, g and b opportunely normalized from spatial domain to color domain, so $0 \le r_{N_A}, g_{N_A}, b_{N_A} \le 1$ and $0 \le r_{N_B}, g_{N_B}, b_{N_B} \le 1$. The value θ, with $0 \le \theta < \pi$, is the angular difference between the pixels with coordinates $\left(x_{N_A}, y_{N_A}\right)$ in N_A and $\left(x_{N_B}, y_{N_B}\right)$ in N_B and it is stored in D as a gray-scale color.

To improve robustness to facial expressions we introduce the *Expression Weighting Mask E*, a subject specific pre-calculated mask whose pixel values assign different relevance to different face regions. Indeed, for each subject enrolled, each one out of ten expression variations (see Fig. 3) is compared to the neutral face, resulting in ten difference maps. We generate the expression variations through a parametric rig based deformation system previously applied to a prototype face mesh, morphed to fit the reconstructed face mesh [15].

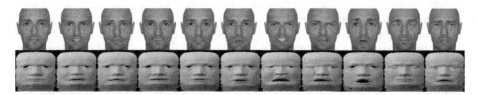

Fig. 3. An example of normal maps of the same subject featuring a neutral pose (leftmost face) and ten different facial expressions

This fitting is achieved via a landmark-based volume morphing where the transformation and deformation of the prototype mesh is guided by the interpolation of a set of landmark points with a radial basis function. To improve the accuracy of this rough mesh fitting we need a surface optimization obtained minimizing a cost function based on the Euclidean distance between vertices. The expression weighting mask E is the average of a set of ten difference maps, with components opportunely normalized from 0 to 1, and it allows to better cope with bending facial regions.

At this point, the histogram *H* resulting from multiplication $D \cdot E$ is analyzed to estimate the similarity score between N_A and N_B. On the X axis we represent the resulting angles between each pair of comparisons (sorted from $0°$ degree to $180°$ degree), while on the Y axis we represent the total number of differences found. The curvature of H represents the angular distance distribution between mesh M_A and M_B, thus two similar faces featuring very high values on small angles, whereas two unlike faces have more distributed differences (see Fig. 4). We define a similarity score through a weighted sum between *H* and a Gaussian function *G*, as in:

$$similarity\_score = \sum_{x=0}^{k} H(x) \cdot \frac{1}{\sigma\sqrt{2\pi}} e^{-\frac{x^2}{2\sigma^2}} \qquad (2)$$

where with the variation of σ and k is is possible to change recognition sensibility.

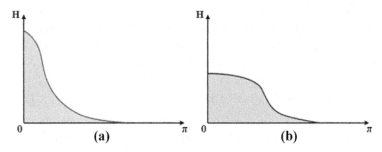

Fig. 4. Example of histogram H to represent the angular distances. (a) shows a typical histogram between two similar Normal Maps, while (b) between two different Normal Maps.

4   Indexing And Accessing Normal Maps

In order to speed up the search for a matching template within large database we rely on *k-d*-tree spatial access method, which allows to classify the entire data set associating an index to each normal map. More precisely, when a query is submitted to the recognition system, the resulting normal map is compressed in order to compute its feature indexes which are subsequently used to reduce the search to a cluster of similar normal maps selected through a visit in the *k-d*-tree.

A normal map index is obtained processing the normal map by a discrete Fourier transform (DFT) and considering only the *k* lower frequency coefficients. It has been empirically verified that typically 3 to 5 complex Fourier coefficients (that is, 6 to 10 numbers) are enough to characterize the index set [14]. The *k-d*-trees is used to represent the index set through a hierarchical structure, managing each index as a *k*-dimensional point. In other terms, we can consider a point in a *k*-dimensional space as an index of a normal map and the answer set as a region in the address space. We used *k-d-trees* solely because of availability; any spatial access method would do, like, e.g. R-tree [15], X-tree [16] or SR-tree [17]. A faster access structure would only make our method run even faster.

The *k-d*-tree [18] is a well know data structure to store an ordered set of record, where at each non-leaf node a different field is tested to determine the direction in which a branch is to be made (see Fig. 5). Suppose we want to index a set of normal maps $M = \{m_1, m_2,\ldots,m_n\}$, let $F_{m_i} = \left\{ f_{m_i}^{(1)}, f_{m_i}^{(2)}, \ldots, f_{m_i}^{(k)} \right\}$ be the set of Fourier k coefficients of normal map m_i. In our case, the level j corresponds to the field $f_{m_i}^{(j)}$ for $j = 1$, 2, …., k, while the level $k + 1$ corresponds to $f_{m_i}^{(1)}$ and so on. If the value of the field $f_{m_i}^{(j)}$ of a node at level j is equal to x, then all its left descendants satisfy the condition $f_{m_i}^{(j)} \leq x$, while all its right descendants satisfy the condition $f_{m_i}^{(j)} > x$. The proposed implementation of *k-d*-tree based search simply operates visiting the aforementioned data structure to find the most similar F_{m_i}, in other terms the nearest neighbor point of a query point.

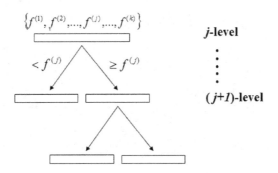

Fig. 5. An example of *k-d*-tree

5   Experimental Results

We had two main experimental goals: 1) Efficacy, to test the recognition performance of the proposed method 2) Efficiency, to validate the speed up in one-to-many modality resulting from database indexing and *k-d*-tree based access.

For the first group of experiments we acquired a front-side pair of face images from 135 different persons (87 males and 48 females, age ranging from 19 to 65) resulting in a database of 135 3D face models, each one augmented with ten expressive variations (see Fig. 6). Experimental results are generally good in terms of accuracy, showing a Recognition Rate of 100% using the expression weighting mask, the Gaussian function with σ=4.5 and k=50 and normal map sized 128×128 pixels.

Since the lack of a reference facial database, such as the FERET [19] is for 2D face recognition, any direct comparison between various 3DFR approaches on different dataset is not conclusive. Nevertheless, in Table 1 we resume the performance of the methods cited in section 2 and the corrispondent database used.

Fig. 7 shows the precision/recall improvement provided by the expression weighting mask both with and without *k-d*-tree. The proposed method proved to be very fast in the recognition process as it required approx. 4 milliseconds on a P4/3.4 Ghz based

PC for a single one to one comparison, a good starting point for one-to-many recognition. As for the second group of experiments we were interested in validating the proposed approach on large face database but we could not afford the enrolment of several thousands of persons, we used a commercial 3D parametric face generation software from Singular Inversion Co., called Facegen, to produce 20.000 faces featuring different race, sex and age. The performance of k-d-tree based spatial access are affected by tree balance, so, to evaluate the average time required to locate the matching node, we consider only the case in which the tree is complete and contains n nodes, as there are several heuristic techniques available to keep a k-d-tree balanced [20]. In this case, each path from the root requires the visit of at most $\log_2 n$ nodes.

Table 1. Some 3D face recognition methods resumed

METHOD	DB Size	No. Subjects	Variations	Recognition Rate
B. Achermann et al [7, 8]	240	24	10 poses	100%
H. T. Tanaka [9]	37	37	-	100%
C. Hesher [10]	185	37	5 facial expressions	90%
G. Medioni [11]	700	100	7 poses	98%
Proposed Method	1485 (1st DB) 20020 (2nd DB)	135 (1st DB) 1820 (2nd DB)	11 facial expressions	100%

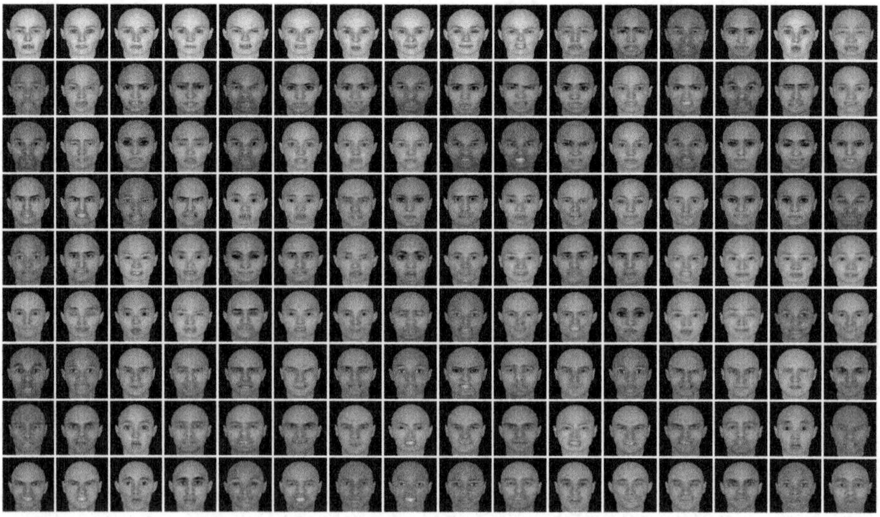

Fig. 6. An example of procedurally generated 3D face models featuring different race, sex, age and expression

We have tested the face recognition method on a P4/3.4 Ghz based PC, considering a database with 20.000 normal maps and a probe gallery of 50 normal maps. It proved to be fast, allowing to work in identification applications even on a large database. As an alternative approach to *k-d*-tree based spatial access we considered the Region-tree (R-tree). The experiments conducted (Fig. 8) showed that R-tree could perform better than k-d-tree only if feature dimensionality was greater than 15-16. As the features extracted by FFT from normal maps have tipically 3 to 5 complex (6 to 10 real) coefficients, the choice of *k-d*-tree is justified.

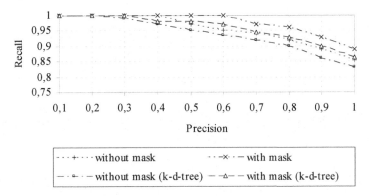

Fig. 7. Precision/Recall Testing without expression weighting mask (the red squares) and with expression weighting mask (the blue rhombuses)

Fig. 9 shows the average response times of sequential and *k-d*-tree searches, as a function of the size of the answer set of normal maps while Fig. 10 shows how time to recognition varies according to different database size.

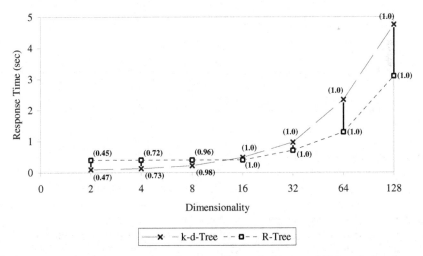

Fig. 8. Average retrieval response time corresponding to k-d-tree and R-tree indexed scan searching (values within brackets refer to recognition rate)

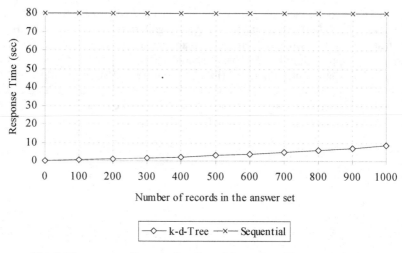

Fig. 9. The response time as a function of the retrieved image set size

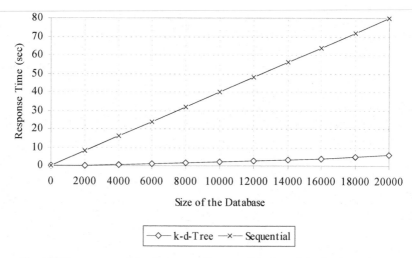

Fig. 10. The average retrieval response time as a function of the database size

6 Conclusions

We presented a 3D face recognition method aimed to identification systems. The proposed approach to face representation and comparison proved to be a valid foundation to one-to-many recognition thanks to high accuracy and recognition speed. The indexing and accessing techniques applied to face descriptors, although based on classic methods (DFT and *k-d*-trees), provided a considerable speed up of time required to find a match, making a search through a large gallery a reasonable task. As the core of the method is the representation of 3D facial features through a color image, we believe that implementing this approach via the new generation of programmable, multi-pipeline GPUs could lead to a huge performance improvement. On another side, a multimodal implementation of the proposed method, working on both 2D (texture) and 3D (geometry) data, could offer a better discriminating power.

References

[1] D. Maltoni, D. Maio, A.K. Jain, S. Prabhakar, "Handbook of Fingerprint Recognition", Springer, New York, 2003.

[2] G. Perronnin, J.L. Dugelay, "An Introduction to biometrics and face recognition", in Proc. of IMAGE 2003: Learning, Understanding, Information Retrieval, Medical, Cagliari, Italy, June 2003.

[3] M. S. Bartlett, J. R. Movellan and T. J. Sejnowski, "Face Recognition by Independent Component Analysis", in IEEE Transactions on Neural networks, vol. 13, no. 6, pp. 1450–1464, November 2002.

[4] J. Zhang, Y. Yan and M. Lades, "Face Recognition: Eigenface, Elastic Matching, and Neural Nets" in Proc. of the IEEE, vol. 85, no. 9, pp. 1423–1435, Sept. 1997.

[5] T. Tan, H. Yan, "Face recognition by fractal transformations", in Proc. of 1999 IEEE Int. Conference on Acoustics, Speech, and Signal Processing, vol. 6, no. 6, pp. 3537–3540, Mar. 1999.

[6] P. J. Phillips, P. Grother, R. J. Micheals, D. M. Blackburn, E. Tabassi, M. Bone, "Face Recognition Vendor Test: Evaluation Report", http://www.frvt.org, Mar. 2003.

[7] B. Achermann, X. Jiang, and H. Bunke, "Face recognition using range images", in Proc. of International Conference on Virtual Systems and MultiMedia, pp. 129–136, 1997.

[8] B. Achermann and H. Bunke, "Classifying range images of human faces with the hausdorff distance", in Proc. of 15th International Conference on Pattern Recognition, Barcelona, Spain, vol. 2, pp. 813-817, 2000.

[9] H. T. Tanaka, M. Ikeda, and H. Chiaki, "Curvature-based face surface recognition using spherical correlation principal directions for curved object recognition", in Proc. of Third International Conference on Automated Face and Gesture Recognition, pp. 372–377, 1998.

[10] C. Hesher, A. Srivastava, and G. Erlebacher, "A novel technique for face recognition using range images", in Proc. of Seventh Int'l Symp. on Signal Processing and Its Applications, Paris, France, Jul. 2003.

[11] G. Medioni and R. Waupotitsch. Face recognition and modeling in 3D. in Proc. of IEEE Int'l Workshop on Analysis and Modeling of Faces and Gestures (AMFG 2003), pp. 232-233, Oct. 2003.

[12] X. Gu, S. Gortler and H. Hoppe, "Geometry images", in Proc. of SIGGRAPH 2002, San Antonio, Texas, ACM, pp. 355-361, Jul. 2002.

[13] W. Lee, N. Magnenat-Thalmann, "Head Modeling from Pictures and Morphing in 3D with Image Metamorphosis based on triangulation", in Proc. of Modelling and Motion Capture Techniques for Virtual Environments (Captech98), Geneva, Switzerland, Lecture Notes in Computer Science, Springer, vol. 1537, pp. 254-267, 1998.

[14] R. Agrawal, C. Faloutsos, A. Swami, "Efficient similarity search in sequence databases," in Proc. Of Foundations of Data Organization and Algorithms (FODO), Evanston, IL, Oct. 1993.

[15] E. G.M. Petrakis, C. Faloutsos, K.-Ip (David) Lin, "ImageMap: An Image Indexing Method Based on Spatial Similarity," in Proc. of IEEE Transactions on Knowledge and Data Engineering, vol 14, no. 15, pp. 979-987, Sept/Oct. 1999.

[16] S. Berchtold, D.A. Keim, H.-P Kriegel, "The X-Tree: An Index Structure for High-Dimensional Data," in Proc. of 22nd Very Large Data Base Conf., pp. 28-39, 1996.

[17] N. Katayama, S. Satoh, "The SR-tree: An Index Structure for High-Dimensional Nearest Neightbor Queries," in Proc. of ACM SIGMOD, pp. 269-380, 1997.

[18] J. L. Bentley, "Multidimensional binary search trees used for associative searching," in Comm. ACM 18, vol. 9, pp. 509–517, 1975.

[19] J. P. Phillips, H. Moon, A. S. Rizvi, P. J. Rauss, "The FERET Evaluation Methodology for Face-Recognition Algorithms," in IEEE Transaction on Pattern Analysis and Machine Intelligence, vol. 22, no. 10, pp. 1090-1104, Oct. 2000.

[20] J.H. Friedman, J.L. Bentley, R.A. Finkel, "An algorithm for finding best matches in logarithmic expected time, " in ACM Trans. Mathematical Software 3, vol. 3, pp. 209-226, 1997.

Information Retrieval from the Web: An Interactive Paradigm

Massimiliano Albanese, Pasquale Capasso,
Antonio Picariello, and Antonio Maria Rinaldi

Università di Napoli "Federico II", Napoli, Italy
{malbanes, pacapass, picus, amrinald}@unina.it

Abstract. Information retrieval is moving beyond the stage where users simply type one or more keywords and retrieve a ranked list of documents. In such a scenario users have to go through the returned documents in order to find what they are actually looking for. More often they would like to get targeted answers to their queries without extraneous information, even if their requirements are not well specified. In this paper we propose an approach for designing a web retrieval system able to find the desired information through several interactions with the users. The proposed approach allows to overcome the problems deriving from ambiguous or too vague queries, using semantic search and topic detection techniques. The results of the very first experiments on a prototype system are also reported.

1 Introduction

The challenging task of a web information retrieval system is that of retrieving from the web all the *relevant* documents to a user query: this operation is considered successful if it returns as few as possible of non-relevant documents. The typical steps thus performed by a user are described as in the following: i) a user submits the query – hopefully written in natural language – to the search engine; ii) the system returns a ranked list of documents; iii) the user reads each document until she finds enough relevant information. From a general point of view, the returned list may be viewed as the *engine's model* of the user's idea of what is considered relevant: in a certain way, we can say that the engine considers the first document as the most relevant one, and so on. The main problem that arises in traditional systems is that in most cases user's interests are either poorly defined or inherently broad. The answer to a typical query is thus a very large set of documents, among which the user has to look for what she is actually interested in. In these cases, we can easily identify another usual user behavior: if, at a certain point, she starts to find that most of the retrieved documents are not relevant, she gives up that returned list and tries to refine the query, adding more specific details. Our vision is that of extending this behavior, in order to give the system the capability of *understanding* if the user query is too much general, thus automatically *trying to refine* the queries and *asking the users* more specific information. In other words, we explicitly accept the user's

K.S. Candan and A. Celentano (Eds.): MIS 2005, LNCS 3665, pp. 17–32, 2005.

feedback in order to adjust the *engine model*. Unfortunately, characterization of the user information need is not a trivial task, and, at the same time, the users want targeted answers to their queries without extraneous information.

Imagine, for example, a user who is looking for a new car. She is interested in the information about different cars, with a primary focus on their prices. Our user turns to a web search engine and types in the simple query $q =$ "car": we surely agree that q is a inherently vague query. In our vision, a great advance in the retrieval process may be obtained if the system could recognize that the required information is poorly specified, thus posing some questions to the user in order to narrow the search. In the above example the user may be explicitly asked to clarify which sense of the word "car" she means, since that word can have multiple meanings (see example 1). Once the user has selected a meaning, then the system may decide if the information for solving the query are sufficient or not. If it is the case, then a set of semantically relevant documents is returned to the user and other questions may be asked, on the basis of the major identified topics, such as "car rental", "car parts", "car prices", and so on, asking the user to specify what she is looking for.

In this paper we propose an approach for designing a web information retrieval system, able to retrieve the desired information through several interactions with the users. The proposed approach allows to overcome the problems deriving from ambiguous or too vague queries, using semantic search and topic detection techniques.

The paper is organized as follows. Next section 2 discusses related works. Section 3 introduces the architecture of the system while section 4 briefly describes the overall retrieval process. Sections 4.1, 4.2 and 4.3 respectively describe in details the three main steps of the process, namely the *user driven keyword extraction*, the *semantic search* and the *topic based query refinement*. First experimental results are reported and discussed in section 5, while conclusions are given in section 6.

2   Related Works

The research community has been devoting huge efforts in the field of information retrieval in the last two decades. Investigations range from traditional document retrieval systems to modern question answering systems, from user relevance feedback to document clustering and classification.

Traditional information retrieval systems [2] usually retrieve and rank documents containing the keywords in the query, irrespective of the context in which those keywords are used. Some attempts have been done to take context into account and retrieve documents that are semantically rather than only syntactically related to the user's query [9,18,25].

In the latest years, the IR community has focused its attention on question answering (QA) systems, whose goal is that of identifying and presenting to the user a concise and precise answer to a question, rather than identifying documents that may be somehow related to the query. Such systems are designed to extract answers from structured knowledge bases or directly from the web. Several question answering systems rely on a variety of linguistic resources – dictionaries, part of speech tagging, syntactic parsing, semantic relations, named entity recognition, etc. [1,5,21] – while many other simpler solutions rely on pattern matching and the inherent redundancy of large text repositories to facilitate answer mining [7,22]. Due to the extreme simplicity of the latter approaches, they are usually more efficient, even if sometimes they may be less reliable.

In most recent works, great importance is also given to the so called 'relevance feedback'. This term is referred to the practice of adapting the retrieval behavior of a search engine, based on some information gathered from the users themselves. The collected information can be used to dynamically refine the current query and speed up future searches. Several ways exist to get feedback from the users. The most common ones rely on asking the user to judge the relevance of each retrieved document w.r.t. her query [23], while many others are based on implicitly inferring users' interests by analyzing browsing logs. Good examples of the latter approach are QueryFind [29] and Takealook [27]: user's interests are captured and document presentation is personalized accordingly.

Independently from the approach, the goal of any feedback strategy is that of overcoming the information overload caused by the great number of documents returned by current web search engines. Search engines themselves commonly provide a simple mechanism to address this issue, ranking documents according to some relevance measure. In order to take into account user requirements, several authors propose document clustering techniques, grouping together similar or related documents into classes. The operation of clustering documents could usually be of two types: global and local. In a global clustering strategy, the entire document collection is clustered off-line and queries are compared with a representation of each cluster instead of a representation of each document. In a local clustering strategy, clustering is applied to the documents that are returned in response to a query (e.g., Carey et al. [4], Wu et al. [30], Zamir and Etzioni [31]). This approach is successfully applied to the web by some search engines, as Northern Light or Vivísimo, to the purpose of making result set browsing easier. Nevertheless, recent works [10,30] about clustering evaluation involving users show no significant differences in effectiveness between interfaces using classic ranked list and post-retrieval clustering. Among others, authors suggested two main reasons: first, the information accompanying clusters (usually a list of keywords) frequently is not enough to specify the content of the documents in a cluster; second, although the organization in clusters helps users to discover groups with a high density of relevant documents, clustering interface does not give further assistance in identifying particular documents with relevant information. Some authors (Mana-Lopez et al. [16]) propose to add to post-retrieval clustering algorithms, some techniques of multi-document summarization, in order to better show the topic related to each cluster and those related to the different documents in it. Kummamuru et al. [13] propose a hierarchical document clustering algorithm for summarizing and browsing search results, based on automatic taxonomy generation.

Despite the great amount of work done, we can state that, at the best of our knowledge, no system is currently able to retrieve only the really relevant documents for each user query. That is why we propose a system that produces a very small answer set for each query, through repeated interactions with the user. The main goal of the user interaction is that of collecting enough information to manage ambiguous or too vague queries. In particular, we apply some kind of clustering to larger answer sets.

It's worth noting that we do not refer to the term *clustering*, like many other authors do, as "grouping data elements such that the intra-group similarities are high and the inter-group similarities are low" [20]. Instead, we agree with Estivill-Castro [8], who more generally defines *clustering* as a "hypothesis to suggest groupings in the data", thus considering the possibility of overlapping document sets. In fact, as described in details in section 4.3, we identify major topics in a document collection and group documents based on such topics.

3   System Architecture

Figure 1 shows at a glance the overall architecture of the system. From a structural point of view, the system acts as a meta search engine, relying on existing general purpose search engines.

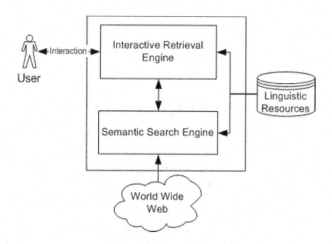

Fig. 1. System architecture

Users submit their queries – sets of keywords or natural language questions – to the *Interactive Retrieval Engine*, whose role is that of analyzing queries, asking appropriate questions to the users if they exhibit some ambiguities and forwarding the clarified queries to the *Semantic Search Engine*, that returns a set of documents semantically matching the queries. The role of the

Interactive Retrieval Engine also consists in asking further questions to the users in order to narrow too wide answer sets.

Both the Interactive Retrieval Engine and the Semantic Search Engine rely on a set of linguistic resources. In our implementation we adopt WordNet [17], since it offers both a dictionary functionality and semantic network capabilities. The latter one are fundamental for the design of a semantic search engine.

During the entire retrieval process, the Interactive Retrieval Engine keeps track of the answers given by the users and updates an internal cache, in order to simplify and speed up future searches.

4   The Retrieval Process

In this section we briefly introduce all the steps of the interactive retrieval process. Figure 2 shows a data flow diagram of the process.

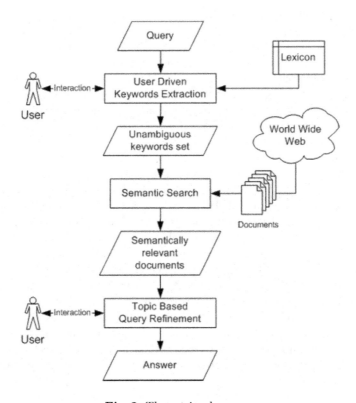

Fig. 2. The retrieval process

First of all a user submits a query to the system expressing her information needs. In its simplest form, a query is composed of keywords, but in our framework we allow more general queries, in the form of natural language phrases or questions (e.g. "The capital of France").

Given the query, a set of keywords must be derived from the query string, as described in section 4.1. This step may require interaction with the user in order to clarify ambiguities.

The unambiguous keyword set built in the previous step is then used in the semantic search phase for retrieving documents that are semantically relevant to the user query, as described in details in section 4.2.

The answer set returned by the Semantic Search Engine may be still too wide to be directly presented to the user for manual inspection and contain non relevant information. Thus the documents in the answer set are further analyzed and main topics are identified, as described in section 4.3. The user is then asked to select which of them she is interested in. At this point the documents covering the selected topic are presented to the user or the latter step is repeated if the the answer set is still too wide.

4.1   User Driven Keyword Extraction

This section describes the steps needed to extract a set of unambiguous keywords from the original user query in a user driven fashion.

As we have previously seen, a query is usually composed of keywords: anyway, we want to allow more general queries, such as natural language sentences. A user who is interested in retrieving information about the capital of France, may just type the sentence "The capital of France", from which the system should identify "capital" and "France" as keywords.

In the simplest cases elimination of stopwords may be enough to achieve the goal. We propose a more general approach based on a preliminary syntactical analysis of the text. To this aim, part of speech tagging is applied to the query text. The tagger is based on a dictionary and a set of heuristic rules that allows to resolve ambiguous part of speech assignment: most words usually have more than a single part of speech, but most ambiguities may be simply resolved (e.g. the word after an article can be a noun but not a verb). In addition to that we also apply *Named Entity Recognition* [3] in order to identify and properly tag the names of entities – people, places, organizations. Based on the part of speech tagging, we can select the keywords by considering named entities and other noun phrases only. It is worth noticing that query strings shorter than 3 or 4 words are unlikely to be natural language questions: they may just be sets of keywords or noun phrases. Given the results of part of speech tagging, we can easily distinguish keyword based queries from natural language queries and correctly identify keywords.

At this point, words that admits more than a single meaning need to be disambiguated. An effective way to address this issue is that of asking the user which sense she intended for each of the ambiguous words. In order to perform this interaction with the user, the system extracts from the dictionary the glosses for the several senses of the ambiguous words and asks the user to select one of them.

Example 1. Consider a query containing the word "car", that is selected as a keyword. Since the word "car", according to WordNet, has five different senses, the user is presented with the following question.

What do you mean by "car"?

1. "4-wheeled motor vehicle; usually propelled by an internal combustion engine"
2. "a wheeled vehicle adapted to the rails of railroad"
3. "a conveyance for passengers or freight on a cable railway"
4. "car suspended from an airship and carrying personnel and cargo and power plant"
5. "where passengers ride up and down"

Similar questions are posed for each ambiguous word in the keyword set.

4.2   Semantic Search

Several techniques have been proposed in the last years [2,6] in order to overcome the limitations of traditional search engines, that are mainly keyword based, and evolve towards semantic search engines. In this work we use a technique based on *ontologies*. A formal definition of ontology can be found in [11] and [19]. According to this definition an ontology can be seen as a set of "terms" and "relations" among them, denoting the concepts that are used in a specific domain.

In our framework the implementation of the ontology is realized through a semantic network that is dynamically built around a term or a set of terms that are central to a specific context. We call this kind of ontology *Dynamic Semantic Network* (DSN) due to the way it is built. Technically speaking the network is built by extracting a subgraph from the complete graph of WordNet. WordNet organizes words into synsets, that are set of synonyms; words having more than a single meaning appear into as many synsets, each representing a different concept. Given a word and chosen a sense, i.e. the synset that represents the concept which the user is interested in, the DSN is built starting from that synset.

In the construction of the DSN we consider all the terms (synonyms) in the synset. Beyond the synonymy, we consider other semantic and lexical proprieties, namely holonymy, meronymy, hyponymy, hypernymy, coordinate terms and domain terms. WordNet manages all the properties we are interested in for building the DSN.

Figure 3 shows an example of DSN built around the synset corresponding to the first sense of the word "car".

After considering the synonyms, we build a hierarchy, only based on the hyponymy property; its last level corresponds to the last level of WordNet hierarchy. After this first step we enrich our hierarchy considering all the other kinds

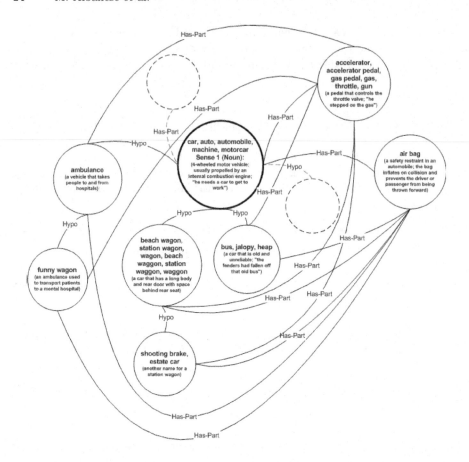

Fig. 3. An example of DSN

of relationships in WordNet. Based on these relations we can add other terms obtaining an highly connected semantic network.

The lexical and semantic properties are represented by arcs between the nodes of the DSN and are assigned a weight σ_i, in order to express the strength of the relation. The concept of strength of a relation is presented in [28] and, following its example, the values of our weights, defined in the [0,1] interval, are set by experiments.

In the worst case, the above described way of building the network leads to a number of completely disconnected subnets equal to the number of keywords in the query. This may be a problem, due the lack of a path between some pairs of nodes. We address this issue by taking advantage of the linguistic propri-eties of WordNet. In particular we consider the single subnets and their roots, representing the keywords in the query, and connect them by finding the first common subsumer and adding all the synsets along the path. We thus obtain a totally connected DSN. We remark that this operation is always possible, given the hierarchical structure of WordNet: in fact each synset has the concept *entity* among its ancestors.

Example 2. Let us consider a user interested in renting a car and suppose she types in the query "rent a car". The user driven keyword extraction step selects as keywords the words "rent" and "car" and attaches to them the desired sense. The system thus builds two DSNs and tries to find some common synset. In the example of figure 4 the module finds as connecting term the word "rental".

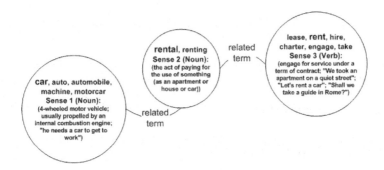

Fig. 4. Connection of two DSNs

At this point we retrieve web pages containing the keywords in the query by means of a traditional search engine and then build a lexical chain [12,26] on them using the DSN; each word in the page which matches any of the terms in the DSN is a lexical chain component and the references between the components are the relations in the DSN.

Using these words and an appropriate metric described in the following, we can measure the semantic relatedness between words in a given context represented by a DSN.

In order to discriminate interesting pages from the others, we propose a re-ranking strategy that takes into account the measure of similarity among words in a given domain. It is expressed by a combination of the length (**l**) of the path between the terms and the depth of their first subsumer (**d**). The correlation between the terms is the semantic relatedness and it is computed through a nonlinear function. The choice of a nonlinear function to express the semantic relatedness between terms derives from several considerations. The values of path length and depth may range from 0 to infinity, while relatedness between two terms should be expressed as a number in the [0,1] interval.

Furthermore when the path length decrease towards 0, the relatedness should monotonically increase towards 1, while it should monotonically decrease towards 0 when path length goes to infinity. We need a scaling effect w.r.t. the depth, because words in the upper levels of a semantic hierarchic express more general concepts than the words in a lower level. We use a non linear function for scaling down the contribution of subsumers in a upper level and scaling up those in a lower one.

Given the above considerations, we selected an exponential function, that satisfies the constraints previously discussed; our choice is also supported by the studies of Shepard et al. [24], who demonstrated that exponential-decay functions are a universal law in psychological science.

Let us give the following preliminary definition.

Definition 1 (Path Length).
The length l of the path between two terms is defined as follows:

$$l = \min_{j} \sum_{i=1}^{h_j} \frac{1}{\sigma_j} \tag{1}$$

where j spans over all the paths between the two considered terms, h_j is the number of hops in the j-th path and σ_j is the weight assigned to the type of relations in the j-th path. In this way we consider the best path between terms.

We are now in a position to define a semantic relatedness metric extending the one proposed in [14].

Definition 2 (Semantic Relatedness Metric).
The Semantic Relatedness of two terms is defined as follows:

$$W = e^{-\alpha l} \frac{e^{\beta d} - e^{-\beta d}}{e^{\beta d} + e^{\beta d}} \tag{2}$$

where l is the length of the path between the terms, d is the depth of their subsumer, $\alpha \geq 0$ and $\beta > 0$ are two scaling parameters whose values have been defined by experiments.

Example 3. Let us consider two terms X and Y, as in figure 5.

Two paths exist between X and Y. They are labelled with their linguistic properties σ and have a common subsumer S having a distance of 8 levels from the WordNet root. We suppose that $\sigma_i = \sigma_j = 0.8$ and $\sigma_t = 0.3$. In this case the best path is the one traversing Z with a value of $l = 1.58$. We note that according to definition 1, the previous path is not the shortest one. Considering definition 2, the semantic relatedness between the considered terms is thus 0.364.

4.3   Topic Based Query Refinement

The documents returned by the semantic search engine may be too many to be manually inspected, even if semantically related to the query. A possible solution is to partition the answer set into smaller sets by means of some local clustering algorithms. What we propose in this paper is slightly different: given the answer set of the semantic search engine, the idea is to identify the main topics covered in the set of documents, then ask the user which topic she is interested in, and

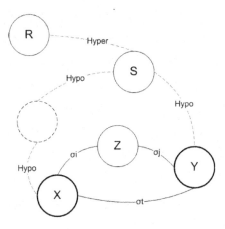

Fig. 5. Best path evaluation

return the documents that cover the selected topic. The process can be repeated several times, until the answer set reaches an affordable size.

First of all, we select candidate topics. To this aim we assume that expressions in the documents such as noun phrases or named entities are appropriate to be considered as topics. We thus adopt a technique similar to that used for extracting keywords from queries.

As an example, topics within documents matching the query "museum" may be "modern art", "science museum" and so on, while topics within documents matching the query "car" may be "car rental", "car parts" or "car prices".

In order to identify candidate topics, retrieved documents undergo part of speech tagging and named entities recognition. Then stopwords, punctuation, verb phrases, adverbs are removed from the text and replaced with a separator. At this point we consider as candidate topics any sequence of words between two consecutive separators.

Example 4. Consider the piece of text *"Founded in 1929 as an educational institution, The Museum of Modern Art is dedicated to being the foremost museum of modern art in the world"*. The described processing produces *"- - - - - educational institution - The Museum of Modern Art - - - - - - museum - modern art - - world"*. "The Museum of Modern Art" is recognized as a named entity and the article "The" is not removed.

Once identified a set of topics, we would like to select and present to the user the ones that best allow to discriminate a small subset of actually relevant documents.

From a preliminary analysis we concluded that three main variables affect the ability of a topic t to effectively group documents: the number of documents containing t, the total number of occurrences of t and the length of t, expressed as the number of words. Let us now explain how to take these variables into account. The greater is the fraction p of documents containing a topic, the worst it can identify small document sets. As regard to the number of occurrences, we observed that the main subjects of a document occur just a few time - say $2 - 5$ - while higher frequencies denote very common terms. As regard to the length of topics, we observed that most meaningful ones contain 2 up to 4 words. We thus need a function as the one in figure 6.a, in order to take into account both frequency and topic length.

We can thus give the definition of *discriminating power* of a topic.

Definition 3 (Discriminating power). *Given a set $\mathcal{D}$ of documents and a topic t_i, we define the discriminating power Δ of t in $\mathcal{D}$ as*

$$\Delta_{\mathcal{D}}(t) = -\log(p) \cdot \frac{\log(f + \Delta f)}{f^{\alpha}} \cdot \frac{\log(w + \Delta w)}{w^{\beta}} \tag{3}$$

p being the fraction of documents containing t, f the average frequency of t over the documents containing t, w the number of words in t; Δf and Δw are used to shift the curve in figure 6.a in order to prevent Δ to be zero when $f = 1$ or $w = 1$; α and β are used to regulate the slop of the curve.

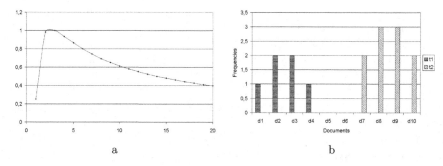

a   b

Fig. 6. a) An example of function used to take into account the effect of frequency and length; b) an example of topic frequency distribution

Example 5. Given two topics t_1 and t_2, let us suppose that their frequency distributions among documents are as in figure 6.b.

Since t_1 and t_2 occurs in the same number of documents, $p_1 = p_2$. However it's also clear that the topic t_2 is more appropriate to discriminate a subset of documents.

The topics are ranked according to descending values of Δ and the system asks the user to choose one among the top-k. Documents containing the selected topic are presented to the user or they are further analyzed and the described process is repeated if the size of the answer set is still too large.

5   Experiments and Discussions

A prototype system has been implemented. In particular, the semantic search module extends the one we introduced in [15]. In this section we report and discuss the results of the very first experiments we carried out in order to evaluate the effectiveness of the approach.

Several very vague single-keyword queries have been submitted to the system. Table 1 lists a subset of those queries and reports the number of documents in the web matching them according to Google.

Table 1. Examples of very vague queries

Query	# documents
car	154,000,000
museum	46,200,000
music	283,000,000
photography	45,500,000
soccer	24,900,000
train	39,600,000

The one presented is clearly the worst case: at the beginning, the user does not clearly specify what she's actually looking for and just types in some general terms. The main goal of our first experiments was to verify that the proposed approach allows to reduce the size of the answer set in a very few iterations, keeping the relevant information.

For each query in the test set, users were asked to specify a meaning for the single term in the query. The semantic search engine then considered the first 100 documents returned by Google, selecting among them the ones whose semantic relatedness w.r.t. the query was higher than a given threshold. An average number of 52 pages were considered relevant. Those pages were then analyzed in order to identify the most discriminating topics.

Table 2 shows the top 8 topics identified in the first step of the refinement of the queries $q_1 = $ "car" and $q_1 = $ "$museum$" respectively. The topics are ranked according to descending values of Δ. The table also reports the number P of documents matching a topic, the total number f of occurrences and the size w of each topic, expressed as the number of words.

The results clearly show that the topic based query refinement is able to identify some meaningful and very discriminating topic, since the first iteration: in fact the maximum number of documents related to each of the top 8 topics in the reported example is 2. In order to evaluate if the relevant information is actually returned in the answer set, we asked a group of students to judge the relevance of each document in the result set w.r.t. the original query plus the selected topic. Around 92% of the documents were considered really relevant while 84% of the answers were considered satisfying.

Table 2. Identified topics

Topic	Δ	P	f	w
used car values	0.623	2	4	3
car reviews	0.612	2	4	2
find new cars	0.599	1	2	3
car loan calculator	0.599	1	2	3
premium cars	0.589	1	2	2
midsize cars	0.599	1	2	3
msn autos	0.573	1	3	2
dollar rent a car	0.560	1	2	4

$$q_1 = \text{``car''}$$

Topic	Δ	P	f	w
national museum	0.736	2	7	2
bishop museum	0.695	1	4	2
nobel prize	0.625	1	5	2
asian art museum	0.617	1	3	3
design museum	0.607	1	3	2
american museum	0.571	2	4	2
san francisco museum	0.509	1	2	3
science museum	0.500	1	2	2

$$q_2 = \text{``museum''}$$

6 Conclusions

In this paper, we have presented a novel information retrieval system from the web based on an interactive paradigm. In particular, we have extended a classic search engine with some semantic capabilities and query refinements techniques, trying to identify the main topics the users are interested in. We have also described some preliminary experiments using a prototypal system. Further investigation should be devoted first to conduct a more extensive experimentation and then to integrate management of multimedia data into the system.

References

1. S. Abney, M. Collins, and A. Singhal. Answer extraction. In *Proceedings of the 6th Applied Natural Language Processing Conference (ANLP 2000)*, pages 296–301, 2000.
2. R. Baeza-Yates and B. Ribeiro-Neto. *Modern Information Retrieaval*. ACM Press, 1999.
3. J. Callan and T. Mitamura. Knowledge-based extraction of named entities. In *Proceedings of the 4th International Conference on Information and Knowledege Management (CIKM'02)*, pages 532–537, November 1998.
4. M. Carey, F. Kriwaczek, and S. Ruger. A visualization interface for document searching and browsing. In *Proceedings of CIKM 2000 Workshop on New Paradigms in Information Visualization and Manipulation*, 2000.
5. J. Chen, A. R. Diekema, M. D. Taffet, N. McCracken, N. E. Ozgencil, O. Yilmazel, and E. D. Liddy. Question answering: CLNP at the TREC-10 question answering track. In *Proceedings of the 10th Text REtrieval Conference (TREC 2001)*, pages 296–301, 2002.
6. H. Chu. *Information Representation and Retrieval in the Digital Age*. Information Today Inc., 2003.
7. S. Dumais, M. Banko, E. Brill, J. Lin, and A. Ng. Web question answering: Is more always better? In *Proceedings of the 25th annual international ACM SIGIR conference on Research and development in information retrieval*, August 2002.
8. V. Estivill-Castro. Why so many clustering algorithms - a position paper. *SIGKDD Explorations*, 4(1):65–75, 2002.

9. L. Finkelstein, E. Gabrilovich, Y. Matias, E. Rivlin, Z. Solan, G. Wolfman, and E. Ruppin. Placing search in context: the concept revisited. In *Proceeding of the Tenth International World Wide Web Conference*, pages 406–414, 2001.

10. M. Fuller, M. Kaszkiel, C. Ng, M. Wu, J. Zobel, D. Kim, J. Robertson, and R. Wilkinson. Ad hoc, speech and interactive tracks at mds/csiro. In *Proceedings of the 7th Text REtrieval Conference (TREC-7)*, pages 465–474, 1998.

11. T. R. Gruber. A translation approach to portable ontology specifications. *Knowledge Acquisition*, 5(2):199–220, June 1993.

12. M. Halliday and R. Hasan. *Cohesion In English*. Longman, 1976.

13. K. Kummamuru, R. Lotlikar, S. Roy, K. Singal, and R. Krishnapuram. A hierarchical monothetic document clustering algorithm for summarization and browsing search results. In *Proceedings of the 13th international conference on World Wide Web (WWW 2004)*, pages 658–665, 2004.

14. Y. Li, Z. A. Bandar, and D. McLean. An approach for measuring semantic similarity between words using multiple information sources. *IEEE Transactions on Knowledge and Data Engineering*, 15(4):871–882, July/August 2003.

15. A. P. M. Albanese and A. M. Rinaldi. A semantic search engine for web information retrieval: an approach based on dynamic semantic networks. In *Proceedings of SIGIR Semantic Web and Information Retrieval Workshop (SWIR 2004)*, July 2004.

16. M. J. Mana-Lopez, M. De Buenaga, and J. M. Gomez-Hidalgo. Multidocument summarization: An added value to clustering in interactive retrieval. *ACM Transactions on Information Systems*, 22(2):215–241, April 2004.

17. G. A. Miller. Wordnet: a lexical database for english. *Communications of the ACM*, 38(11):39–41, November 1995.

18. D. I. Moldovan and R. Mihalcea. Using WordNet and lexical operators to improve internet searches. *IEEE Internet Computing*, 4(1):34–43, 2000.

19. R. Neches, R. Fikes, T. Finin, T. Gruber, R. Patil, T. Senator, and W. R. Swartout. Enabling technology for knowledge sharing. *AI Magazine*, 12(3):36–56, September 1991.

20. P. Pantel and D. Lin. Clustering: Document clustering with committees. In *Proceedings of the 25th annual international ACM SIGIR conference on Research and development in information retrieval (Tampere)*, pages 199–206, August 2002.

21. D. Paranjpe, G. Ramakrishnan, and S. Srinivasan. Passage scoring for question answering via bayesian inference on lexical relations. In *Proceedings of the 12th Text REtrieval Conference (TREC 2003)*, pages 305–310, 2004.

22. D. Roussinov and J. Robles. Web question answering through automatically learned patterns. In *Proceedings of the 4th ACM/IEEE-CS joint conference on Digital libraries*, pages 347–348, June 2004.

23. G. Salton and C. Buckley. Improving retrieval performance by relevance feedback. *Journal of the American Society for Information Science*, 41(4):288297, 1990.

24. R. N. Shepard. Towards a universal law of generalisation for psychological science. *Science*, 237:1317–1323, 1987.

25. A. Sheth, C. Bertram, D. Avant, B. Hammond, K. Kochut, and Y. Warke. Managing semantic content for the web. *IEEE Internet Computing*, 6(4):80–87, 2002.

26. M. Stairmand. *A Computational Analysis of Lexical Cohesion with applications in Information Retrieval*. PhD thesis, Centre for Computational Linguistics, UMIST, Manchester, 1996.

27. K. Sumi, Y. Sumi, K. Mase, S. ichi Nakasuka, and K. Hori. Takealook: Personalizing information presentation according to user's interest space. In *Proceedings of the IEEE International Conference on Systems, Man and Cybernetics (SCM'99)*, volume 2, pages 354–359, October 1999.

28. M. Sussna. Word sense disambiguation for free-text indexing using a massive semantic network. In *CIKM '93: Proceedings of the second international conference on Information and knowledge management*, pages 67–74, New York, NY, USA, 1993. ACM Press.

29. P.-H. Wang, J.-Y. Wang, and H.-M. Lee. QueryFind: Search ranking based on users'feedback and expert's agreement. In *Proceedings of the 2004 IEEE International Conference on e-Technology, e-Commerce and e-Service (EEE'04)*, 2004.

30. M. Wu, M. Fuller, and R. Wilkinson. Using clustering and classification approaches in interactive retrieval. In *Inf. Proc. Manage*, volume 3, pages 459–484, 2001.

31. O. Zamir and O. Etzioni. Web document clustering: a feasibility demonstration. In *Proceedings of the 21th Annual International ACM/SIGIR Conference on Research and Developement in Information Retrieval*, pages 46–54, 1998.

A Rule Based Approach to Message Board Topics Classification

Fabrizio Antonelli and Maria Luisa Sapino

Università degli Studi di Torino
`antonelli.fabrizio@educ.di.unito.it, mlsapino@di.unito.it`

Abstract. The importance of web discussion boards is growing with the interest of sharing knowledge and doubts with colleagues in a working/studying environment. The challenge is to organize the structure of discussion boards, to make the navigation easier, and to effectively extract relevant information. Message hierarchies in web discussion boards, manually organised by users participating into the discussion, might grow uncontrolled, thus making navigation more and more difficult for users. The goal of this paper is to develop a technique to organise messages in a message board, by automatically classifying and annotating pairs of postings to guide users through discussion segments relevant to their navigational goals.

1 Introduction

The World Wide Web is the widest source of information for users and many, organizations (such as companies, universities, schools, e-learning societies) are developing tools to enable their users share and exchange internal information and to improve on their working /study activity. One of the most important tools in this category is the discussion board, a place where every user can post a message to start a discussion, to provide answers to questions, etc. It is very common for the discussion boards to contain postings about several different topics at the same time and it is difficult for a user to latch on if there is one specific topic which he can contribute to or can extract information from. Suppose a user of a discussion board wants to know if anybody knows the answer to a specific question or can provide suggestions about a specific subject. It would be very convenient for the user if the system could assist by providing her with a list of postings matching her interests (based on the criteria she gave), without making her scan the entire board.

Text mining techniques [LCN03] [Cohen96] have been successfully developed and applied in many business intelligence applications. Discussion records, however, cannot fully benefit from these techniques, because of their subtle, often implicit, dependences upon each other. It is often the case that an individual posting carries a very limited amount of information (which makes text mining techniques of very little use on such postings), whereas a collection of inter-related postings in the board forms a context, which carries more information, if properly identified. Moreover, standard text mining techniques and indexing solutions do not apply to message boards since the collections of messages are highly dynamic.

K.S. Candan and A. Celentano (Eds.): MIS 2005, LNCS 3665, pp. 33–48, 2005.
© Springer-Verlag Berlin Heidelberg 2005

The challenge, in this case, is the discovery and organization of such information possibly coming from different messages, given the fact that (i) several different topics can be discussed in a single message, whose title/subject is not necessarily required to match the message content, and (ii) different aspects of the same topic may be found in various postings.

In this paper, we address the problem of *knowledge discovery from message-boards*. More specifically, we concentrate on the problems of classifying the posted messages and discovering different relationships among messages posted on the board. Based on the resulting classification, appropriate indexing techniques can be developed to improve the information accessibility.

As an important step towards information extraction from message boards, an innovative technique for topic segmentation of message hierarchies has been developed in [KCD05]. The method is mainly based on the information explicitly given in the postings, i.e., the relevant keywords and quotations. We propose to couple this type of analysis with a pre-processing phase in which informative elements, which are implicit in the messages, are extracted [CKP04]. These informative elements include, information coming from the document format, from the presence of links within the text, from the number of messages already written by the author, etc.

The logical organization of the messages is described by means of a labeled graph, whose nodes are associated to the postings and whose labeled edges characterize the different inter-dependency relations existing between messages. The use of the graph, as opposed to the original tree structure, makes navigation more flexible. The insertion and labeling of the edges are realized by means of a rule based system (JESS), which associates (possibly multiple) scores to the automatically extracted interdependency relations between pairs of messages. Among all possible labels for a given pair, the one with the highest score is chosen as the assigned classification for the relationship between messages. One of the advantages of the use of a rule based system is its dynamic adaptation to the board content [LKVT00]: at any point in time, the arrival of new messages might fire some previously inhibited rules and induce an appropriate revision /update of the classification for some message, on the basis of the newly added information.

The paper is organized as follows. In Section 2 we give a brief overview of the related work. In Section 3 we introduce the architecture of the proposed system. Section 4 formalizes the data structure we use to address the classification problem. The rule based classification module is presented in Section 5. Section 6 discusses the implementation issues and Section 7 illustrates experimental results. Finally, Section 8 contains concluding remarks.

2   Related Work

The problem of classifying and indexing messages in a message board is strongly related to the one of classifying and indexing web documents or pages. Postings in discussion boards are in general much more heterogeneous and their informative content is not always structured and easily available. Thus, it is hard (or even impossible), in general, to extract keywords and detect a structure over the messages, to make them accessible through search engines [YP97]. Furthermore, what users are usually looking for is a conceptual relationship [CL01] among postings, such as "an answer to...", not just keywords. Unfortunately, postings do not embed in the text their explicit relationships with the others.

The problem of identifying the boundaries of topics in discussion boards and their inner classifications has been addressed by Murakami, Nagao and Takeda in [MTN01]. Based on the idea of extracting information from the postings by analyzing the relationships among fragments of text contained in the messages, they compute the distance among quoted texts in messages. The goal is to relate the quoted parts of different postings to discover their mutual correlation. We expand on this idea and try to go beyond the simple comparison of quoted text (which, in some cases, does not even exist or does not contain enough informative content, since users are not necessarily required to use quotations) to capture a number of additional elements to recognize the relationships among the postings in a thread. Like [MTN01], we use a graph as the data structure to represent the available knowledge.

A relevant work on topic segmentation in message boards is [KCD05], where the authors define the segmentation problem as "searching for special nodes – which are the entry points to new, general, or specific topics – within a single hierarchy of dynamically evolving web content". The core of the approach is to first identify the boundaries of topics, by analyzing the keyword vectors of the postings, and then segmenting the topics to discover specialization /generalization relationships between directed linked postings. Our main enhancement over this work is the introduction of an automated offline system to highlight the topic boundaries and their internal organization, based on additional structural aspects. In addition to the aspects considered in [KCD05], we take into account the fact that, even if certain postings might be too short to have a large informative content (and to be characterized in terms of significant keyword vectors [MG98]), they might still carry information, if considered with respect to some other message. Also, a classification only based on specialization/generalization might not necessarily capture the conceptual organization of the board.

Another approach to classifying message board content has been presented in [AK04]. This approach suggests the use of a formal representation of documents as linear combination of term vectors extracted from the entire corpus of postings. Each term is assigned a frequency and a weight. These are combined to compute a posting score to be used as a discriminator in classification. The paper aims at identifying postings about the increase or decrease of a company's trading volume; therefore, there are only two interesting classes. The intuition of using special terms for analysis is interesting, but the approach has three main limitations. First, each posting is evaluated in isolation from the others; second, the method relies on a set of 15 different parameters to evaluate every single posting, which makes it very complex in practice; and third, the method can not be generalized to other domains or purposes.

3   System Architecture

In this section, we introduce the overall architecture of the proposed system, which is partially based on the one proposed in [KCD05]. Our system differs from [KCD05],

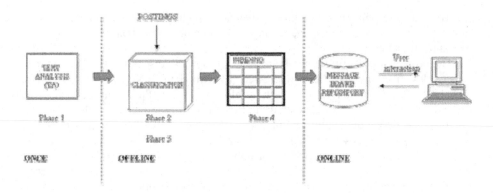

Fig. 1. A representation of the 4-phase architecture of the system

because of (i) the introduction of the first step, devoted to the statistical analysis of the text in postings and (ii) the choice of using the rule based system to assign (multiple) classification labels to messages. The architecture we describe here represents the global plan of the work we are conducting on this topic. In this paper, we only focus on the first two steps of the classification process. These represent the main innovations over the approach in [KCD05]. Figure 1 schematically represents the architecture.

The **Text Analysis** module performs a statistical analysis of the text of the postings in the message board, to discover the patterns contained in the different postings. The goal of the statistical analysis is to extract a set of rules that can describe the general behavior of the authors of the board (see Figure 2). The analysis takes into account the possible use of some specific words, relevant to the application domain, their repetition, etc. The analysis has to be conducted *manually,* or semi-automatically, with the help of a domain expert.

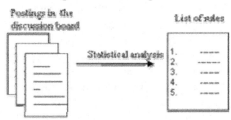

Fig. 2. The Text Analysis process

Extracted rules should be as general as possible. Therefore, we require the analysis to be done across-the board, instead of being done per-user. The challenge is to use to the best posting patterns and to extract the most informative content (rules) from them. In this paper, we consider message boards of a university course discussion forum. In this context, based on the analysis of a few hundred messages, we identified eleven different rules (which we will discuss in section 5.2). Each rule is based on a different aspect of the analyzed postings (words used, presence of HTML tagged terms, presence of URL links, etc.)

The rules codifying the patterns extracted by the domain experts are further analyzed with the goal of measuring their extent and validity. The result of this step is an *assignment function*, which associates to every rule a numeric value representing the degree of discrimination it carries. To do this, we represent the discussion board as a

graph, in which the nodes represent the postings and the edges represent the relationship between them (Figure 3). The existence of an edge between any pairs of nodes represents the fact that the two messages are related to each other in some way. Many different reasons may support the relationships between two messages. To take them into account, we associate to every edge a list of pair-labels *<tag,score>*, in which *tag* qualifies the type of relationship and *score* is a numeric value which represents the confidence associated to this tag.

Given the University course domain we are considering, we choose to consider the following tags: *ANNOUNCEMENT* for postings introducing an announcement, like a news on an event, a discovery, an experience, etc...; *QUESTION*, for postings containing one or more requests on a specific topic; *ANSWER*, for postings that give a direct answer to any question that had been posted earlier; *CUE*, for a suggestion on a topic introduced by someone else. Differently from an ANSWER message, a CUE does not necessarily give the final information asked by a question, while it provides relevant information and suggestions about doubts coming from previous messages. Finally, *RELATED,* captures for postings giving relevant information related to the topics mentioned in previous messages.

The **Classification** module organizes the information on which the indexing will be based. First, the **Rule-based classifier** applies the rules, extracted in the previous step to classify the relationship among different postings, on the basis of their informative content. For this purpose, the postings are formalized as facts populating the working memory of the rule-based system. Relevant information (to be coded in the working memory) is semi-automatically extracted from the messages, by parsing tools (e.g. STPT, SAS® Text Miner, TextPipe Pro). During the analysis, the labeling can dynamically change: the scores associated to different tags can be updated as the result of the application of the classification rules. The rule based classifier can revise the scores associated to the initial tag. More interestingly, it can discover new relationships that were not evident to the initial manual annotator.

The **commitment of the relationships among postings** completes the classification. After having tagged each edge in the original graph G (associated to the discussion board), a new graph G' is created. The new graph is derived from the initial one by the addition of the tags according to the results of the rule-based systems. The addition of those edges represents newly discovered relationships, detected by the inference engine. Notice that some existing *parent-child* edges in the original tree-structured graph might not be assigned any meaningful classification tag. In these cases, the child node corresponds to a new *entry point* of discussion. In this graph, some nodes might be shared among different topic discussion threads.

The last module of the architecture is the **Message board indexing** module. As a side effect of the classification process, a number of entry points are identified in the message board. These entry points will be the targets pointed by the corresponding topic in the index structure. Therefore, boundaries of the topics will be easily detected during navigation in the graph. Therefore, the navigation is more informed. In particular, it is reduced to a two-level access. First, the external index is used to access a specific topic through its entry point (for example a topic leading with an integrative course of Security, having as entry point a posting titled "An extension to the Security course program"). Then, following the tagged edges (manually or through a query to the system), the user will access the information of interest.

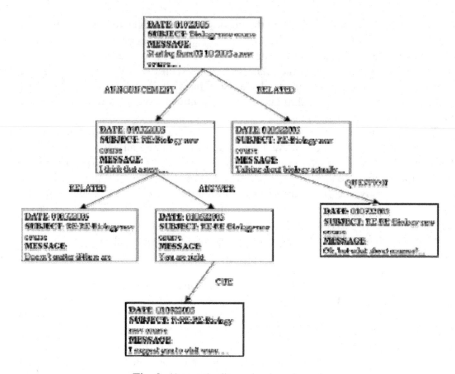

Fig. 3. A` sample discussion board graph

4   Structure of the Discussion Board

In this section we formalize the problem we are addressing and the data structure on which our classification algorithm is based.

Definition: (**Discussion Graph**)   The discussion graph is a (non labeled) directed acyclic graph G=(P,E) where P = {p_1 , p_2, ... , p_n}, the set of vertices, represents single postings populating the board. E = { (p_i,p_j) / p_i, p_j ∈ P} is the set of edges, which connect different postings (see Figure 4).

The Discussion Graph represents the initial structure of the discussion board. It has a tree structure, since the only inter-node relationship known at the beginning represents the fact that a given posting p_j has been written in reply to message p_i. In this case, p_i is the parent of p_j.

Initially, the graph is not labeled. Labels will be added by the classification engine and will qualify the role that the different postings play with respect to the other related postings. While we can assume that the author of a posted message explicitly lists (and maybe quotes) the previously posted messages that he is referring to in his contribution (thus further enriching the structure of the graph), we cannot expect any explicit contribution to the classification. In principle, the author is not even aware of the classification process being conducted and is not required to declare the meaning of the relationship between the posting he is writing and the one he is replying to.

The classification process will derive an enriched discussion graph from the given discussion graph.

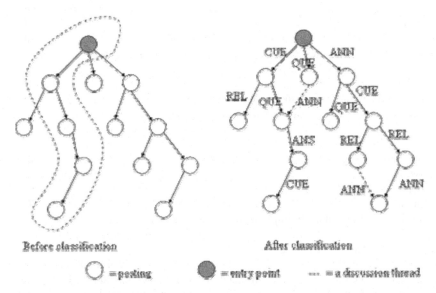

Before classification   After classification

○ = posting   ● = entry point   --- = a discussion thread

Fig. 4. The graph G, on the left, before the classification of edges. The graph G' on the right.

Definition: (***Enriched Discussion Graph***) Given a discussion graph $G=(P,E)$, its *enriched* version is the labeled graph $G'=(P',E')$, where $P' = P$, and $E' \supseteq E$. Edges in E'- E reflect relationships discovered during the classification process. Edges in E' are labeled to capture the semantic role the target node plays in the relationships with the source node. The labeling induces a partition of the edges,

$$E' = E_A \cup E_C \cup E_S \cup E_Q \cup E_R \cup E_E, \quad \text{where}$$

$E_A = \{(p_i,p_j) \mid p_i, p_j \in P, \quad p_j \text{ ANNOUNCEMENT } p_i \}$

$E_C = \{(p_i,p_j) \mid p_i, p_j \in P, \quad p_j \text{ CUE } p_i \}$

$E_S = \{(p_i,p_j) \mid p_i, p_j \in P, \quad p_j \text{ ANSWER } p_i \}$

$E_Q = \{(p_i,p_j) \mid p_i, p_j \in P, \quad p_j \text{ QUESTION } p_i \}$

$E_R = \{(p_i,p_j) \mid p_i, p_j \in P, \quad p_j \text{ RELATED } p_i \}$

$E_E = \{(p_i,p_j) \in E, \quad p_j \text{ ENTRY\_POINT } p_i \}$

The enriched graph G' for the discussion graph G is likely to loose the original tree structure since the classification engine is likely to find interesting connections between pairs of postings at different, non necessarily consecutive, levels.

On the enriched graph, edges are labeled as entry points if (i) they are parent-child edges appearing in the given discussion graph and (ii) no semantically meaningful relationships between the two connected nodes have been discovered.

5 The Rule Based Classification Module

In our approach, we aim at mimicking the reasoning patterns adopted by human be-ings, when they try to classify the messages. We aim at discovering pairs of related messages in the board and partitioning these relationships into 5 classes. Considering a message *m*, any other message referring to it can be interesting because of the event it talks about (ANNOUNCEMENT message), because of a question it asks (QUESTION message), because of a suggestion it gives (CUE message), because it strongly confirms or denies some statement in the message it replies to (ANSWER message), or just because it has a related content (RELATED message).

It is important to note that even for human beings, the relevant class for a given in-ter-message relationships is not always uniquely determined. Consider, for example, a message containing the following sentence: *"Did you look at the paper http://www.bibliosite/file.pdf ?"*, which might come in reply to a help request. We could have good reasons (the syntactical form, with the question mark at the end of the sentence) to think of the message as a QUESTION message. On the other hand, the question can be seen as an implicit way to give an advice: *"in case of negative re-ply, please have a look at the recommended paper..."*, which would support the clas-sification of the message as a CUE message.

Such potential multiple classifications of relationships is one of the motivations for the choice of a rule based system as the core of our architecture. Rules allow to assign the same pair to multiple classes, with different confidence for distinct classes, and to dynamically adapt the confidence values to take into account the information avail-able at any future point in time. The representative class for a pair will be the one with the higher confidence.

5.1 Introduction to Rule Based Systems

In rule based systems, the reasoning mechanisms typically adopted by human domain experts are coded in a set of *if-then-statements, i.e,* the rules of the system. These rules are used to infer new knowledge on the basis of the currently available informa-tion, expressed by means of a set of initial assertions. A rule based system has the fol-lowing fundamental components.

(i) A set of assertions collectively forms the '**working memory**' and represents the knowledge/information on which the reasoning is based. The initial working memory is a set of facts which describe the initial data on which the system will base its reasoning activity. In our case, the facts in the initial working memory represent a formal description of the postings contained in the message board.

(ii) A set of **rules** specifies how to act on the assertion set. Rules can be seen as *if-then statements*, which encode the knowledge of a domain expert, with the goal of reproducing the reasoning schema that a human expert would apply in the presence of the data currently available. In our case, the rules are used to classify the relationships among different postings (e.g. message m_1 is a reply to message m_2).

(iii) A **termination condition** determines that a solution has been found or con-cludes that no solution exists. In our case, the termination condition represents the fact that all currently available postings have been analysed.

The activity of a rule based system can be described as a loop, which ends when the termination condition is reached. Every iteration of the loop acts through the following steps. First, all (IF) conditions of the rules are checked to isolate the set of conditions which are satisfied with respect to the current working memory. If the identified set is empty, the system stops (even if the specified termination condition is not reached yet). Otherwise, from the set of applicable rules (called the conflict set), one candidate will be chosen to be fired. The choice of the rule, among all the candidates in the conflict set, to be triggered depends on the conflict resolution strategy employed by the system. In our case, we use the **Best rule** as the conflict resolution strategy: each rule is given a 'salience', which specifies how strong it should be considered over the alternatives; therefore, the rule with the highest salience is chosen. When the selected rule is fired, all the actions specified in its THEN clause are carried out. These actions can have multiple effects on different targets. In some cases, they simply modify the working memory. In other cases, they also update the rule-base or execute any other actions coded by the system programmer in the THEN clause.

5.2 The Classification Algorithm

Based on the text analysis of our postings, from a university course discussion board, we have extracted a set, R, of rules containing eleven *if-then-statements* each one dealing with a different aspect of the postings' structure. These are the rules of our classifier module. Each edge connecting two contiguous vertices (i.e., postings) will be classified as an ANNOUNCEMENT, a QUESTION, an ANSWER, a CUE, a RELATED edge, or an ENTRY_POINT. In principle, the same message can belong to more than one of the listed classes, with a different degree of membership. We use scores for labels (representing classes) to denote the confidence associated to the membership to the corresponding class. The final use of the scores is in the choice of the classification for each given edge: we use the classification with the highest score.

Each rule can contribute to the definition/update of the score of the edges in the enriched graph being constructed. In particular, any rule r considers a specific aspect (or a specific set of aspects) of the posting structure being analyzed and being related to the other existing postings. As a consequence, the rule will affect the classification of the relationships between that posting and the other ones, with respect to the specific aspects being taken into account. The contribution that a rule can give is associated to the rules by means of a *labeling contribution matrix*, as follows.

Definition: **(Labeling contribution matrix)** Given a set of rules $R = \{r_1, r_2, ..., r_k\}$, and a set of *labels* $L = \{l_1, l_2, ..., l_m\}$, a labeling contribution matrix for R and L is a k×m matrix, Δ, such that $\Delta [r,l]$ represents the contribution that the rule r can give to the score of an edge with label l ($\Delta [r,l]=0$ whenever the rule r is not contributing to the score of any edge labeled l, since the aspects it is considering are completely unrelated to the semantic meaning associated with the label).

Intuitively, a value $\Delta [r,l]$ in the labeling contribution matrix can be seen as a parameter for a function that, when the rule r is fired, determines the new score for the label l on an edge, based on the previously existing value, and $\Delta [r,l]$. In our classifier, we have 11 rules and 5 labels Therefore, the labeling contribution matrix is an 11×5 matrix (See Table 1).

Definition: **(Scoring function)** Given a discussion graph G (P,E), a set of rules $R = \{r_1, r_2, ..., r_k\}$, a set of *labels* $L = \{l_1, l_2, ..., l_m\}$, and the corresponding labeling contribution matrix Δ, the scoring function *Score*: $L \rightarrow (P{\times}P \rightarrow Real)$ is defined as

$$\text{Score (1) } (p_i, p_j) = \sum_{r \in R} \Delta[r, l] \bullet C_r ,$$

where $C_r \in \{0, 1\}$, is used to distinguish the rules that have been fired ($C_r = 1$) from the ones which have not been fired ($C_r = 0$).

Table 1. The Labeling Contribution Matrix values table

Rule	Δ_A	Δ_C	Δ_S	Δ_Q	Δ_R
1. Similarity among posting keywords (n is the number of equal keywords)	0	+10*n	+10*n	+3*n	+10*n
2. Existence of a URL link	+8	+8	0	0	+8
3. Existence in the URL link path of special words (domain dependent – e.g. education, course, etc.)	+6	+10	0	0	0
4. Similarity among the keywords of a posting and the title of the web page linked by a URL link	+8	+4	0	0	+8
5. Similarity among the HTML tagged words of a posting and the title of the web page linked by a URL link	+5	+2	0	0	+5
6. Similarity among the keywords of a posting and the meta-tag of the web page linked by a URL link (n is the number of equal keywords)	+4	0	+7	0	0
7. Number of intervention of the author of the posting (p is the number of posting written)	0	0	0	+p	+p
8. The author of the posting is the author of the entry point too	+5	0	0	+5	0
9. Number of the question marks in the posting (q is the number of the question marks)	0	0	0	+4*q	0
10. Presence of quotations in the text*	0	0	+30%	+20%	0
11. Short answers, containing special terms like thanks, I agree, yes, etc.*	0	0	+30	0	0

* The Δ is applied only if in the (p_i, p_j) edge, p_j is the direct father or p_i in the graph G

Table 1 contains a compact representation of the classification rules applicable to any edge (p_i, p_j) in the discussion graph. In the first column of the table the aspects/criteria checked by the eleven rules are listed. The following five columns are each associated to a specific class: ANNOUNCEMENT, CUE, ANSWER, QUESTION, RELATED. These five columns are our labeling contribution matrix.

For the sake of space, we do not comment exhaustively on all of the eleven rows of the table. Instead, we only comment on a sample rule, Rule #2, summarized in the second row:

- Rule #2 is activated if in the text of the posting, a URL link has been recognized (other than the link to the sender's home page, possibly appearing in his signature). Usually URL links are inserted in the postings to suggest a reading, to give information about something new, or to notify about an event. Hence, the more appropriate classification for the edges having that posting as destination is ANNOUNCEMENT, CUE, or RELATED. We assume that the three mentioned classes are equally likely and associate to them the value +8, meaning that when the rule is fired the corresponding scores should be increased 8 units. Nothing can be inferred for the other classes with this rule, thus the corresponding increments are zero.

It is important to note that the values appearing in the matrix depend on the considered domain (the same classification rules can result in very different classification parameters if applied to a different domain) and reflect the sensitivity and the experience of some domain expert who set their initial values. For this reason, before the actual classification on the entire discussion board, the classifier needs to go through a training phase, in which a subset of heterogeneous messages are classified and the matrix values are properly adjusted by means of a relevance feedback module (see Figure 5).

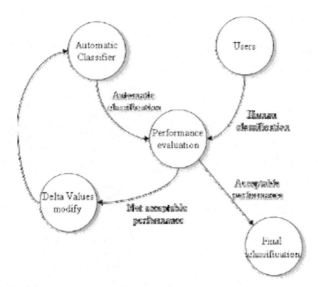

Fig. 5. The relevance feedback based improving process

6 Implementation

The inferential engine of the classification system has been developed using Jess, a rule engine and scripting environment written in Sun's Java™ language, inspired by the CLIPS expert system shell. The code is available at the link http://www.di.unito.it/~mlsapino/message-board/classify.txt. Figure 6 shows example rule, Rule#2 discussed earlier.

```
(defrule #2_exists_URL_link
      (declare (salience 18))
      (url_link (post_ID ?id))
      ?f1<-(score (post_ID ?id)(type announcement)(value ?v1))
      ?f2<-(score (post_ID ?id)(type cue)(value ?v2))
      ?f3<-(score (post_ID ?id)(type related)(value ?v3))
      (not (done (op link_check)(arg1 ?id)))
   =>
      (modify ?f1 (value (+ ?v1 8)))
      (modify ?f2 (value (+ ?v2 8)))
      (modify ?f3 (value (+ ?v3 8)))
      (assert(done (op link_check)(arg1 ?id))))
```

Fig. 6. An example of classification rule

To describe the actual behaviour of the classifier we rely on a pseudo-code description of the module, containing the rules that can be applied (see Fig.7).

MAIN
max_value , min_value $\in N$
CHOOSE ENTRYPOINT
level L = 0;
EP = a new entry-point
If (there is no new entry point)
{end classification}
CONTROL LEVEL
L = L + 1
CREATE SCORE
∀ p_i of level L with entry-point EP
{∀ p_j of level L-1 with entry-point EP
{ new $S_A(p_i,p_j) = 0$
new $S_C(p_i,p_j) = 0$
....
new $S_R(p_i,p_j) = 0$ } }
If (there are no scores to create)
{pop-focus to NEW ENTRYPOINT}

CLASSIFY
∀ rule $r_i \in R$)
{ ∀ (p_i,p_j) having a score

{ $S_A(p_i,p_j) = S_A(p_i,p_j) + \Delta[r,A] * C_r$
$S_C(p_i,p_j) = S_C(p_i,p_j) + \Delta[r,C] * C_r$
...
$S_R(p_i,p_j) = S_R(p_i,p_j) + \Delta[r,R] * C_r$}}

CHOICE
∀ score $S_t(p_i,p_j)$
{choose highest $S_h(p_i,p_j)$}
If (p_j is the father of p_i in G)
{ If ($S_h(p_i,p_j) < min\_value$)
{ focus NEW ENTRYPOINT }
else {classify (p_i,p_j) as type h}}
Else
{If ($S_h(p_i,p_j) > max\_value$)
{classify (p_i,p_j) as type h}
Else
{discard classification for (p_i,p_j)}
pop-focus to CONTROL LEVEL
NEW ENTRYPOINT
∀ p_i reachable from new entry point
{$p_i.level=p_i.level$ new_entrypoint.level
$p_i.ep=$ new_entrypoint }

Fig. 7. The algorithm in pseudo-code

In the **CHOOSE ENTRYPOINT** module, the choice of the candidate entry points is made on the basis of the title. Each posting having a title with no reference to any other previously existing postings (e.g. "Program of lessons of Prof. Kert") is considered as an entry point and the other postings in the hierarchy are analyzed starting from it. The level number for postings is derived from the number of nested REPLY tags as "R:" or "Re:" in the title. Thus, a posting having title "Re: Re: Program of lessons of Prof. Kert" is assigned level 2.

In the **CREATE SCORE** module, a score is created for every possible classification and for every edge connecting a posting of the selected level to another in the previous level. If no more score can be created, we conclude that the maximum depth of the hierarchy for the selected entry point has been reached. At this point, another entry point will be chosen for classification.

During classification, a new entry point can be identified if no connection with his direct parent is strong enough (i.e., is above a given threshold). The **NEW ENTRYPOINT** module records the posting to be identified as entry point and changes all the postings reachable from this on, to have a new entry point and a coherent level.

7 Experimental Results

For evaluation purposes, we have compared the rule based classification results for a computer science course discussion board, with the human classification obtained from a user study on 18 computer science students. Users were asked to classify a discussion board (100 messages from a course messageboard for a course at the Arizona State University). During their survey, users could only select one of the possible classes (QUESTION, ANSWER, CUE, ANNOUNCEMENT, RELATED) on the basis of the most relevant features of each posting in the context of the thread it belongs to. Students taking part to the experiment had been informed about the meaning we assign to the different labels, but did not know about the underlying scoring mechanism.

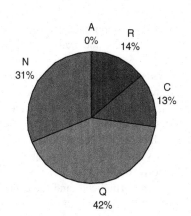

Fig. 8. Class Distribution in the Discussion Board used for experimentation

The distribution of the classes (according to the users) among the postings was not uniform (see Figure 8). A relevant aspect is the lack of postings classified as ANNOUNCEMENT: most of the potential ANNOUNCEMENT postings have been recognized as RELATED by the users. This can be caused by the fact that the (Italian) users did not tell clearly the difference between the two classes or to the fact that during their standard use of a discussion board, these users would not pay any attention to this distinction. We are currently investigation ways to improve the classification scheme.

For each class c_i the precision value has been computed as

$$prec(c_i) = \frac{users\_posting\,(c_i) \cap system\_posting\,(c_i)}{users\_posting\,(c_i)}$$

The comparision of the user's classification and the system results are quite satisfactory: the system is well aligned with the users when question/answer relation ships are considered (representing the 73% of the total postings), with an agreement exceeding 80%. The overall precision is 77,14%: a user could expect to have a correct matching between his query and the system answer almost 8 times out of 10.Table 2 shows the precision values calculated for each different class.

Table 2. Precision values

Class	Precision
Question (Q)	0,972
Answer (N)	0,719
Cue (C)	0,725
Related (I)	0,667

8 Conclusions

In this paper, we have presented an architecture to simplify the access to messages in a (university) discussion board and proposed an effective approach for the first two steps of the architecture, concerning message text analysis and automatic message classification.

Our approach relies on a rule based system. In this paper, we have commented on the classification algorithm, whose core aspects are (i) the detection of the relevant labels for the considered domain; (ii) the formalization of the classifying rules, and (iii) the choice of the proper values to be used in score update functions. The choice of a rule based system as the classification engine has the important advantage of allowing a high degree of modularity in the system development. If a new label is identified to be relevant to the considered domain, the corresponding label can be added to the system, the criteria characterising this label can be formalized, and the classification rules whose IF condition tests the aspects which are relevant to the new criteria can be inserted to the rule-base. The overall classification will self-adjust with the firing of those rules which are triggered as a consequence of the new ones. Similarly, the insertion of new messages in the board will result in an incremental application of the rules to relate the new message to the currently existing ones. The user studies we conducted provided encouraging results and suggested a number of possible extensions: for example, we plan to merge (by identifying them) independent entry points which are about the same topic; we also plan to check, during the format analysis, the presence of attachments, and to further detail the classification of the entry points, by means of a second level of classification on these messages, to better qualify postings that are not related to their ancestors (and thus are entry-points) but can be further partitioned based on their content. For example, we plan to distinguish entry-points which are questions from entry-points which are announcements. As a longer term future work, we also plan to (a) implement a user-friendly interface to make it easier for the trainer user to provide feedback during the definition of the contribution matrix, (b) to develop a new training phase for the system, in which the values in the matrix are automatically assigned on the basis of a compiled training set. Of course, our ultimate goal is integrating these modules in the general architecture, along with an appropriate indexing mechanisms and user friendly interfaces for access and navigation.

Acknowledgements

We thank Prof. Piero Torasso for introducing Fabrizio Antonelli (who started working on the project as an undergraduate student) to rule based systems and for the discussion on their appropriateness for classification purposes. We are especially grateful to the students of the course of " Multimedia Databases" at the *Computer Science Department* of *University of Torino*, who took part to the user evaluation session of the project.

References

[AK04] – Aasheim, C. and G.J. Koehler, "Mining Message Board Content on the World Wide Web for Organizational Information," Organizational Data Mining: Leveraging Enterprise Data Resources for Optimal Performance, Editors C. Barko and H. Nemati, 2004, Idea Group, Inc., pp.188-200.

[CL01] – K. S. Candan and W.-S. Li, "Reasoning for web document associations and its applications in site map construction", Int. Journal of Data and Knowledge Engineering, 2002.

[Cohen96] – W. W. Cohen, "Learning rules that classify e-mail", AAAI Spring Symposium on Machine Learning in Information Access, 18—25, 1996

[CKP04] – Elisabeth Crawford, Irena Koprinska, and Jon Patrick. "Phrases and Feature Selection in E-Mail Classification", In the Proceedings of the Australasian Document Computing Symposium,2004.

[KCD05] – Jong Wook Kim, K. Selcuk Candan, Mehmet E. Donderler "Topic Segmentation of Message Hierarchies for Indexing and Navigation Support", WWW2005, Japan, 2005

[LKVT00] – Wen-Syan Li, Okan Kolak, Quoc Vu, and Hajime Takano, "Defining Logical Domains in a Web Site", In Proceedings of the 2000 ACM Hypertext Conference, San Antonio, Texas, USA, May 2000.

[LCN03] - Bing Liu, Chee Wee Chin, Hwee Tou Ng "Mining topic-specific concepts and definitions on the web", Proceedings of the twelfth international conference on World Wide Web, WWW2003, May 20-24, 2003, Budapest, Hungary.

[MG98] – D. Mladenic and M. Grobelnik. "Feature selection for classification based on text hierarchy." In Working notes of Learning from Text and the Web, Conference on Automated Learning and Discovery CONALD-98, Pittsburg, USA, 1998.

[MTN01] – Murakami, A., Takeda, K. and Nagao K. "Discussion Mining:Knowledge Discovery from Online Discussion Records", NLPRS Workshop XML and NLP, 2001

[YP97] – Yang, Pedersen "A Comparative Study on Feature Selection in Text Categorization", Proceedings of the Fourteenth International Conference on Machine Learning table of contents, Pages: 412 – 420, 1997

A Proposal for a Multimedia Data Warehouse

Anne-Muriel Arigon[1,2], Anne Tchounikine[1], and Maryvonne Miquel[1]

[1] LIRIS (Laboratoire d'InfoRmatique en Images et Systèmes d'information),
UMR CNRS 5205,
Bâtiment Blaise Pascal, INSA, 7 avenue Capelle,
69621 Villeurbanne Cedex, France
{anne.tchounikine, maryvonne.miquel}@insa-lyon.fr
[2] LBBE (Laboratoire de Biométrie et Biologie Evolutive) - UMR CNRS 5558,
Université Claude Bernard – Lyon 1, 43 bd. du 11 novembre 1918,
69622 Villeurbanne Cedex, France
arigon@biomserv.univ-lyon1.fr

Abstract. The traditional multidimensional models have a static structure where members of dimensions are computed in a unique way. However, data (particularly multimedia data) is often characterized by descriptors that can be obtained by various computation modes. We define these computation modes as "functional versions" of the descriptors. We propose a Functional Multiversion Multidimensional Model ("F2M model") by integrating the concept of "version of dimension". This concept defines dimensions with members computed according to various functional versions. In order to allow the user to choose the best representation of data, this new approach integrates a choice of computation modes of these members into the model. We implement a multimedia data warehouse in the medical field by integrating the multimedia data of a therapeutic study into a multidimensional model. We formally define a conceptual model and we present a prototype for this study.

1 Introduction

Data Warehouse is a "subject-oriented, integrated, nonvolatile and time-variant collection of data in support of management's decisions" [1]. The aim is to extract relevant data from production databases and to organize them according to an adapted model to improve decision making. Decisional analyses are based on OLAP processes (On-Line Analytical Processing) as defined in [2]. In this approach, information is organized around major subjects and is modeled to make possible precomputation and fast and easy access to summarized data. OLAP treatments refer to analysis functionalities used to explore data. According to Kimball [3], the data-modeling paradigm for a data warehouse must comply with requirements that are very different from the data models in OLTP (On-Line Transactional Processing) environments. Data models have to be easy to understand for the end-user so that the user can write queries easily, and also must maximize the efficiency of queries. These models are called multidimensional models or hypercubes and have been formalized by [4]. They are designed to represent measurable facts or indicators along the various dimensions that characterize these facts. A dimension can be organized according to a hierarchy

K.S. Candan and A. Celentano (Eds.): MIS 2005, LNCS 3665, pp. 49–62, 2005.

and can present various granularities (various degrees of precision) in order to drill-down to a more precise analysis or roll-up to a more abstract analysis (operators roll-up and drill-down) [5]. A dimension is represented by a schema that defines various levels of granularity that are connected by hierarchical links. Each level of dimension is composed of members that represent the entities of the considered dimension. These members are also connected by hierarchical links; this hierarchical structure is the instance of the considered dimension. Aggregated data is the facts computed by using the functions ("count, sum, min, max, avg") according to different granularities. Data aggregations are computed from the fact table and the links between the members. There are several representations of multidimensional structures such as the "star model" and the "snowflake model".

Multidimensional models [3], [4], [6] usually consider facts as the dynamic part of data warehouses, and dimensions as static entities [7]. In such data warehouses, members of dimensions are computed in only one way. However, this can restrict the data analysis, particularly in the case of multimedia data. The multimedia data is bulky data, with various formats (text, graph, video, sound,…). It is generally stored in sequences of bit of different length. This data is generally described by some descriptors and is stored so as to improve their indexing and exploration. So, that requires a specific treatment, adapted visualisation tools and a new definition of aggregated functions relating not on alphanumeric data but on multimedia facts. In multimedia data warehouses, descriptors of multimedia data are the dimensions of the multidimensional model. These descriptors are extracted from the multimedia data. They characterize the data and allow its identification. Two kinds of systems of indexation and research of multimedia documents exist. They are based on different types of descriptors of multimedia data. The first one, called "description-based retrieval system", uses descriptors defined from the description of the data (description-based descriptors) (ex., for images, it can be key words, date of acquisition and in the case of videos it can be author, topic). The second one, called "content-based retrieval system", is based on descriptors representing the content of the data and is computed directly on data (content-based descriptors) [8], [9] (ex., for images, it can be color, texture and in the case of videos, it can be sound, quality). These descriptors are very diversified and the same descriptor can be extracted from multimedia data in various ways. Several algorithms make it possible to compute a descriptor and several classifications provide the possibility to order the values of a descriptor. These computation modes can define functional versions of a descriptor, which makes possible the characterization of the data by various ways. In this case, dimension data should not represent a pre-defined information and must integrate multiple methods to represent data according to the various functional versions of each descriptor. Therefore, it seems to us that the integration of functional versions of dimension (corresponding to the data descriptors computed by different functions) into the model can improve data characterization: this can enable the user to choose the computation modes for each descriptor in order to define the best representation of the data. The aim of our study is to define a multidimensional conceptual model capable of managing multimedia data characterized by descriptors obtained by various computation modes. This model is illustrated by a case study on a medical multimedia data warehouse.

The remainder of the paper is organized as follows. Section 2 provides a study of related work in this research area. Section 3 presents the case study. Section 4 proposes the general principle of our approach and formally defines a conceptual model. In section 5, we present a developed prototype for this study by describing its architecture, a way of adapting our model to a logical and physical level, and its implementation on the case study. Finally, we conclude in section 6.

2 Related Work

Some works about the design of multimedia data cubes were undertaken to improve multidimensional analysis of large multimedia databases. In [10], the authors seek to extend the concept of traditional data warehouses and multimedia databases so as to store and to represent the multimedia data. Another example is the multimedia data analysis system, MultiMediaMiner, which uses a multimedia data cube [11] making it possible to store multidimensional data and to incorporate them on different granularities. In the medical domain, the problems of exploration and analysis of huge multimedia data are omnipresent. For example, we can mention a study undertaken within the domain of breast cancer detection in which the aim is development of a data warehouse of numerical mammography for diagnostic help [12]. Another study [13] deals with the problem of storage and restitution of medical image data from a warehouse. This study compares the data warehouse with a pyramid of means of storage. Some other studies were made particularly on cancer by making multidimensional analysis of an epidemiological spatio-temporal data set [14]. These works are based on the multimedia database modelling and on descriptors that define the data. Design of multimedia data cubes is the same as the design of traditional data cubes. A star or snowflake schema is used to model multimedia data warehouses. The fact table gathers multimedia data and only links on this data are generally stored. Dimensions represent descriptors of this data. Aggregated data is computed thanks to specific functions and the storage of these aggregations requires a great volume. All these models are static since the descriptors are fixed, i.e. each descriptor is computed in only one way when the data warehouse is loaded.

Dynamic aspects in multidimensional models can be found in studies that deal with evolutions of the analysis structures. When data changes in the course of time, dimensions and their attributes evolve through time and the multidimensional structure changes. In order to take evolutions of the analysis structures into account two types of approaches are proposed: the first one consists in updating models [15], [16], [17], [18] that focus on mapping data into the most recent version of the structure; the second is based on tracking history models [7], [19], [20] that keep trace of evolutions of the system. This last model is particularly interesting because it makes it possible to analyze data in their various versions and their evolutions. Several authors have proposed models which take the handling of evolutions into account. The models of Mendelzon and Vaisman [7], Pedersen et al. [20] Eder and Koncilia [19] take into account the user needs of both accurately tracking history and comparing data, and provide a way of mapping data in an "unchanged structure", chosen by the user. [19] proposes mapping functions, [20] proposes a conceptual model focusing on imprecision and complex dimension structures and [7] defines a temporal multidimensional model that uses valid times to build the TOLAP Query Language. Recently, the multiversion and multidimensional model of Body et al. [21], [22] integrates the concept of version in dimensions and gathers the data in a fact table, called multiversion fact table, according to various temporal modes of presentation (MTP). This model makes it possible to take temporal evolutions in data warehouses into account. However, this model provides a limited navigation because the user chooses only the temporal version. In the case of multimedia data and functional versions, this solution is too restricted because the user must be able to choose the functional version, for each data descriptor (i.e. each dimension).

Finally, in real-life, data has often been organized in complex hierarchies. It seems to be interesting to consider complex hierarchies (multiple, non-onto, non-strict and non-covering hierarchies) in order to be closer to reality and to improve the analysis of the data, particularly the analysis of multimedia data. In the same way, explicit hierarchies are useful to improve guidance for the user navigating in the cube. The majority of models makes it possible to define explicit hierarchies but they only partially treat the complex hierarchies [5], [7], [17], [18], [23], [24]. Some models cover all the characteristics of the complex hierarchies [20], [21], [22]. They are based on relations named "parent-child" (i.e. hierarchical links that can be multi-valued), between the levels and the dimension members. A graph defines the instance of the dimension from which the "parent-child" relations are defined by indicating the child-like member of a level and the parent-like member of the higher level to which it is connected [20]. Some authors [21], [22] propose to deduce the dimension schema and its hierarchy from the instance and the links that exist between various members of the dimension, whereas others [20] define both, i.e. the dimension schema and the instance of this corresponding dimension. This "parent-child" representation makes it possible to support complex hierarchies whereas star models and snowflake models do not treat the non-strict and non-onto hierarchies.

3   Case Study

This work was done in a collaboration with a team of INSERM (ERM 107) specialized in the methodology of cardiological information. In cardiology, a commonly used diagnostic is the Electrocardiogram (ECG) which is an important information for the follow-up of the patient and the diagnostic. An ECG is a signal recorded on 3 lines (dimension of space X,Y,Z).We propose to integrate this multimedia data and associated information of patients into a data warehouse. This example makes it possible to underline the difficulties and the needs linked to this kind of data.

The team ERM107 worked specifically on data of the therapeutic study named EMIAT (European Myocardial Infarct Amiodarone Trial). The EMIAT study is carried out to evaluate the effects of "amiodarone" compared with a placebo among patients that have survived a myocardial infarct. As a result this study provides data to be exploited and analyzed. Among this data, there is multimedia data: the ECGs signals of the various patients who participated in the study. From an ECG, several descriptors or indicators can be computed to characterize the cardiac health state of a patient. The QT interval measure (time after which the ventricles are repolarized) and the noise level (interferences on the ECG at the time of its acquisition) are the most studied. Other information are associated with these ECGs, such as pathology with the patient and hour of the medical examination. Thus, two types of descriptors characterize ECGs: description-based descriptors (principal pathology, age, gender of the patient, ECG acquisition date and ECG acquisition slot, technology with which the ECG is obtained) and content-based descriptors (the duration of the QT and the noise level of the ECG). The facts are ECGs characterized by descriptors (corresponding to the dimensions) organized in complex hierarchies. As an example, the ECG acquisition slots can be classified in hours and then in periods (night, waking, day). Some sets of hours (ex., 6 am) can belong to several periods (waking and night). The dimension Time corresponding to this descriptor is then organized in non-strict hierarchy. A simple multidimensional model of the data warehouse shows the fact table (ECGs Signal) and the dimensions we use (Time, Duration of QT, Gender, ...) (Fig. 1). This data warehouse will be used in order to analyze the ECGs of a population with selected age, pathology.... Furthermore, some descriptors can be computed by various computation modes. As an example, the duration of the QT can be obtained using several algorithms. It is necessary for the user to choose the relevant computation mode (or the functional version) of each descriptor in order to select the wanted representation or view of data.

On the one hand, our model will incorporate the versions of dimension that we define as dimensions with members that are calculated according to various functional versions of descriptors. On the other hand, we will integrate explicit hierarchies and complex hierarchies.

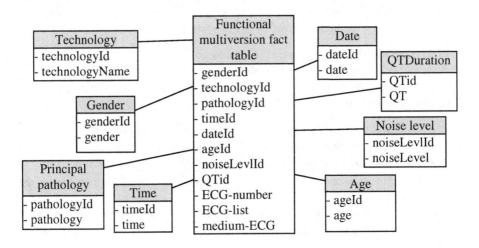

Fig. 1. Schema of the data warehouse

4 Conceptual-Level Approach

4.1 General Principle of Our Approach F2M

Our approach is based on a fact table that groups the set of measures which represent the data to analyze (references on multimedia data) and dimensions that represent the descriptors of this multimedia data. To take the problem of functional multiversion into account, we redefine the multidimensional structure by adding the concept of functional version. Thus, we introduce the concepts of version of dimension, multiversion dimension, functional multiversion fact table and function of version of dimension. A multiversion dimension is composed of several versions of a dimension, each one being a dimension for a given version with its own schema and its own instance. The functional multiversion fact table gathers all data by combining the various versions of dimension of a multiversion dimension with the others. Finally, the functions of versions of dimension correspond to the computation modes that make it possible to obtain its members. We define the schemas of various dimensions by describing the hierarchical levels and the links that bind them. We also describe the instances of these dimensions by describing the set of members belonging to a hierarchical level and their parent-child relationships. Thus, our approach makes it possible to have explicit dimensions since the schemas of dimension are defined explicitly. Our model also supports complex hierarchies (multiple, non-onto, non-strict and non-covering hierarchies) since the instances of dimensions are built from the members and the hierarchical links.

4.2 Concept Definition

Definition 1 (Schema of version of dimension). A schema of version of dimension is a schema of dimension for a given version. A version is a computation mode used to obtain the members of a dimension. The schema S_{VD} of the version of dimension VDid, is defined by the tuple $< VDid,\ \mathcal{N},\ <_{VDid} >$ where:

- $VDid$ is the identifier of the version of dimension
- $\mathcal{N} = \{n_j,\ j=1,...,k\}$ is the set of levels of S_{VD}. A level in S_{VD} represents a set of values with the same granularity associated with the same version of dimension. A level n_j is defined by the tuple $< levelId_j,\ levelName_j,\ [\mathcal{A}_j],\ [\ description_j] >$ where:
  - $levelId_j$ is the identifier of the level of version of dimension
  - $levelName_j$ is the name of the level of version of dimension
  - $\mathcal{A}_j$ is an optional property representing descriptive attributes of this level
  - $description_j$ is an optional property representing textual information on the level n_j
- $<_{VDid}$ is a partial order on the set $\mathcal{N}$ which defines the hierarchical links between the levels of schema S_{VD}. The partial order $<_{VDid}$ is defined such as: $\forall\ (n_1,n_2) \in \mathcal{N} \times \mathcal{N}$ if $n_1 <_{VDid} n_2$ then n_1 has a granularity finer than n_2.

Thus, a schema of version of dimension can be seen as a directed graph, where nodes are elements of the set $\mathcal{N}$ and arcs are relations according to $<_{VDid}$. This graph must be acyclic in order to enable aggregations to the finest hierarchical levels. One defines a level ALL as the root of the hierarchy, i.e. the highest level of granularity.

Example 1. Suppose we want to analyze the influence of age on ECG. Age is a dimension of the data warehouse but its members can be ordered in various ways, the ages can be classified by intervals of age, i.e. five years interval, ten years, fifty years. Let $S_{agePerInterval}$ be a schema of the version of dimension " *agePerInterval* " of which $VDid = 1$. The schema of this version of dimension is defined by:

$S_{agePerInterval} = <1,\{n_1,n_2,n_3\},<_1>$ with
$n_1 = <1,"IntervalOf5">$, $n_2 = <2,"IntervalOf10">$, $n_3 = <3,"IntervalOf50">$
and the following order: $n_1 <_1 n_2$, $n_2 <_1 n_3$ and $n_3 <_1$ ALL
The schema of the version of dimension $S_{agePerInterval}$ can be represented by the following graph (Fig. 2).

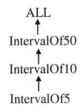

Fig. 2. Schema of the version of dimension $S_{agePerInterval}$

In a 2nd way, one can group these ages in age classes (young child, child, teenager, young adult, adult, senior) then in categories (minor, major) and one can define the schema of this version of dimension $S_{agePerClass}$.

Now let us regard the duration of the QT of these electrocardiograms as another dimension of the data warehouse. It can be computed by several algorithms, i.e. algo1 and algo2. The schema of dimension characterizing the duration of the QT has as hierarchies, the values of the duration of the QT for the finest level, grouped into an interval of 100ms, then in an interval of 400ms. So one can define the schemas of these two versions of dimension $S_{Qtalgo1}$ and $S_{Qtalgo2}$.

Definition 2 (Version of dimension). A version of dimension is a dimension for a given version. The version of dimension VD of schema $S_{VD} = < VDid, \mathcal{N}, <_{VDid} >$ is defined by the tuple $< VDid, VDname, \mathcal{M}, <_{VD}, [VDdescription] >$ where:

— $VDid$ is the unique identifier for the version of dimension
— $VDname$ is the name for the version of dimension
— $\mathcal{M} = \{m_j, j=1...l\}$ is the set of members of this version of dimension. A member of version of dimension is a member computed by the computation mode corresponding to the version of dimension. It belongs to one of the levels of the schema S_{VD}. Thus, one gathers in a level the members with the same granularity. A member m_j is represented by a tuple $< id_j, val_j, [a_j], levelId_j >$ where:

- id_j is a unique identifier for this member of version of dimension
- val_j is the value for this member of version of dimension.
- a_j is an optional property which contains the set of values of the attributes related to this member (corresponding to the level). If this property is defined for the level corresponding to the member, then it must be defined for the member.
- $levelId_j$ is the identifier for the hierarchical level to which this member of version of dimension belongs.

– $<_{VD}$ is a partial order on the set M which defines hierarchical links between the members of the same version of dimension VD. For each pair of levels (n_1,n_2), such as $n_1 <_{VDid} n_2$, there exist at least a couple $(m_1, m_2) \in M \times M$, such as $m_1.levelId_1 = n_1$ and $m_2.levelId_2 = n_2$ and $m_1 <_{VD} m_2$. Thus, it is said that m_1 is a member of the level lower than m_2, i.e. m_1 has a finer granularity than m_2.

– $VDdescription$ is an optional property containing possible comments on the version of dimension.

Thus, a version of dimension can be represented by an acyclic directed graph, where nodes are elements of the set M and arcs are relations according to $<_{VD}$. In the rest of the paper, we will call leaf member, a member of a version of dimension that has no children. Moreover, one defines the member "all" like the unique member contained in level "ALL". One notes LM_{VD} the set of leaf member of the version of dimension VD. This set is defined by:

$$LM_{VD} = \{ \ m_j \mid m_j \in M \ and \ \neg \exists m_i \in M \ such \ as \ (i \neq j \ and \ m_i <_{VD} m_j) \}.$$

Example 2. The version of dimension "$agePerInterval$" whose the schema $S_{agePerInterval}$ is presented in the previous example is defined by:
$agePerInterval = < 1, \ " \ agePerInterval \ ", \ \{m_1,......,m_7 \}, <_{agePerInterval} > with$
$m_1 = < 1, \ 0\text{-}5,1 >$, $m_2 = < 2, \ 6\text{-}10,1 >$, $m_3 = < 3,11\text{-}15,1 >$, $m_4 = < 4,16\text{-}20,1 >$,
$m_5 = < 5,0\text{-}10,2 >$, $m_6 = < 6,11\text{-}20,2 >$, $m_7 = < 7,0\text{-}50,3 >$
and the following order: $m_1 <_{agePerInterval} m_5$, $m_2 <_{agePerInterval} m_5$, $m_3 <_{agePerInterval} m_6$, $m_4 <_{agePerInterval} m_6$, $m_5 <_{agePerInterval} m_7$, $m_6 <_{agePerInterval} m_7$ and $m_7 <_{agePerInterval} all.$
So, the members of the level n_1 ("$IntervalOf5$") are $\{m_1, m_2, m_3, m_4\}$, those of the level n_2 ("$IntervalOf10$") are $\{m_5, m_6\}$ and that of the level n_3 ("$IntervalOf50$") is $\{m_7\}$.
The set of $LM_{agePerInterval}$ is defined by: $LM_{agePerInterval} = \{m_1, m_2, m_3, m_4\}$
The version of dimension "$agePerInterval$" can be represented by a graph (Fig. 3).

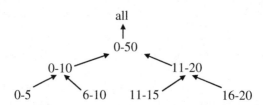

Fig. 3. Instance of the version of dimension "$agePerInterval$"

In the same way, one can also define the versions of dimension "*agePerClass*", "*QTalgo1*" and "*QTalgo2*" whose the schemas are $S_{agePerClass}$, $S_{QTalgo1}$, $S_{Qtalgo2}$ as well as the sets $\mathcal{LM}_{agePerClass}$, $\mathcal{LM}_{QTalgo1}$ and $\mathcal{LM}_{Qtalgo2}$.

Definition 3 (Multiversion dimension). A multiversion dimension *MVD* is a dimension that contains 1 to n versions of dimension. It is defined by the tuple < *MVDId, MVDname, VD, [MVDdescription]* > where:

- *MVDId* is the unique identifier for the multiversion dimension
- *MVDname* is the name for the multiversion dimension
- $VD = \{ VD_i, i=1,...,n \}$ is the set of versions of dimension associated with this multiversion dimension
- *MVDdescription* is an optional property containing textual information on the multiversion dimension.

One notes $\mathcal{LM}_{MVD}$ the set of leaf members of the versions of dimension contained in the multiversion dimension *MVD*. This set is defined by:

$$\mathcal{LM}_{\mathrm{MVD}} = \bigcup_{i=1}^{n} \mathcal{LM}_{VD_i}$$

with *n* being the number of versions of dimension contained in the multiversion dimension *MVD*.

Example 3. The versions of dimension "*agePerInterval* " and "*agePerClass*" defined previously belong to the multiversion dimension "*Age*" with the identifier *1*. This multiversion dimension is defined by:
Age = < *1, "Age", { " agePerInterval", "agePerClass" }>*
In the rest of the paper we will use the names of the members of versions of dimension to identify them. One defines the set $\mathcal{LM}_{Age}$ by: $\mathcal{LM}_{Age}$ = *{ 0-5, 6-10, 11-15, 16-20, young child, child, teenager, young adult, adult, senior }*
The versions of dimension "*QTalgo1*" and "*QTalgo2*" belong to multiversion dimension "*DurationQT*" with the identifier 2. This multiversion dimension is defined by: *DurationQT* = < *2, QT, { QTalgo1, QTalgo2 }* >
In the same way, one defines the set $\mathcal{LM}_{DurationQT}$.

Definition 4 (Functional multiversion fact table). A functional multiversion fact table provides the measurements according to various versions of dimension. Let $\{ \mu_i, i=1,...,m \}$ be the set of measurements, a functional multiversion fact table *ft* is defined by a function such as:

$$ft : MVD_1 \times MVD_2 \times ... \times MVD_n \rightarrow dom(\mu_1) \times ... \times dom(\mu_m)$$

$$m_1, m_2, ..., m_n \rightarrow v_1, ..., v_m$$

where *n* is the number of multiversion dimensions of the data warehouse, $mi \in \mathcal{LM}_{MVD_i}$ with $i=1,...,n$ and $dom(\mu_k)$ is the range for the measure μ_k . This function associates the set of the values v_k of measurements μ_k with a set of leaf members of the versions of dimension of each multiversion dimension.

Definition 5 (Function of version of dimension). The functions of version of dimension are the computation modes that make it possible to obtain the members of a version of dimension *VD* from the data of the production database. A function of version of dimension f_{VD} is defined by the tuple $< functionId_{VD},\ VDid,\ functionName_{VD},\ functionDefinition_{VD} >$ where:

- $functionId_{VD}$ is the identifier for the function of version of dimension *VD*
- *VDid* is the identifier for the version of dimension *VD* whose members are computed by using this function of version of dimension
- $functionName_{VD}$ is the name for the function of version of dimension
- $functionDefinition_{VD}$ is the definition for the function of version of dimension

These functions are of the form:

$$f_{VD} : \mathcal{DB}_f \to \mathcal{LM}_{VD}$$

$$d \to m$$

where $\mathcal{DB}_f$ is the set of data of the production database restricted to f_{VD} i.e. used to compute the members of *VD*. f_{VD} associates with a value of the production database, a leaf member of the version of corresponding *VD*.

Example 4. Suppose that in the production database, one has a 12-year-old patient. Let the function $f_{agePerClass}$ be defined for the version of dimension "*agePerClass*" and the defined function $f_{agePerInterval}$ for the version of dimension " *agePerInterval* ". Then, one obtains respectively for the versions of dimension, the members:
$f_{agePerClass}(12) = "young"$ and $f_{agePerInterval} (12) = "11\text{-}15"$.
In the same way, suppose an electrocardiogram "*ECG5*" of the production database. Let the function $f_{Qtalgo1}$ be defined for the version of dimension "*Qtalgo1*" and the defined function $f_{Qtalgo2}$ for the version of dimension "*Qtalgo2*". Then, one obtains respectively for the versions of dimension, the members:
$f_{Qtalgo1} (ECG5) = 100$ and $f_{Qtalgo2} (ECG5) = 110$.

Definition 6 (Functional multiversion multidimensional structure). A functional multiversion multidimensional structure *F2M* is defined by the tuple $< \mathcal{MVD}, ft,\ \mathcal{F} >$ where:

- $\mathcal{MVD} = \bigcup_{i=1}^{s} MVD_i$ is the set of all multiversion dimensions
- *ft* is the functional multiversion fact table
- $\mathcal{F} = \bigcup_{j=1}^{r} f_{VD_j}$ is the set of all functions of the versions of dimension

Définition 7 (Aggregation of data). Aggregations of data can be computed from the multiversion fact table and the schema of the versions of dimension. Let an aggregation function $\bigoplus_{\mu_k}$ be defined for each measurement μ_k, m a non-leaf member of the version of dimension VD of the multiversion dimension MVD_l and $m_1^1, m_2^1, ..., m_J^1$ its children (leaf member) i.e. such as:

$$(m_1^1, m_2^1, ..., m_J^1) \in \mathcal{L M}_{VD} \times ... \times \mathcal{L M}_{VD} .$$

One has the following relation:

$$\forall j \in [1, J], ft(m_j^1, m_2, ..., m_n) = v_1^j, ..., v_m^j$$

where n is the number of multiversion dimensions of the data warehouse. Thus, one can obtain the aggregated values for m as:

$$ft(m, m_2, ..., m_n) = \bigoplus_{\mu_1}^{J} v_1^j, ..., \bigoplus_{\mu_m}^{J} v_m^j .$$

An aggregation function can be classic a function of OLAP technology (sum, min, max, avg) for numeric measures or a more specific function (statistic average,...) for signal or image type measures.

5 Prototype

5.1 Architecture

We use Microsoft SQL Server and Analysis Services to implement our prototype. The aggregations functions are implemented in Visual Basic ; an interface using Proclarity 4.0 is built for navigation. The 3-tier architecture is the following:

- a functional multiversion multimedia data warehouse in which the multiversion dimensions and the functional multiversion fact table are stored,
- an OLAP cube built from the functional multiversion multimedia data warehouse, using aggregations, which enables requests against the functional versions of the dimensions,
- a tool for data navigation and visualization.

Data is loaded from the production database to the functional multiversion multimedia data warehouse using the functions of versions of dimension.

5.2 Application on EMIAT Study

The data of the EMIAT study have been integrated in the prototype. The data warehouse contains a functional multiversion fact table and eight multiversion dimensions. The facts are ECGs signals from the EMIAT study. Multiversion dimensions represent the description-based descriptors and the content-based descriptors of these ECGs. Among the multiversion dimensions, three dimensions are related to the patient (principal pathology, age, gender), three to ECG acquisition (date, time (acquisition slot) and technology) and two to the content of the ECGs (the duration of the QT, the noise level). Aggregations of data are computed from the functional multiversion fact table and the hierarchical links between the members of the versions of dimension. The aggregation functions make it possible to compute aggregated data according to granularities of the versions of dimension (the levels of the corresponding schemas). In our data warehouse, we define the following aggregation functions:

– "ECG-count": this function counts the number of ECGs that correspond to the characteristics selected by the user.
– "ECG-list": this function returns the list of ECGs that correspond to the characteristics selected by the user.
– "Medium-ECG": this function gives the "medium-ECG" calculated on the ECG-list.

The user can visualize in a frame the hierarchies and the members of the versions of dimensions and build his request choosing the appropriate data aggregation operator ("ECG-count", "ECG-list" or "medium-ECG"). The result is a multidimensional table. It is also possible to visualize several versions of dimension of a multiversion dimension in order to make comparisons. The selected multimedia data can be visualized in a frame. Moreover, metadata can be visualized in order to have a global view of all versions of dimension and to navigate the data cube more easily (ex., the schemas and the instances of each version of dimension are represented for each multiversion dimension).

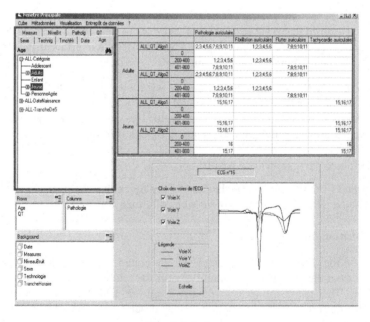

Fig. 4. Interface

6 Discussion and Conclusion

We present a new model that takes functional versions into account. The model helps to manage multimedia data and allows the user to choose different views that represent various functional versions of the descriptors. We define the concept of version and multiversion in dimensions in order to compare results obtained by various versions. This model is particularly well suited to multimedia data because they require various computation modes. We also use specific aggregation functions for multimedia data that are integrated into the data warehouse. This model is used to develop an OLAP application for the navigation into a hypercube integrating signal data. We propose a tool to explore this complex data which improves navigation in the multidimensional data cube. Thus, we enable the visualization of data according to several methods of analysis and we provide the possibility to visualize the representation of this multimedia data.

However, the data storage of our model could be improved. It is possible to have some redundancy in the schemas of versions of dimension, the functional multiversion fact table storage is not optimised, and the treatment of non-strict and multiple hierarchies implies duplications. Our model could be extended by associating the notion of functional version with the facts, in the same way that our model associates functional versions with dimensions. This could be possible by adding a version of fact dimension so as to enable the user to choose the version of fact.

References

1. Inmon, W.H.: Building the Data Warehouse. 3rd Edition, Eds.Wiley and Sons, 1996
2. Vassiliadis, P., Sellis, T.: A Survey of Logical Models for OLAP Databases. SIGMOD Record Volume 28, Number 1, March, 1999
3. Kimball R.: The Data Warehouse Toolkit. J.Wiley and Sons, Inc, 1996.
4. Cabibbo, L. and Torlone, R.: A Logical Approach to Multidimensional Databases. Proocedings of the 6th International Conference on Extending Database Technology (EDBT'98), Valencia, Spain, 1998.
5. Agrawal, R., Gupta, A., Sarawagi, S.: Modeling Multidimensional Databases. IBM Research Report, IBM Almaden Research Center, September 1995. 25p.
6. Lehner, W.: Modeling large OLAP scenarios. Proceedings of the 1998 International Conference on Extending Database Technology, Valencia, Spain, 1998.
7. Mendelzon, A.O. and Vaisman, A.: Temporal Queries in OLAP. Proceedings of the 26th VLDB'00 Conference, Cairo, Egypt, 2000.
8. Han, J., Kamber, M.: Data mining, concepts and techniques. Morgan Kaufmann Publishers, 2001.
9. Zaïane, O.R.: Resource and knowledge discovery from the internet and multimedia repositories. Ph.D., Simon Fraser University, 1999.
10. You, J. and al.: On hierarchical multimedia information retrieval. IEEE International Conference on Image Processing (ICIP), 2001.
11. Zaïane, O. R., Han, J., Li, Z.H., Hou, J.: Mining Multimédia Data. CASCON'98: Meeting of Minds, pp 83-96, Toronto, Canada, November 1998.
12. Zhang, H. and al.: Developing a digital mammography data warehouse. Medical Imaging 2001.

13. Tikekar, R.V., Fotouhi, F. : Storage and retrieval of medical images from data warehouses. Digital Image Storage and Archiving Systems, 1995.
14. Kamp, V., Wietek, F.: Database system support for multidimensional data analysis in environmental Epidemiology. IEEE Computer Society , 1997.
15. Blaschka, M., Sapia, C. and Höfling, G.: On Schema Evolution in Multidimensional Databases. Proceedings of DaWak'99 Conference, Florence, Italy, 1999.
16. Blaschka, M.: FIESTA: A Framework for Schema Evolution in Multidimensional Information Systems. Proceedings of 6th Doctoral Consortium, Germany, 1999.
17. Hurtado, C. , Mendelzon, A.O. and Vaisman, A.: Maintaining Data Cubes Under Dimension Updates. Proceedings of the IEEE/ICDE'99 Conference, 1999.
18. Hurtado, C., Mendelzon, A.O. and Vaisman, A.: Updating OLAP Dimensions. Proceedings of the ACM Second Int. Workshop on Data Warehousing and OLAP, USA, 1999.
19. Eder, J. and Koncilia, C.: Evolution of Dimension Data in Temporal Data Warehouses. Proceedings of the DaWaK'01 Conference, Munich, Germany, 2001.
20. Pedersen, T.B., Jensen, C.S. and Dyreson, C.E.: A foundation for capturing and querying complex multidimensional data. Information Systems (2001), Vol 26, No 5, 383-423.
21. Body, M., Miquel, M., Bédard, Y., Tchounikine A.: A multidimensional and multiversion structure for OLAP applications. ACM Fifth International Workshop on Data warehousing and OLAP (DOLAP 2002), McLean, VA, USA, November 8th 2002.
22. Body, M., Miquel, M., Bédard, Y., Tchounikine, A.: Handling Evolutions in Multidimensional Structures. ICDE 2002, the 19th International Conference on Data Engineering, Sponsored by the IEEE Computer Society, Bangalore, India, March 5-8 2003.
23. Jagadish, H. V., Lakshmanan , L. V. S., Srivastava, D.: What can hierarchies do for warehouses? Proc. Of the 25th VLDB Conference, Edinburgh, Scotland, 1999.
24. Kimball R.: Is Your Dimensional Data Warehouse Expressive? Intelligent Enterprise, volume 3, no. 8, May 2000.

An Indexing Approach for Representing Multimedia Objects in High-Dimensional Spaces Based on Expectation Maximization Algorithm

Giuseppe Boccignone[1], Vittorio Caggiano[2], Carmine Cesarano[2],
Vincenzo Moscato[2] and Lucio Sansone[2]

[1] University of Salerno, Dipartimento di Ingegneria dell'Informazione,
via Ponte Melillo 1, 84084, Fisciano (SA), Italy
boccig@unisa.it
[2] University Federico II, Dipartimento di Informatica e Sistemistica,
via Claudio 21, 80125, Naples, Italy
{vcaggian, carmine.cesarano, vmoscato, lucio.sansone}@unina.it

Abstract. In this paper we introduce a new indexing approach to representing multimedia object classes generated by the Expectation Maximization clustering algorithm in a balanced and dynamic tree structure. To this aim the EM algorithm has been modified in order to obtain at each step of its recursive application balanced clusters. In this manner our tree provides a simple and practical solution to index clustered data and support efficient retrieval of the nearest neighbors in high dimensional object spaces.

1 Introduction

The emerging technologies based on repositories of heterogeneous information (such as images, video, audio, time series and DNA sequences) require general search models and algorithms in order to deal with such complex and large-scale multidimensional data sets. In this context a "key-problem" is the development of fast and efficient access techniques.

A viable solution to perform queries on multimedia and complex data is the introduction, in the objects domain, of a distance function, pointing out the dissimilarity between two objects and satisfying non-negativity, symmetry and triangular inequality properties. When a distance function with the above features is defined, it is said to be a metric function, the domain is said to be metric, and metric access methods [8] can be used to indexing and retrieving data by means of the "similarity query" search paradigm. Its essence is to find in a given collection of objects those which better fit (i.e., which are more similar to) a given query specification.

An efficient index for a large data set, where data are described in high dimensional feature space, should allow to prune comparisons between data during the similarity search process by taking advantage from distance properties. To this end, the overall data distributions can be considered for "grouping" similar objects in the same "similarity-class", and each class represented by a particular object called "centroid", "pivot" or "routing object". Then, during retrieval, it is possible to reduce necessary comparisons by calculating the similarity between the query objects and each class through their representatives. In this way, complex and multimedia data retrieval can be accelerated and improved using both classes-based index structures and the similarity query concept.

Probably, the first general solution to search in metric spaces was presented by Burkhard and Keller [6]. They propose a tree (thereafter called the "Burkhard Keller Tree", or BKT), which is suitable for discrete-valued distance functions. ¿From the opposite the "vantage-point trees" or VPT is proposed in [16] as a tree data structure designed for continuous distance functions. The "bisector trees" (BST) are proposed in [13] as binary trees built recursively segmenting the data space. In [15], is also proposed the "generalized-hyperplane tree" (GHT), identical in construction to a BST. The GHT is extended in [5] to an m-ary tree, called GNAT ("geometric near-neighbor access tree"), keeping the same essential idea, but also using a Voronoi-like partition. Eventually, the "M-tree" (MT) data structure is presented in Ciaccia et al., [9] aiming at providing dynamic capabilities and good I/O performance in addition to few distance computations.

Clustering [12] represents the most diffused analysis technique for discovering interesting data patterns in the underlying data set: given a set of n data points in a d-dimensional metric space, a clustering approach assigns the data points to l ($l << n$) classes or groups, maximizing object similarity within the same class. The clustered data structure can be efficiently used (e.g., by means of a recursive application on the data space) to build indexes (e.g., search-trees) for high dimensional data sets, which support efficient queries. Interestingly enough, many statistical clustering techniques (e.g., k-means, fuzzy k-means) can be considered as special cases of the Expectation-Maximization (EM) algorithm [3].

Different approaches were proposed in literature for represinting clustered data by indexing structures. In [11], the clusters are organized in a tree structure CF^*tree and a representative called "clusteroid" is chosen from each cluster. While searching, the query object is compared against the clusteroid and the associated cluster is eliminated from consideration in the case in which a similarity criterion does not hold. The problems connected to the inserting of new objects are solved by introducing a "inter-cluster" distance. An advantage of the clustering approach respect to the other ones is the possibility of generating classes of objects that are independent: such feature can be used to simplify the pruning conditions in the query process. In [17] a new indexing approach to representing clusters generated by any existing clustering algorithm in a tree structure called "ClusterTree" is presented.

In this paper we introduce a new indexing approach to represent multimedia object classes, generated by a variant of the EM algorithm, in a balanced and dynamic tree structure. To this aim the EM algorithm has been modified in order to obtain at each step of its recursive application balanced clusters (BEM, Balanced EM). In this way our tree provides a simple and practical solution to index clustered data and support efficient retrieval of the nearest neighbors in high dimensional object spaces.

2 Preliminary Definitions

Similarity queries can introduced using the concept of a dissimilarity measure, or distance function, which can be defined as a function that compare two objects belonging to the class of objects $\mathcal{O}$ and determines a positive real number denoting their dissimilarity. Formally:

$$\delta : \mathcal{O} \times \mathcal{O} \to \mathcal{R}^+ \tag{1}$$

In the multimedia realm, to make possible a comparison between any two objects, a "feature-based" solution is usually proposed. The basic idea is to extract important features from the multimedia objects, represent the above features by high-dimensional vectors and search the database objects having the most similar features. Thus, we assume that objects are mapped into points of a "multi dimensional features vector space" with a fixed and finite dimension d.

The introduced distance function must satisfy some particular properties that characterize a metric. Formally a metric space is a pair $\mathcal{M} = (\mathcal{S}, \delta)$ where $\mathcal{S}$ is a domain of feature values and δ is a distance function having the following properties:

1. $\delta(\mathcal{O}^x, \mathcal{O}^y) = \delta(\mathcal{O}^y, \mathcal{O}^x)$ (symmetry);
2. $\delta(\mathcal{O}^x, \mathcal{O}^y) > 0$ with $(\mathcal{O}^x \neq \mathcal{O}^y)$ (non negativity); and $\delta(\mathcal{O}^x, \mathcal{O}^x) = 0$
3. $\delta(\mathcal{O}^x, \mathcal{O}^y) < \delta(\mathcal{O}^x, \mathcal{O}^z) + \delta(\mathcal{O}^z, \mathcal{O}^y)$ (triangle inequity).

The types of queries that can be usefully used to search objects in a generic metric space are defined as follows.

Definition 1 (Range Query).

$$RangeQuery(DB, \mathcal{O}^q, \varphi, \mathcal{M}) = \{\mathcal{O} \in DB | \delta_{\mathcal{M}}(\mathcal{O}, \mathcal{O}^q) \leq \varphi\}$$

where DB is a set of n points in a d-dimensional data space, $\mathcal{O}^q$ is the query object, φ is a distance value and $\mathcal{M}$ is a generic metric space.

The result of this function is the set of all object-points having a distance smaller than or equal to φ from $\mathcal{O}^q$, according to the metric δ

Definition 2 (Nearest-Neighbor Query).

$$NNQuery(DB, \mathcal{O}^q, \mathcal{M}) \subseteq \{\mathcal{O} \in DB | \forall \mathcal{O}' \in DB : \delta_{\mathcal{M}}(\mathcal{O}, \mathcal{O}^q) \leq \delta_{\mathcal{M}}(\mathcal{O}', \mathcal{O}^q)\}$$

where DB is a set of n points in a d-dimensional data space, $\mathcal{O}^q$ is the query object and $\mathcal{M}$ is a generic metric space.

The result is an object-point chosen among those points having minimal distance from the query object $\mathcal{O}^q$. In particular if a user wants to get the first k closest points to the query object, the notion of Nearest-Neighbor query could be expanded with the definition of k-NN Query.

Definition 3 (K-Nearest-Neighbor Query).

$$kNNQuery(DB, \mathcal{O}^q, k, \mathcal{M}) = \{\{\mathcal{O}^1..\mathcal{O}^k\} \in DB | \neg \exists i, \ 0 \leq i < k :$$
$$\delta_{\mathcal{M}}(\mathcal{O}^i, \mathcal{O}^q) > \delta_{\mathcal{M}}(\mathcal{O}', \mathcal{O}^q)\}$$

where k indicates the number of closer points to the query point Q.

Note that the queries introduced above can be performed using either a "sequential" scan of the objects present in the database or a "smart scan" that permits to locate and analyze only the relevant objects. A drawback of sequential scanning is time complexity, which is directly related to the size and number of stored objects [19].

To improve retrieval efficiency, features should be organized into indexing data structures that support efficiently the query process. Generally speaking, an index consists of a collection of entities, one for each object, containing the key for that object, and a reference pointer which allows immediate access to that object [9]. Different indexing mechanisms have been proposed in the literature to facilitate fast feature-based retrieval of multimedia objects in very large database. A formal definition is:

Definition 4 (Index mechanism for feature based retrieval). *Let Σ be a set of multimedia objects (O_i) and $\Omega = \omega_1, \omega_2, ..., \omega_m$ a set of m classes to which Σ is to be classified where ω satisfies the following:*

1. *$\omega_i \neq \Sigma \forall i = 1, 2, 3...m;$*
2. *$\cup_{1 \leq i \leq m} \omega_i = \Sigma;$*
3. *$\omega_i \neq \omega_j \ for \ i \neq j;$*

The indexing process consists of the application of a mapping $\Sigma \to \Omega$ denoted by $T = \eta(R, \Omega)$, where R is a set of parameters to define the mapping, and classes in Ω represent the categories of multimedia object set Σ.

If the clusters are organized according to the classical tree structure, we have the following indexing association $\{\omega_1, \omega_2, ..., \omega_m\} \to \{N_1, N_2, ..., N_m\}$, N_i being a generic tree-node [20].

3   Indexing Multimedia Objects via Balanced Cluster Tree

3.1   Generating Balanced Objects Clusters Using a Balanced EM Algorithm

We are interested in a procedure capable to find, in a generic data space S, the number of interesting objects respect to a test object $O^t \in S$; in probabilistic terms we want to determine for each database object in our space $O^i \in S$, the probability $P(\mathcal{O}^i | \mathcal{O}^t)$.

An obvious and efficient solution to this problem is to partition all our space objects into particular subgroups, called clusters $\mathcal{C}^l$. Note that each object $\mathcal{O}$

can be seen as a feature vector and the problem of calculating its cluster can be reduced to the problem of searching, in a high dimensional space, the coordinates of the minimum-distance point from other space-points, which could be accomplished by classical clustering algorithms [12].

Thus, the first step of the process is to cluster data-space ($\mathcal{S}$) in order to determine the subgroups of similar objects. More precisely, the aim is to assign a label l to the different $\mathcal{O}$, where $l \in [1, \ldots, L_n]$ identifies a particular cluster $\mathcal{C}^l$ that can be selected with a certain probability $P(l)$.

Denote $\mathcal{O} = \{\mathcal{O}^1, \cdots, \mathcal{O}^N\}$ the objects data set generated by sampling independently from the generative model, namely a mixture model $p(\mathcal{O}|\Theta) = \sum_{l=1}^{L} \alpha_l p_l(\mathcal{O}|\theta_l)$, where $\Theta = \{\alpha_1, \cdots, \alpha_L, \theta_1, \cdots, \theta_L\}$, α_l being the mixing proportions subject to constraints $\alpha_l \geq 0$, $\sum_{l=1}^{L} \alpha_l = 1$ and the distribution $p_l(\mathcal{O}|\theta_l)$ is a single multivariate gaussian distribution with parameters (mean and covariance) $\theta_l = \{\mathbf{m}_l, \mathbf{\Sigma}_l\}$, $p_l(\mathcal{O}^i|\mathbf{m}_l, \mathbf{\Sigma}_l) = \frac{exp(-\frac{1}{2}(\mathcal{O}^i - \mathbf{m}_l)^T \mathbf{\Sigma}_l^{-1}(\mathcal{O}^i - \mathbf{m}_l))}{(2\pi)^{(d/2)}|\mathbf{\Sigma}_l|^{1/2}}$; here d denotes the dimension of the space.

Let $\mathcal{Z} = \{z_1, \cdots, z_N\}$ be the corresponding set of hidden random variables such that $z_i = l$ when $\mathcal{O}^i$ has been generated following $p_l(\mathcal{O}|\theta_l)$. Then, the *complete* log-likelihood of the observed data is given by:

$$\log \mathcal{L} = \log p(\mathcal{O}, \mathcal{Z}|\Theta) = \sum_{i=1}^{N} \log(\alpha_{z_i} p_{z_i}(\mathcal{O}^i|\theta_{z_i})), \tag{2}$$

from which maximum likelihood parameter estimates can be obtained.

Since, in terms of the mixture model we are dealing with an incomplete data problem (i.e., we must simultaneously determine the labelling $p(\mathcal{Z}|\mathcal{O}, \Theta)$ given distribution parameters Θ and viceversa), a suitable choice for the maximization of the likelihood is the Expectation Maximization algorithm (EM) [10]. The EM algorithm starts with some initial guess at the maximum likelihood parameters θ_l^0, and then proceeds to iteratively generate successive estimates, $\theta_l^1, \theta_l^2, \cdots$ by repeatedly applying the following two steps for $t = 1, 2, \cdots$ [14]:

1. **E-step**: compute a distribution $\tilde{p}^t$ over the range of $\mathcal{Z}$ such that $\tilde{p}^t = p(\mathcal{O}|\mathcal{Z}, \Theta^{t-1})$
2. **M-step**: set Θ^t to maximize the expectation of the complete log–likelihood $E_{\tilde{p}^t}[\log p(\mathcal{O}, \mathcal{Z}|\Theta)]$

Note that the expectation of $\log \mathcal{L}$ over the given distribution p is [3]:

$$E_p[\log p(\mathcal{O}, \mathcal{Z}|\Theta)] = \sum_{i=1}^{N} E_{p(z_i|\mathcal{O}^i, \Theta)}[\log(\alpha_{z_i} p_{z_i}(\mathcal{O}^i|\theta_{z_i}))] = \tag{3}$$

$$= \sum_{i=1}^{N} \sum_{l=1}^{L} p(l|\mathcal{O}^i, \Theta) \log(\alpha_l p_l(\mathcal{O}^i|\theta_l)) =$$

$$= \sum_{i=1}^{N} \sum_{l=1}^{L} h_{il} \log(\alpha_l) + \sum_{i=1}^{N} \sum_{l=1}^{L} h_{il} \log(p_l(\mathcal{O}^i|\theta_l))$$

where $h_{il} = p(l|\mathcal{O}^i, \Theta)$ denotes the posterior distribution of the hidden variables given the set of parameters Θ and the observed $\mathcal{O}^i$.

Under this setting, the standard EM algorithm for gaussian mixtures with parameters $\theta_l = \{\mathbf{m}_l, \Sigma_l\}$ can be computed in close form. The E-step computes the distribution of hidden variables as $h_{il}^t = \frac{\alpha_l^t p(\mathcal{O}^i|l, \mathbf{m}_l^t, \Sigma_l^t)}{\sum_l \alpha_l^t p(\mathcal{O}^i|l, \mathbf{m}_l^t, \Sigma_l^t)}$, while the M-step given the distribution of the hidden variables, obtain the parameters Θ_l that maximize the expectation of $\log \mathcal{L}$ as $\alpha_l^{t+1} = \frac{1}{N}\sum_i h_{il}^t$, $\mathbf{m}_l^{t+1} = \frac{\sum_i h_{il}^t \mathcal{O}^i}{\sum_i h_{il}^t}$, and $\Sigma_l^{t+1} = \frac{\sum_i h_{il}^t [\mathcal{O}^i - \mathbf{m}_l^{t+1}][\mathcal{O}^i - \mathbf{m}_l^{t+1}]^T}{\sum_i h_{il}^t}$. Both steps are iterated t times until convergence criteria are met.

It can be shown that the *incomplete* data log-likelihood $\log p(\mathcal{O}|\Theta)$ is non-decreasing at each iteration of the update [10]. Thus, a suitable convergence criterion is $|\log \mathcal{L}^{(t+1)} - \log \mathcal{L}^{(t)}| < \epsilon$, were ϵ is a threshold experimentally determined. Once the learning step is completed and the parameters Θ of the Gaussian mixture model have been obtained, the object O_i of a given cluster $\mathcal{C}$ can be partitioned in subclusters $\mathcal{C} = \{\mathcal{C}^1, \mathcal{C}^2, \ldots, \mathcal{C}^{L^n}\}$, where object O_i is assigned to the cluster $\mathcal{C}^l$ with probability $p(l|\mathcal{O}^i, \Theta)$

The cluster representation previously discussed, beyond its generality, has some drawbacks when exploited for a very large database. On the one hand the labelling of the image has a computational cost which is linear in time with the number of clusters L. On the other hand, for retrieval purposes, such solution is not efficient with respect to indexing issues, since the clusters obtained are in general not balanced. To overcome such drawbacks, we introduce a variant of the EM algorithm which provides a balanced clustering of the observed data, so that clusters can be organized in a suitable data structure, namely a balanced tree [17]. The idea is to constrain, along the E-step, the distribution of the hidden variables so as to provide a balanced partition of the data, and then perform a regular M-step. This is equivalent to provide a mapping $p(\mathcal{Z}|\mathcal{O}, \Theta) \rightarrow q(\mathcal{Z}|\mathcal{O}, \Theta)$ so that $\log p(\mathcal{O}|\Theta)$ is non-decreasing at each iteration of the update.

To make this clear define, following Neal and Hinton [14], the free energy:

$$F(\tilde{p}, \Theta) = E_{\tilde{p}}[\log p(\mathcal{O}, \mathcal{Z}|\Theta)] + H(\tilde{p}) \tag{4}$$

where:

$$H(p) = E_p[\log p(\mathcal{Z}|\mathcal{O}, \Theta)] = \sum_{i=1}^N \sum_{l=1}^L h_{il} \log(h_{il}) \tag{5}$$

is the entropy of the hidden variables. It has been shown [14] that this function is maximized by the E- and M- steps of the EM algorithm. In particular when the distribution of the hidden variable is computed according to the standard E-step, then $\tilde{p} = p$ gives the optimal value of the function, which is exactly the *incomplete* data log-likelihood $F(p, \Theta) = \log p(\mathcal{O}|\Theta)$. For any other distribution $\tilde{p} = q \neq p$ over the hidden variables,

$$F(q, \Theta) \leq F(p, \Theta) = \log p(\mathcal{O}|\Theta) \tag{6}$$

Basically, what we need is to design a distribution q so that objects $\mathcal{O}^i$ are hard-assigned to clusters, so that effectively each of the hidden variables has a distribution which has probability 1 for one of the mixture component and zero for all the others [2].

Denote $\mathcal{Q}$ this class of distributions. Remark that for $q \in \mathcal{Q}$, a partition of $\mathcal{O}^1, \cdots, \mathcal{O}^N$ is defined where for each $\mathcal{O}^i$, there exists $l(1 \leq l \leq L)$ such that $q(l|\mathcal{O}^i, \Theta) = 1$, thus $q(l|\mathcal{O}^i, \Theta) \log q(l|\mathcal{O}^i, \Theta) = 0$ for all $1 \leq l \leq L$ and $1 \leq i \leq N$ (since $0 \log 0 = 0$). Hence $H(q) = 0$ and we have:

$$F(q, \Theta) = E_q [\log p(\mathcal{O}, \mathcal{Z}|\Theta)] \leq F(p, \Theta) = \log p(\mathcal{O}|\Theta) \qquad (7)$$

which shows that the expectation over q lower bounds the likelihood of the data. Further, it has been shown [2] that for some choices of q (e.g., $q = 1$, if $l = \arg\max_{l'} p(l|\mathcal{O}^i, \Theta)$ and $q = 0$ otherwise) is a tight lower bound, $E_p [\log p(\mathcal{O}, \mathcal{Z}|\Theta)] \leq E_q [\log p(\mathcal{O}, \mathcal{Z}|\Theta)]$.

Thus, due to Eq. 7, we can set up an E-step in which the free energy is maximized by maximizing $E_{\widetilde{p}} [\log p(\mathcal{O}, \mathcal{Z}|\Theta)]$ given Θ where, taking into account Eq. 4, and discarding the penalty term $\sum_{i=1}^{N} \sum_{l=1}^{L} h_{il} \log(\alpha_l)$,

$$E_{\widetilde{p}} [\log p(\mathcal{O}, \mathcal{Z}|\Theta)] = \sum_{i=1}^{N} \sum_{l=1}^{L} h_{il} \log(p_l(\mathcal{O}^i|\theta_l)) \qquad (8)$$

Following [18], balanced partitioning can be achieved through by solving the optimization problem:

$$\max E_{\widetilde{p}} = \max_{h} \sum_{i=1}^{N} \sum_{l=1}^{L} h_{il} \log(p_l(\mathcal{O}^i|\theta_l)), \qquad (9)$$

subject to $\sum_{l=1}^{L} h_{il} = 1, \forall i, \sum_{i=1}^{N} h_{il} = \frac{N}{L}, \forall l$, and $h_{il} \in \{0, 1\}, \forall i, l$.

Since the solution of such optimization problem is an integer programming problem, which is NP-hard in general, in [18] a greedy heuristics has been suggested which gives a locally optimal solution to such problem. The procedure assign N/L data samples to one of the L clusters at each iteration, by selecting the first N/L samples with higher h_{il} probability with respect to the cluster. For instance, for $L = 2$, this gives a $\{N/2, N/2\}$ bipartition that maximizes $E_{\widetilde{p}}$. Eventually, the given partition provides the hard assigned distribution $q \in \mathcal{Q}$. Denote $q_{il} = q(l|\mathcal{O}^i, \theta_l^t)$; the balanced EM algorithm is thus the following.

Note that the algorithm introduces a sort of classification within the E-step in the same vein of the CEM algorithm [7]. In figure 1.a an example of balanced clustering is shown.

3.2 Building the Balanced Cluster Tree

Our data-space can thus be represented in terms of clusters by mapping the data onto the tree-structure shown in Fig. 1.b, which we denote Balanced Cluster Tree (BCT).

Given a space $\mathcal{S}$ a BCT of depth Υ is obtained by recursively applying the BEM algorithm at each level $v = 0, \cdots, \Upsilon - 1$ of the tree. Each tree node of

---

Algorithm 1 Balanced EM

Initialize all $\alpha_l, \theta_l, l = 1, \cdots, L$
$t \leftarrow 1$
repeat
  {E-step}
  for $(i = 1, ..., N)$ **do**
    for $(l = 1, ..., L)$ **do**
      $h_{il}^t \leftarrow \frac{\alpha_l^t p(O^i | l, \mathbf{m}_l^t, \boldsymbol{\Sigma}_l^t)}{\sum_l \alpha_l^t p(O^i | l, \mathbf{m}_l^t, \boldsymbol{\Sigma}_l^t)}$
      $q_{il}^t \leftarrow 1$ if h_{il}^t is in the N/L highest values for class l, $q_{il}^t \leftarrow 0$ otherwise
  {M-step}
  for $(l = 1, ..., L)$ **do**
    $\alpha_l^{t+1} \leftarrow \frac{1}{N} \sum_i q_{il}^t$
    $\mathbf{m}_l^{t+1} \leftarrow \frac{\sum_i q_{il}^t O^i}{\sum_i q_{il}^t}$
    $\boldsymbol{\Sigma}_l^{t+1} \leftarrow \frac{\sum_i q_{il}^t [O^i - \mathbf{m}_l^{t+1}][O^i - \mathbf{m}_l^{t+1}]^T}{\sum_i q_{il}^t}$
  Compute $\log \mathcal{L}^{(t+1)}$
  $t \leftarrow t + 1$
until $|\log \mathcal{L}^{(t+1)} - \log \mathcal{L}^{(t)}| < \epsilon$

---

level v is associated with one of the discovered clusters at the $v + 1^{th}$ iteration of the BEM algorithm. New discovered clusters are recursively partitioned until each cluster contains a number of points/object lower than a fixed threshold B, representing the desired filling-coefficient (capacity) of tree leaves. This induces a coarse-to-fine representation, namely $\mathcal{C}(v) = \{\mathcal{C}^1(v), \mathcal{C}^2(v), \ldots, \mathcal{C}^L(v)\}_{v=0,\cdots,\Upsilon-1}$.

In particular, as shown in Fig. 1.b, the root node is fictitious and the tree maintains a certain number of entry points for each node dependent on the number L of wanted clusters for each tree-level; we represent the non-leaves node $\{\mathcal{C}^1(v), \mathcal{C}^2(v), \ldots, \mathcal{C}^L(v)\}_{v=0,\cdots,\Upsilon-1}$, at level v by using the parameters $\mathbf{m}^l(v)$ and $|\boldsymbol{\Sigma}_n^l(v)|$; whereas leaves contain the object pointers.

Formally we can define the tree-nodes ("pivots","routing nodes") and the leaves of our structure nodes as $N_r = \langle \mathbf{m}, \boldsymbol{\Sigma}, Ptr \rangle$ and $N_f = \langle \Gamma \rangle$, respectively, where $(\mathbf{m}, \boldsymbol{\Sigma})$ are the features representative of the current routing node, Ptr is the pointer to the parent tree-node and Γ is the set of pointer to the objects on the secondary storage system. The procedure to build our tree is outlined in 2,

3.3 Traversing the Balanced Cluster Tree

When a query object O^q is proposed the BCT representing cluster $\mathcal{C}$ can be traversed for retrieving the N_I target objects O_t, by evaluating the similarity between O^q and clusters $\mathcal{C}_n^l(v)$ at the different levels v of the tree. Recall that each cluster $\mathcal{C}^l(v)$ is represented through its mean and covariance, respectively $\mathbf{m}^l(v)$, $\boldsymbol{\Sigma}^l(v)$. To this end, it is possible to define the distance $d(O^q, \mathcal{C}_n^l(v))$ by computing the distance between O^q and the cluster center $\mathbf{m}^l(v)$, and if we want, weighted by covariance $\mathcal{C}^l(v)$. For example we can use a distance function based on the Mahalanobis formulation,

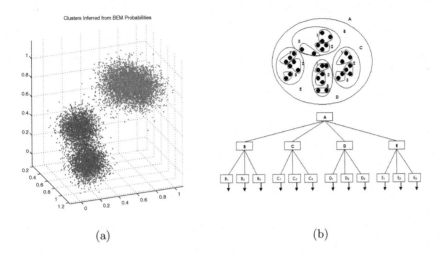

(a)   (b)

Fig. 1. Generating BCT: (a) Balanced Clusters obtained by BEM in a 3-dimensional space, (b) A 2-D example of BCT

Algorithm 2 Building the BCT

Given the current level v and the pointer Ptr to the parent node
lev$=\left[log_{|\mathcal{C}(v-1)|}\left(\frac{n}{B}\right)\right]$ //n being the number of objects
if $v \leq$ lev **then**
  for $(i = 1, ..., |\mathcal{C}(v)|$ **do**
    $\mathbf{m}_i^v, \boldsymbol{\Sigma}_i^v \leftarrow BEM_{Algorithm}$
    $N_{r_i}^v \leftarrow \{\mathbf{m}_i^v, \boldsymbol{\Sigma}_i^v, Ptr\}$
    Building Cluster Tree $(v + 1, Ptr(N_{r_i}^v))$
else
  $N_{f_i}^v \leftarrow \Gamma$ // Γ being the pointers set to the objects of current cluster

---

$$\delta(\mathcal{O}^q, \mathcal{C}^l(v)) = e^{-(\mathcal{O}^q - \mathbf{m}^l(v))^T \boldsymbol{\Sigma}^l(v)^{-1}(\mathcal{O}^q - \mathbf{m}^l(v))}. \tag{10}$$

This distance is real-valued, finite and nonnegative and satisfies symmetry and triangle inequality properties, so that δ is a metric on the our space $\mathcal{S}$ and the pair $(\mathcal{S}, d)$ is a metric space. The distance δ has score 1 if the blobs are identical in all relevant features while decreasing as the match becomes less perfect.

In general we want a BCT defined as metric balanced tree to support operations of classic multidimensional access methods [9]. Then, a search can be performed through a range query. In [9] the tree-search is based on a simple concept: the node related to the region having as center $\mathbf{m}^l(v)$ is visited only if $d(\mathbf{m}^l(v), \mathcal{O}^q) \leq \varphi) + r(\mathbf{m}^l(v))$, where $r(\mathbf{m}^l(v))$ is the radius of the analyzed region. More in details, the range query algorithm starts form the root node and recursively traverses all paths which cannot be excluded from leading to objects because satisfying the above inequality. The φ value is usually evaluated in an experimental way; in particular, we can choose $\varphi = \sqrt[d]{s}/2$, d being the number of dimensions of the metric space and s the wanted selectivity [9].

In our formulation the query radius takes into account, for each tree level, the maximum and the minimum distance between the query object and each cluster distribution. For a given tree level $\nu >= 1$, only the clusters $\mathcal{C}^l(v)$ that satisfy the following condition are traversed:

$$\delta(\mathcal{O}^q, \mathcal{C}^l(v)) < \varphi) \tag{11}$$

with $\varphi = \alpha_q \cdot (\max_l \delta(\mathcal{O}^q, \mathcal{C}^l(v)) - \min_l \delta(\mathcal{O}^q, \mathcal{C}^l(v))) + \min_l \delta(\mathcal{O}^q, \mathcal{C}^l(v))$, $\alpha_q \in [0, 1]$ being the parameter to decide the search width. Algorithm 3 describes a range query using our approach.

Algorithm 3 Range Query on Cluster $\mathcal{C}(v)$

Given α_q, $\mathcal{O}^q$ and v
$maxDist \longleftarrow \max_{l \in \{1,\dots,L\}} \delta(\mathcal{O}^q, \mathcal{C}^l(v))$ and $minDist \longleftarrow \min_{l \in \{1,\dots,L\}} \delta(\mathcal{O}^q, \mathcal{C}^l(v))$
$\varphi = \alpha_q \cdot (maxDist - minDist) + maxDist$
for $(i = 1, \dots, |\mathcal{C}(v)|$ **do**
  if $v = \Upsilon - 1$ **then**
    Save Object Pointers Γ
    break
  else if $\delta(\mathcal{O}^q, \mathcal{C}^l(v)) < \varphi$ **then**
    Range Query$(\mathcal{C}^l(v + 1))$

Eventually, it is worth remarking that, for what concerns the tree updating procedures, a naive strategy would simply re-apply the classification step of BEM algorithm. However, a more elegant and efficient solution is to exploit the cluster detection step to assign the new item to cluster $\mathcal{C}$ and then exploit an on-line, incremental version of the BEM algorithm to update the related tree; the incremental procedure updates the sufficient statistics of the expected log-likelihood only as a function of the new data item inserted in the database, which can be done in constant time [14].

4   Performance Evaluation on an Image Database

4.1   Experimental Setting

The experiments on our BCT have been performed using a dataset composed by about 50000 images collected from the Internet, experimental databases and several commercial archives. In our system the images are coded in the JPEG format at different resolution and size, and stored into a commercial object relational DBMS.

To exploit the BEM algorithm, each image is represented by means of its features vector. As representative image-features we have chosen the image HSV histogram (color information), and the covariance signatures of image wavelet transform (shape-texture information, see [4] for details). More precisely the color histogram is obtained on the HSV components quantized using $256, 128, 64$ levels for H S and V components, respectively, while, the covariance signatures of wavelet transform are represented through using 18 components. Eventually the clustering space becomes a 466-D (high dimensional) space.

For what concerns the BCT building step, at each level $\nu \geq 1$ of the tree (we assume the root node related to level 0), a number L of fixed clusters was used in the recursive application of BEM algorithm. Note that we assume L fixed, in that we are not concerned here with the problem of model selection, in which case L may be selected by Bayesian information criterion (BIC).

Non uniform initial estimates were chosen for $\alpha_k^{(0)}, \mu_l^{(0)}, \Sigma_l^{(0)}$ parameters; $\{m_l^{(0)}\}$ were set in the range from minimal to maximal values of $\mathcal{O}^i$ in a constant increment; $\{\Sigma_l^{(0)}\}$ were set in the range from 1 to $\max\{\mathcal{O}^i\}$ in a constant increment; $\{\alpha_l^{(0)}\}$ were set from $\max\{\mathcal{O}^i\}$ to 1 in a constant decrement and then normalized, $\sum_l \alpha_l^{(0)} = 1$. We found that convergence rate is similar for both methods, convergence being achieved after $t = 300$ iterations (with $\epsilon = 0.1$). Fig. 2 shows how the *incomplete* data log-likelihood $\log p(\mathcal{IP}|\Theta)$ as obtained by the BEM algorithm is non-decreasing at each iteration of the update, and that convergence is faster than with classic EM.

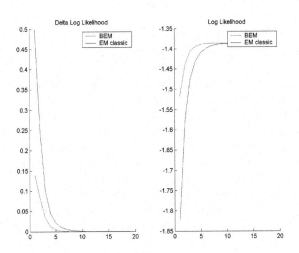

Fig. 2. Behavior of $\log p(\mathcal{IP}|\Theta)$ for $t =$ iterations of the BEM algorithm and comparison with EM

4.2   Retrieval Efficiency

Our BCT index structure can be evaluated from the efficiency point of view by considering its capacity to quickly response to a given user query. Retrieval efficiency is usually measured by evaluating the time elapsed between query formulation and presentation of results. In our case the total search time is obtained from the tree search (traversing) time $\mathbf{t}_{tree}$. The tree search time accounts for the CPU time $\mathbf{t}_{CPU}$ for computing the range query distances while traversing the tree, and the I/O time $\mathbf{t}_{IO}$ needed to retrieve from the disk the image $\mathcal{O}$s and to transfer them to central memory:

$$\mathbf{t}_{tree} = \mathbf{t}_{CPU} + \mathbf{t}_{IO}. \tag{12}$$

Usually, by allocating the images of a leaf node in contiguous disk sectors (exploiting the appropriate operating system primitives) it is possible to reduce the time and number of disk accesses, so that $\mathbf{t}_{CPU} \gg \mathbf{t}_{IO}$, and $\mathbf{t}_{tree} \approx \mathbf{t}_{CPU}$ holds. The parameters that influence the traversing tree time are the range query radius (in our case α_q), the number of clusters (L) that is fixed for each level of the BCT, the tree capacity (B) and the number n of total images. More precisely, for computing the total search time, we have set $\alpha_q = 1$, obtaining:

$$\mathbf{t}_{tree} = \mathbf{t}_{CPU} + \mathbf{t}_{IO} \approx \sum_{k=0}^{[log_L(\frac{n}{B})]} t_d \cdot L^k \tag{13}$$

here t_d is the time for computing a single Mahalanobis distance (dependent on the hardware platform).

We want to notice that the described $\mathbf{t}_{tree}$ is an upper upper bound for the total search time (its complexity is using a L fixed $O(L^{log_L \frac{n}{B}})$), in other terms we are considering the worst case: in fact, the number of evaluated distances, in the tree traversing step, is greater than the average case since, to simplify, we are not considering that in practice at each tree-level many pruned nodes occur. In fact, by setting $\alpha_q = 1$, all nodes of the tree are explored: the number of evaluated distances is equal to the total number of such nodes and the number of retrieved leaves that satisfy the range query is equal to the total number of tree leaves; on the contrary by choosing $\alpha_q < 1$, at each tree-level, using our range query approach, there are many pruned nodes.

For the experiments we have adopted a PENTIUM IV 3GHz Server (1 GB RAM) using the Windows 2003 Server operating system. To create the full BCT index on the entire database (50000 images) our system requires about 2 hours. Moreover for such hardware configuration the time required for computing t_d is about $0.5e - 4$ secs. (about 25000 CPU floating operations are necessary). In Fig. 3 we have shown the $\mathbf{t}_{tree}$ times obtained considering a variable range query radius (we have fixed $B = 20, L = 4$). In this last case the equation 13, is not more valid, moreover there is an extra CPU time spent to evaluate minimum and maximum distances at each tree level and necessary to execute the comparisons among calculated distances. Results refer to the case in which the query image

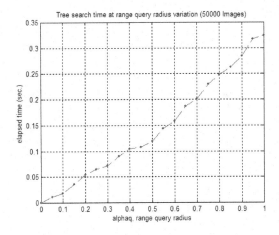

Fig. 3. Tree search time at α_q variation

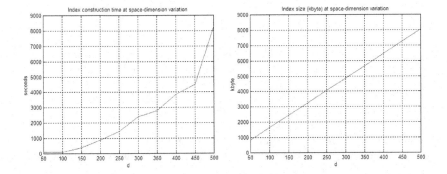

Fig. 4. Index Construction Time and Index Size at d variation

is in the database; if the query image is not in the database, one extra second of CPU time is spent to extract from the query image features.

In order to have an idea of BCT performances respect to other access methods, in figure 4 we report the index construction time and index size at d (space-dimension) variation.

We compared BEM access method with M-Tree and R*-Tree ones in terms of *Query Processing Time*, using our data set and metric. To this end, we have observed a performance improvement of 0.05 sec. respect to M-tree, of 0.07 sec. respect to R*-Tree and of about 2 sec. respect to sequential scan approach.

Eventually considering equation 13, it is possible to calculate the scalability of our system and estimate the total search times for very large databases. For a database of 1000000 images images for each category), choosing $L = 4, B = 25$, we have a tree search time of about 5 sec., in other terms, in the worst case, our system spends about 5 seconds to execute a user query.

5 Conclusions

In this paper, we have presented an indexing approach (BCT) to representing clusters in a hierarchical structure using EM algorithm. By integrating the cluster representation with the index structure, the BCT can enhance the performance of the nearest-neighbor search because it can effectively exploit the structure of the data set and the preliminary results encourage to go on in this direction. Future works will be devoted to enlarge our experimentation using more exhaustive approaches and compare our results with the other ones present in literature.

Acknowledgments

This work has been carried out partially under the financial support of the Ministero dell' Istruzione, dell' Universita' e della Ricerca (MIUR) in the framework of the FIRB Project Middleware for advanced services over large-scale, wired-wireless distributed systems (WEB-MINDS).

References

1. R. Baeza-Yates, W. Cunto, U. Manber, and S. Wu, Proximity matching using Fixed-queries trees, *The 5th Combinatorial Pattern Matching*, volume 807 of Lecture Notes in Computer Science, 198-212, 1994.
2. A. Banerjee, I. S. Dhillon, J. Ghosh, and S. Sra, Clustering on hyperspheres using Expectation Maximization, *Technical Report TR-03-07*, Department of Computer Sciences, University of Texas, February 2003.
3. J. A. Bilmes, A Gentle Tutorial of the EM Algorithm and its Application to Parameter Estimation for Gaussian Mixture and Hidden Markov Models, *Technical Report*, U.C. Berkeley, April 1998
4. G. Boccignone, A. Chianese, V. Moscato and A. Picariello, Fovaeted Shot Detection for Video Segmentation, *IEEE Trans. on Circuits and Sistems for Video Technology*, vol. 15, n.3, March 2005
5. S. Brin, Near neighbor search in large metric spaces, *In Proc. of VLDB95*, 574-584, Switzerland, 1995.
6. W. A. Burkhard, and R. M. Keller, Some approaches to best-match file searching, *Comm. of the ACM*, 16(4):230236, 1973.
7. G. Celeux, and G. Govaert, A classification EM algorithm for clustering and two stochastic versions, *Computational Statistics and Data Analysis*, 14:315-332,1992.
8. E. Chavez, G. Navarro, R. Baeza-Yates, and J. L. Marroquin, Searching in Metric Spaces, *ACM Computing Surveys*, 1999.
9. P. Ciaccia, M. Patella, and P. Zezula, M-tree: An efficient Access Method for Similarity Search in Metric Spaces, *In Proc. of 23rd International Conference on VLDB*, 426-435, 1997. FQ tree 0..5825 FQ tree (with bag distance) 0.4124
10. A.P. Dempster, N.M. Laird, and D.B. Rubin, Maximum likelihood from incomplete data, *Journal of the Royal Statistical Society*, 39:1-38, 1977.
11. V. Ganti, R. Ramakrishnan, J. Gehrke, A. Powell, and J. French, Clustering large datasets in arbitrary metric spaces, *In the Proceedings of International Conference on Data Engineering*, 1999.

12. Anil K. Jain, and Richard C. Dubes, Algorithms for Clustering Data, *Prentice Hall, Englewood Cliffs*, New Jersey, 1998.
13. I. Kalantari, and G. McDonald, A data structure and an algorithm for the nearest point problem, *IEEE Transactions on Software Engineering*, 9(5), 1983.
14. R.M. Neal and G.E. Hinton, A view of the EM algorithm that justifies incremental, sparse, and other variants, *Learning in Graphical Models*, M.J. Jordan ed., 355-368, MIT Press, 1998.
15. J. Uhlmann, Satisying general proximity/similarity queries with metric trees, *Information Processing Letters*, 40, 175-179, 1991.
16. Peter N. Yianilos, Data structures and algorithms for nearest neighbor search in general metric spaces, *Proceedings of the fourth annual ACM-SIAM Symposium on Discrete algorithms*, p.311-321, Jan. 25-27, 1993.
17. D. Yu, and A. Zhang, ClusterTree: Integration of Cluster Representation and Nearest-Neighbor Search for Large Data Sets with High Dimensions, *IEEE Trans. on KDE*, 15(5), 1316-1330, 2003.
18. S. Zhong and J. Ghosh, A Unified Framework for Model-based Clustering, *Journal of Machine Learning Research*, 4:1001-1037, 2003.
19. Jian-Kang Wu, Content-Based Indexing of Multimedia Databases, *IEEE Transactions on Knowledge and Data Engineering*,9(6),1997.
20. C.Bohm, S.Berchtold, D.A. Keim, Searching in High-Dimensional Spaces-Index Structures for Improving the Performance of Multimedia Databases, *ACM Computing Surveys*,33(3),2001.

The MX Formalism for Semantic Web Compatible Representation of Music Metadata*

S. Castano, A. Ferrara, G. Haus, L.A. Ludovico, S. Montanelli,
G. Racca, and G. Vercellesi

Università degli Studi di Milano,
DICo - Via Comelico, 39, 20135 Milano - Italy
{castano, ferrara, haus, ludovico, montanelli, racca,
vercellesi}@dico.unimi.it

Abstract. Music description is nowadays considered an important matter in Information and Communication Technology. The encoding formats commonly accepted and employed are often characterized by a partial view of the whole problem: they describe music data or metadata for score, audio tracks, computer performances of music pieces, but they seldom encode all these aspects together. In this paper, we present the MX formalism that aims to address this limitation of the existing formats, by providing a Semantic Web compatible representation of music information in terms of structural and semantic features, by means of XML and OWL.

1 Introduction

Music description is nowadays considered an important matter in Information and Communication Technology. The encoding formats commonly accepted and employed are often characterized by a partial view of the whole problem: they describe music data or metadata for score, audio tracks, computer performances of music pieces, but they seldom encode all these aspects together. Many encoding formats have been proposed aimed at a precise characterization of different specific music aspects. For example, MP3, AAC and PCM formats encode audio recordings; MIDI represents a well known standard for computer-driven performance; TIFF and JPEG files can contain the results of a scanning process of scores; finally, NIFF and Sibelius formats are aimed at score typing and publishing. The purpose of these file formats is the description of music data and, in a certain measure, also of metadata. Let us consider for example an MP3 file. It describes both music contents (e.g., frequencies, loudness, and other audio characteristics) and the corresponding metadata (e.g., author, song title, album). In general terms, common file formats usually include not only a detailed description of one musical aspect - logical, structural, aural, interpretative, typographic,

---

* This paper has been partially funded by "Wide-scalE, Broadband, MIddleware for Network Distributed Services (WEB-MINDS)" FIRB Project funded by the Italian Ministry of Education, University, and Research.

K.S. Candan and A. Celentano (Eds.): MIS 2005, LNCS 3665, pp. 78–92, 2005.

or graphical - but also more abstract information about the piece. In order to appreciate the richness of music communication, we can point out that music - in its most general meaning - can stimulate different senses: the sense of hearing, the sense of sight and even the sense of touch. Music language is made up of many different and complementary aspects. A complete analysis of music richness and complexity is provided in [1], where six different levels of description are identified - namely general, structural, logical, notational, audio and performance layers. This multi-layer structure could answer the request of completeness in music description, as the layers we listed can be considered a good coverage of the different domains of music. They take into account the evidence that music is the composition itself as well as the sound a listener hears, and music is the score that a performer reads as well as the execution provided by a computer system. In this paper, we describe the MX Format that provide a XML-based support for the representation of the different layers composing music information. In particular, we focus on the top layer, devoted to the representation of music metadata and their semantics. We propose the use of ontologies in order to address the requirement of a flexible and meaningful description of music metadata, and of genre in particular.

The paper is organized as follows. In Section 2 we provide a short description of the MX format, and we point out the main limitations of the actual metadata description and the requirements for a richer representation of the metadata layer. In Section 3, we describe our approach to the representation of the music metadata by means of an ontology that describes the MX Semantic Layer. In Section 4, we point out the applicability issues related our work, and, in Section 5, we discuss the related work with respect to our approach. Finally, in Section 6, we give conclusions and we focus on the future work.

2   A Comprehensive XML-Based Format for Music

We have developed a new XML-based format, called MX. Currently, MX is undergoing the IEEE standardization process, as described in [2]. Our approach is different from the aforementioned partial perspectives in music description, in particular because we represent music information according to a multi-layer structure and to the concept of space-time construct. In our opinion, music information can be (and should be) structured by using a layer subdivision model, as shown in Figure 1. Each layer is specific to a different degree of abstraction in music information. In our proposal for a common and exhaustive format, we distinguish among General, Structural, Music Logic, Notational, Performance and Audio layers (see Figure 1a). For example, MusicXML could be integrated in the more comprehensive MX format to implement the Logical Organized Symbols layer, that is score symbolic information (e.g., notes, rests), whereas other common file types can be linked to represent other layers: TIFF for the Notational layer, MP3 and WAV for the Audio layer and so on. The issue of the integration between MX and other formats is covered in [3].

The main advantage of MX is the richness of our descriptive format, which is based on other commonly accepted encodings aimed at more specific descriptions.

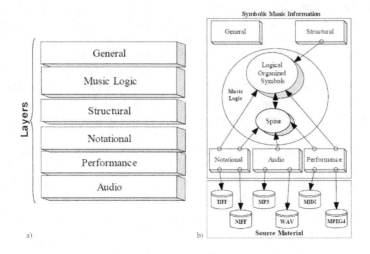

Fig. 1. (a) Music information layers and (b) relations among them

Considering music structure as a multi-layered information, we need a sort of glue to keep together the heterogeneous contributions that compose it. Accordingly, we introduced the concept of *spine*. Spine is a structure that relates time and spatial information (see Figure 2), where measurement units are expressed in relative format. Through such a mapping, it is possible to fix a point in a layer instance (e.g. Notational) and investigate the corresponding point in another one (e.g. Performance or Audio).

2.1 A MX Encoding Example

In the following, we provide a series of significant portions of MX encoding the different layers, together with some comments for demonstration purpose. The complete DTD of MX 1.5 format is available at http://www.computer.org/-standards/1599/par.htm

The Logic layer contains information referenced by all other layers, and represents what the composer intended to put in the piece. It is composed of two elements: i) the Spine description, used to mark the significant events in order to reference them from the other layers and ii) the LOS (Logically Organized Symbols) element, that describes the score from a symbolic point of view (e.g., chords, rest). The second example below illustrates how notes, chords and rests can be represented in MX notation.

Fig. 2. Spine: relationships between Notational, Performance and Audio layer

```
<spine>
        <event id="e0" timing="0" hpos="NULL"/>
        ...
</spine>

<measure number="1">
     <voice ref="violin_1">
            <rest event_ref="v1_e0" staff_ref="staff_1">
                    <duration den="1" num="2"/>
            </rest>
            <chord event_ref="v1_e1">
                    <notehead staff_ref="staff_1">
                            <pitch step="C" octave="6"/>
                            <duration num="1" den="2"/>
                    </notehead>
            </chord>
     </voice>
</measure>
```

The Structural layer contains explicit descriptions of music objects together with their causal relationships, from both the compositional and musicological point of view, i.e. how music objects can be described as a transformation of previously described music objects. The Notational layer links all possible visual instances of a music piece. Representations can be grouped in two types: notational and graphical. A notational instance is often in a binary format, such as NIFF or Enigma, whereas a graphical instance contains images representing the score. Usually, the latter is in a binary format too (e.g., a JPEG image or a PDF file), but it can also be a vector image encoded in SVG. The information contained in this layer is tied to the spatial part of the Spine structure, allowing its localization. The Performance layer lies between Notational and Audio layers. File formats grouped in this level encode parameters of notes to be played and parameters of sounds to be created by a computer preformance. This layer supports symbolic formats such as MIDI, Csound or SASL/SAOL files. Finally, the Audio layer describes properties of the source material containing music audio information. It is the lowest level of the layered structure.

```
<audio>
    <clip>
        <clip_format file_name="Beethoven_Symphony#7_4.mp3" file_format="MP3"
        encoding_format="MPEG1">
            <frequency type="constant" avg_value_Hz="44100"/>
            <bitrate type="CBR" avg_value_bitsec=""/>
            <channel channel_number="2" LFE="no"/>
        </clip_format>
        <clip_indexing>
            <clip_marker timing_type="sec">
                <clip_marker_event timing="0.00" spine_ref="v1_e0"/>
                ...
        </clip_indexing>
    </clip>
</audio>
```

2.2   The MX General Layer and Its Limitations

Recalling the previous subsection, MX format is rich in information and description possibilities. One of its layers, the so-called General layer, is not directly related to score and audio contents. This layer simply describes some fundamental alphanumeric information about the coded music work. The situation is shown in Figure 1, where the General block is clearly separated from other levels, even if it belongs to Symbolic Music Information as well. A particular importance is given to sub-element Description, devoted to author, genre and piece information. Such music metadata, even if not related to music symbols or audio performances, are particularly important for music classification and retrieval. In detail, the MX 1.5 DTD description of metadata can be shown by means of the following example:

```
<general>
    <description>
        <work_title>Symphony No.7 in A major</work_title>
        <work_number>7</work_number>
        <movement_title>Allegro con brio</movement_title>
        <movement_number>4</movement_number>
        <genre>
            <genre_spec name="Classic" weight="40"/>
            <genre_spec name="Preromantic" weight="60"/>
        </genre>
        <author type="composer">Ludwig van Beethoven</author>
    </description>
</general>
```

In particular the Description element contains 6 sub-elements, corresponding to 6 metadata categories: This structure is aimed at the general description of the original score, as the author(s) conceived it. In the Audio layer, for instance, we will find similar information (and a similar structure) about the audioclips related to the score itself. Some elements would be redundant, so they are not present in the audio instances: typically, the data about the composition itself (e.g., composer, title). Other elements are naturally related only to performances-it is the case of the performers list. Finally, some elements are repeated as their value can differ from the original score: potentially we can conceive a jazz cover version of a classical piece or a rock performance of a baroque music work. Apparently, this schema seems to be complete and powerful. The characteristic information about a single score and its performances can be represented, and all these data are organized in a multi-layered structure. However, even in the General layer, a number of problematic issues arise and pose a number of requirements to be addressed. First, we have general metadata to describe the score and partially different metadata to describe related score performances. Second, the schema and the names we gave to elements are meaningful only for a certain kind of music: if the concepts of movement and work can be useful for a traditional composer's production, it would be difficult to classify a pop song according to this terminology. Besides, the concept of genre is vague. Genre could represent something related to a historical period, to a geographical area, to a musical style, to a musicological classification, and, more generally, different people give usually different meanings to the concept of genre and refer to different genre descriptions. As a consequence, the final key problem is represented by the wide possibilities of classification left to the user who encodes a music piece by MX. For example, a description of the genre in natural language could provide informative richness, but on the other hand it could have dramatic repercussions on music information retrieval. Imagine a query to extract all the baroque pieces from a huge database where each piece was described in natural language and using no conventions about terminology and classification features.

2.3   Ontologies for Classification and Management of Music Metadata

There is no consensus about *what* belongs to *which* genre, and about the taxonomy itself. For example, two users may agree that certain values associated to certain characteristics define a single genre, but they could give two different names to that genre (e.g. Easy Listening music is also called Variety). It is possible to define a piece of music through several style levels. For example, II sang Dixie by Dwight Yoakam is defined as Popular music, or Country music, or Hard Honky Tonk as well, where each genre is a subset of the previous one. Moreover, a piece of music could change the associated genre, and a definition of a genre could change in time (e.g. Underground was a kind of independent music, now the same term defines a kind of disco music). Unfortunately a stable and commonly accepted definition for every genre does not exist. In other terms, the concept of genre is non-well-defined, and in many cases ambiguous. The problems related to the classification and the management of music metadata in a MIR context are well covered in [4]. This is also the result of a study (see [5]) that compared three Internet genre taxonomies - allmusic.com, amazon.com and mp3.com - coming to an important result: there is no consensus in the name used in these classifications, and no shared structure. However, from our point of view, the genre is particularly important, as this information could help music consumers and MIR systems to identify, classify and retrieve music pieces, using genre as a criterion of query or as a base for similarity measures. Our goal is to provide a tool for classifying and describe genre, and music metadata in general, that: i) does not impose a shared and common definition; ii) provides a flexible mechanism that, at the same time, supports different users to give their own description of music; iii) supports a discovery service and provides matching functionalities for comparing different descriptions in order to find similarities among them. These goals can be achieved by using an ontology that describes music metadata.

3   Ontology-Based Representation of the MX Semantic Layer

Ontology is generally defined as a explicit representation of a conceptualization [6]. In our approach, a *Music Ontology* is used for enriching the MX Format by providing a semantic description, called Semantic Layer, of the layer General of MX.

3.1   Conceptual Specification of the MX Semantic Layer

The music ontology that we create to express the semantic information within the MX general layer is specified in OWL [7]. In this paper, in order to give a more comfortable representation and a clearer view of objects involved as well as their relations, we decided to use ER formalism for describing the ontology conceptualization of the semantic layer, and then to describe the OWL implementation of this conceptualization. The ER diagram of our ontology is shown in Figure 3. The ontology has to satisfy three main requirements: i) to separate informa-

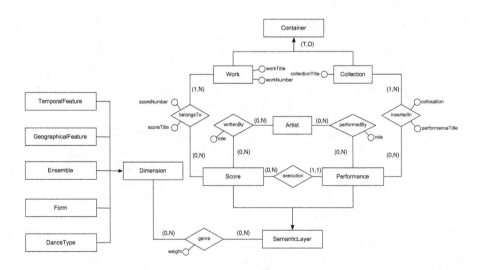

Fig. 3. ER diagram for the music ontology

tion regarding scores and performances; ii) to adequately express the complex relationships among artists and scores/performances; iii) to adequately model the genre classification. The first requirement refers to the need to express the conceptual separation between a score and its (possibly) multiple performances, as well as the logical relationship between a score and all its performances. This distinction is one of the main features of the MX Format. The second requirement refers to the complex relationships between a score and its authors as well as between a performance and the artists involved. A score may have many authors with different roles (e.g. music author, lyrics author), an artist may be the author of a particular score, but we may not have any performance of that score involving its author. Moreover the same artist may be involved in a particular performance with different roles (e.g. vocals and guitar). The third requirement refers to the classification of a performance or score with respect to its genre. In order to deal with this complexity we can think to the genre as a classification along different dimensions. Each dimension refers to a particular set of features and each score or performance can be classified along one or more of these dimensions. Moreover, when we associate a particular score or performance with a particular dimension, we want to specify the strength of the relationship. In the ER diagram shown in Figure 3 we see the entities of our representation as well as their main attributes. Some attributes are not shown to mantain the figure cleaner (e.g. first and last name of artists, creation date of a score). Semantic information contained into the MX general layer is enriched by associating it to an instance of the SemanticLayer entity. This entity is a total and exclusive generalization of semantic information related to scores (the Score entity) and performances (the Performance entity). Each score may be related to its performances. Each score may be related to its authors that are instances of the Artist entity. While associating an artist with a score we must specify a role, that represents the particular kind of authorship (e.g. Composer, Librettist). In the same way, we associate an artist to a particular performance (e.g. Conductor, Orchestra). We also decided to introduce a generic container that would allow to group together scores or performances. This container will be useful for retrieval or classification purposes. We can group scores within works and performances within collections. Since the hierarchy is total but overlapped, works and collections are not disjoint. A Work refers to way the author of the score originally released it, while a Collection refers to all the containers in which a particular performance can be found. A Bach fugue will be contained in an instance of the Work entity, typically referring to its paper-publication, while "Helter Skelter" will be contained in an instance of the Work entity representing "The White Album". Beside, we can have a particular recording of "Helter Skelter" song that can be contained in the instance of the Collection entity referring to "The White Album" as well as in the instance referring to the "Beatles' complete work". In order to deal with the complexity of genre classification, we decided to model the genre as an association between a score or performance and a dimension. This association must be enriched by a value (weight) that specify the strenght of the relation. The Dimension entity is a generalization, since we have specific entities expressing the five dimensions that we decided to include in this first implementation of our ontology. Each dimension refers to a particular feature of the score or performance. The five entites representing genre dimensions are: i) TemporalFeature: this entity describes historical periods (e.g. Pre-Romantic, 80's); ii) GeographicalFeatures: this entity describes countries and regions; iii) Ensamble: this entity elements involved in a particular performance (e.g. String Quartet); iv) Form: this entity describes relations among elements (e.g. melodic themes) of a score. A form instance can be a Fugue or a Sonata; v) DanceTypeFeature this entity describes rhythmic reatures about accents disposition (e.g. Waltzer, Polka). A particular instance of the Score or Performance entity will be associated to one or more instances of the Dimension hierarchy. For each genre association we will have also to express a weight. We can classify our scores and performances focusing our attention to one or more dimension. Moreover, this kind of classification allows us to associate the same score instance to multiple instances of the same dimension, overcoming the limitations of tipical classification methods based on predefined genre attribution.

3.2   OWL Representation of the MX Semantic Layer

To ensure Semantic Web compatibility, the music ontology is represented by means of OWL. The idea is to define an OWL ontology describing the conceptualization of the semantic layer in terms of concepts, properties and semantic relations. In terms of OWL, the music ontology is associated with the MX semantic layer by means of a XML Namespace, denoted as mxsl and available at http://islab.-dico.unimi.it/ontologies/mx-semantic-layer.owl. A graphical representation of this approach is shown in Figure 4.The music ontology includes the OWL representation of the concepts described in Figure 3. In the ontology we have defined an OWL class for each entity, and appropriate OWL properties for representing the attributes and the relations reported in the ER model. The hierarchies have been represented by means of the OWL subClassOf construct, specifying an explicit disjunction between the Score and the Performance elements. The problem of representing attributes of the relations (e.g., the attribute weight of the relation genre) in OWL has been addressed as suggested in [8]. The problem is due to the fact that OWL provides constructs for representing only binary relations, without attributes. In order to address this limitation, we have defined a class for each attribute featured relation and a set of properties for representing the relation attribute as well as its second argument. An example of this approach is provided in Figure 5 where we show the OWL description of the class Genre that represents the genre relation of the ER model. The attribute weight and the argument Dimension of the genre relation are represented by means of the restriction mechanism of OWL, which states that the values of the dimension for a genre must be an instance of the class Dimension and that each instance of the class Genre has exactly one dimension associated with one weight. The result is that each genre featuring a semantic layer description is seen as a pair of the form $< Dimension, Weight >$. Each genre feature is then associated with a semantic layer description by means of a property genre, as specified in the class

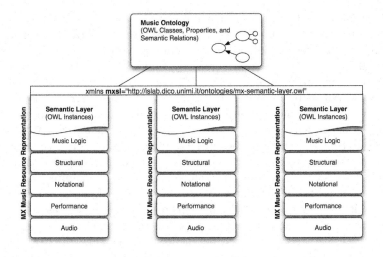

Fig. 4. The music ontology and the MX Semantic Layer

SemanticLayer by an appropriate OWL restriction. A complete description of the music ontology is shown in Figure 6, where the OWL features are represented graphically by means of the HOE (H-MODEL Ontology Editor) developed for ontology management in the context of the HELIOS project [9]. In the logical view provided by the HOE tool, the concepts are represented by rectangular labels, while properties are represented by circles. Solid lines and dashed lines represent the domain and range of the properties, respectively, while arrows represent subClassOf relations. By referring to the music ontology, each MX semantic

```
<owl:Class rdf:about="#Genre">
   <rdfs:subClassOf>
     <owl:Restriction>
       <owl:onProperty rdf:resource="#dimension" />
       <owl:allValuesFrom rdf:resource="#Dimension"/>
       </owl:Restriction>
   </rdfs:subClassOf>
   <rdfs:subClassOf>
     <owl:Restriction>
       <owl:onProperty rdf:resource="#dimension" />
       <owl:cardinality rdf:datatype="&xsd;int">1</owl:cardinality>
     </owl:Restriction>
   </rdfs:subClassOf>
   <rdfs:subClassOf>
     <owl:Restriction>
       <owl:onProperty rdf:resource="#weight" />
       <owl:cardinality rdf:datatype="&xsd;int">1</owl:cardinality>
     </owl:Restriction>
   </rdfs:subClassOf>
</owl:Class>
```

Fig. 5. Example of the OWL description of the genre concept

description is an OWL document that imports the ontology and defines a set of instances for describing a music resource represented with MX. The OWL document starts with a declaration of the mxsl namespace that is used for linking the semantic description to the music ontology, and with the owl:Ontology element that imports the music ontology elements. Each score or performance modeled by MX is described by means of an instance of the class Score or Performance, respectively. The instances describe a MX resource in terms of its properties that are associated with other instances describing information about the artists and the role that they have played in the present MX resource, the containers the resource belongs to, the genre classification, and, in the case of scores, the performances associated with the present resource. As an example, we consider the 4th movement of the Symphony No.7 in A major by Ludwig van Beethoven. The score title depends on the title that this resource have when associated with a work as well as its number in that work. These dependences are represented by creating an instance of the class BelongsTo, that describes the work in which the score is inserted, and the title and number of the score within that context. The main advantage of this approach is that we can associate with a score a multiple set of containers, in the case that the author have inserted the score in more than a work. Moreover the title and number of the score can be different for each work it belongs to. A similar approach has been used for artists. In fact, each score is associated with a number of artists with different roles (e.g., author, composer). A possible solution is to associate with a score a predefined set of roles. The disadvantage is that the score statement is not flexible, in that we cannot add a new role to it. Our solution is based on the idea to define an instance for each pair composed by an artist and its role. In that way, we have two advantages: i) we can create such an information for each kind of role, without limitations, and ii) we create a portion of information that can be reused in further score descriptions. The score genre is represented by instances of the class Genre, each representing the weight set for a dimension. In the example, we state that the score is classic and preromantic. Moreover, we state that the preromantic feature is more relevant than the classic one for this score, by means of a weight associated with the two dimensions. Once these genres are set, we can reuse them for further classifications. An example of genre definition and its use in a score description is shown in Figure 7. Finally, a score is associated with one or more performances that are described by means of the same properties used for the score. The complete description of the example is available at http://islab.dico.unimi.it/ontologies/mxsl-description-example.owl. The approach used for the MX resource description has two main advantages: i) we have a high level of flexibility in describing the features of music information in that there is an extensible mechanism for enriching the set of available instances and the capability of capturing the fact that different people describe music in a high number of different ways; ii) while each description is composed, a new set of reusable instances is defined. In this way, each new description enriches the ontology by adding new features that can be used for further descriptions.

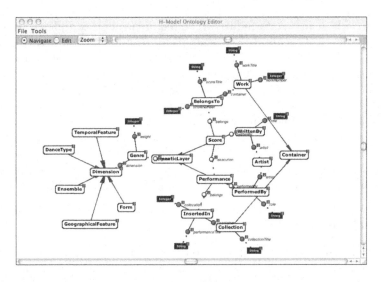

Fig. 6. Graphical representation of the MX semantic layer ontology

```
<mxsl:Genre rdf:ID="Preromanticism_60">
    <mxsl:weight rdf:datatype="&xsd;int">60</mxsl:weight>
    <mxsl:dimension rdf:resource="#Preromanticism"/>
</mxsl:Genre>
<mxsl:Genre rdf:ID="Classicism_40">
    <mxsl:weight rdf:datatype="&xsd;int">40</mxsl:weight>
    <mxsl:dimension rdf:resource="#Classicism"/>
</mxsl:Genre>
<mxsl:Score rdf:ID="Symphony_N_7_A_major_Allegro_con_brio">
    ...
    <mxsl:genre rdf:resource="#Classicism_40"/>
    <mxsl:genre rdf:resource="#Preromanticism_60"/>
    ...
</mxsl:Score>
```

Fig. 7. An example of genre definition

4   Applicability Issues

In this section, we discuss main applicability issues of using the proposed ontology for semi-automated music resources retrieval and classification according to semantic criteria.

4.1   Semantic Retrieval of Music Resources

The MX semantic layer can be used to improve music pieces retrieval from the traditional keyword-based approach to a semantics-based approach. According to the keyword-based approach, a query can contain one or more equality constraints represented by pairs $< metadata\_name = value >$ to be satisfied. Each music piece whose metadata fulfills all the requirements is considered to be relevant for the query. This approach is suitable for searches related to unambiguous metadata, such as Title and Author. Nevertheless, the semantics-based approach allows to take into consideration the different representation of subjective metadata, such as Genre, during the retrieval process. Given a query, a music piece is found to be relevant if the values of its metadata match the query requirements according to some similarity criteria. The meaning of similarity can be user-defined and depends on the context of the search. In general, the semantic retrieval of music can be improved by using ontology-based matching techniques for evaluating the similarity between two different music piece description. An example of this kind of similarity evaluation is provided in [10,11].

4.2   Semi-automated Classification of Music Resources

Some features about genres can be automatically extracted from score features. Melodic profiles, persistent rhythms, voices texture, declared ensemble are only some examples of music characteristics that can be extracted from MX format. Sometimes, this information provides a direct mean of classification: consider a row (or series) identified by a trivial melody analysis, which is an unambiguous proof for serial music. However, in general terms the extractable information is not intended for an automatic classification, rather it is helpful to exclude several possibilities. For instance, a simple harmony analysis could roughly date the composition: some harmonic behaviors are typical of jazz music and can not be applied to baroque pieces. Similarly, it is difficult to classify a piece as a string quartet if the ensemble includes more than four instruments, or those instruments differ from violin, viola, and cello. Our idea is to exploit the rich description provided by MX in describing the structural features of music information, in order to semi-automatically support the classification of music with respect to its semantic description. The application of such a technique is particularly relevant for the publication of catalogues of music that can potentially contain a high number of music items.

5   Related Work

XML is an effective way to describe music information. Nowadays, there is a number of good dialects to encode music by means of XML, such as MusicXML, MusiXML, MusiCat, MEI, MDL (see [3] for a thorough discussion). In particular, we have at least two good reasons to mention MusicXML [12]. MusicXML is a comprehensive way to represent symbolic information. As a consequence, MusicXML was integrated in a number of commercial programs. Among them, its worthwhile to cite one of the leading applications for music notation: Coda Music Finale. One of the key advantages of MusicXML over other XML-based formats is represented by its popularity in the field of music software. However, all the encoding formats we listed before are not interested in semantic descriptions of metadata, and do not contain an ontology approach similar to our. In MPEG-7 context, currently there are initiatives to integrate OWL ontologies in a framework opportunely developed for the support of ontology-based semantic indexing and retrieval of audiovisual content. This initiative follows the Semantic Level of MPEG-7 MDS (*Multimedia Description Schemas*), and TV-Anytime standard specifications for metadata descriptions. Despite of MX Semantic Layer, MPEG-7 Semantic Level describes music information from the real world perspective, giving the emphasis on Events, Objects, Concepts, Places, Time in narrative worlds and Abstraction. Therefore, MPEG-7 ontology is only aimed at the description of music performance and not of score information, as in the case of MX. The methodology of OWL ontology integration and the interoperability methodology and tools have been based on a core OWL ontology, which fully covers the Semantic Part of the MPEG-7 MDS and a methodology for the definition of domain-specific ontologies that extend the core ontology in order to fully describe the concepts of specific application domains, together with two sets of rules, used for the transformation of semantic metadata (formed according to the core ontology and its domain-specific extensions) to MPEG-7 and TV-Anytime compliant XML documents respectively. A complete discussion of the matter is in [13]. Genre, an intrinsic property of music, is probably one of the most important descriptor used to classify music archives. Traditionally, genre classification has been performed manually but many automatical approaches are provided by the state of art. In [14], three different categories of genre classification are proposed: i) manual approch based on human knowledgment and culture; ii) automatic approch based on automatic extraction of audio features; iii) automatic approch based on objective simliraty measures. Taxonomy use is the main difference beetwen the two automatic approaches: in the first a given taxonomy is necessary, in the second is not required. Further methods to classifiy music genre working on audio signals can be found in [15]. In MX, we have tried to classify genres by an OWL ontology, in order to get a taxonomy as flexible as possible and capturing the complexity of real world genre classifications.

6   Concluding Remarks

In this paper, we have presented the MX format for music representation, together with a proposal of enrichment of MX to achieve a flexible and Semantic Web compatible representation of the metadata associated with MX resources. The metadata representation is realized by means of an OWL ontology that describes music information and proposes three main direction for future work. A first activity is the enrichment of the ontology with new classes and properties that capture further features of music information. A particular attention will be devoted to the structure of music and its relations with the problem of genre classification. A second activity will be devoted to the definition of the functionalities of a music retrieval system based on the ontological description of scores. The idea is to adapt ontology matching techniques to capture the similarity among different music resources and to exploit it for retrieval purposes [11]. Finally, a third activity will be devoted to semi-automated, ontology-driven, classification of music resources, with respect to their genre. The idea is to exploit the rich description provided by MX in describing the structural feature of music in order to automatically identify in the music ontology the genre of a given music item and classify it accordingly.

References

1. Haus, G., Longari, M.: Towards a Symbolic/Time-Based Music Language Based on XML. In: Proc. of Musical Application Using XML (MAX 2002), Milan, Italy, IEEE (2002)
2. XML Musical Application Working Group: Recommended Practice for the Definition of a Commonly Acceptable Musical Application Using the XML Language. IEEE SA 1599, PAR approval date 09/27/2001 (2001)
3. Longari, M.: Formal and Software Tools for a Commonly Acceptable Musical Application Using the XML Language. PhD thesis, Dipartimento di Informatica e Comunicazione, Università degli Studi di Milano (2003)
4. Diana, L.: An XML-based Querying Model for MIR Applications Within a Multi-layered Music Information Environment. PhD thesis, Dipartimento di Informatica e Comunicazione, Università degli Studi di Milano (2004)
5. Pachet, F., Cazaly, D.: A taxonomy of musical genres. In: Proc. of Content-Based Multimedia Information Access (RIAO), Paris, France (2000)
6. Gruber, T.: A Translation Approach to Portable Ontology Specifications. Knowledge Acquisition (2003) 199–220
7. Smith, M.K., Welty, C., McGuinness, D.L.: OWL Web Ontology Language Guide. Technical report, W3C Recommendation (10 February 2004)
8. Noy, N., Rector, A.: Defining n-ary relations on the semantic web: Use with individuals. Technical report, W3C Working Draft (21 July 2004)
9. ISLab Università degli Studi di Milano: The HELIOS Project. http://islab.dico.unimi.it/helios/ (2003)
10. Castano, S., Ferrara, A., Montanelli, S., Racca, G.: Matching Techniques for Resource Discovery in Distributed Systems Using Heterogeneous Ontology Descriptions. In: Proc. of the Int. Conference on Coding and Computing (ITCC 2004), Las Vegas, Nevada, USA, IEEE Computer Society (2004)
11. Castano, S., Ferrara, A., Montanelli, S., Racca, G.: From Surface to Intensive Matching of Semantic Web Ontologies. In: DEXA Workshops 2004, IEEE (2004) 140–144
12. Good, M.: MusicXML for Notation and Analysis. In: The VirtualScore: Representation, Retrieval, Restoration. MIT Press (2001) 113–124
13. Tsinaraki, C., Panagiotis, P., Christodoulakis, S.: Integration of owl ontologies in mpeg-7 and tvanytime compliant semantic indexing. In: Proc. of the 16th International Conference on Advanced Information Systems Engineering (CAiSE), Riga, Latvia (2004)
14. Aucouturier, J.J., Pachet., F.: Respresenting musial genre: A state of the art. Journal of New Music Research **32** (2003) 83–93
15. Tzanetakis, G., Essl, G., Cook, P.: Automatic musical genre classification of audio signals. In: Proc. of 2nd Annual International Symposium on Music Information Retrieval, Indiana University Bloomington, Indiana, USA (2001)

Icon Language-Based Auxiliary Communication System Interface for Language Disorders

Kyonam Choo, Yoseop Woo, Hongki Min, and JuYeon Jo[*]

Dept. of Information and Telecommunication Engineering, University of Incheon,
402-749, 177 Dowha-Dong, Nam-Gu, Incheon, Korea
{kyonam, yswooo, hkmin}@incheon.ac.kr
[*]Computer Science Department College of Engineering and Computer Science,
California State University, Sacramento
joj@ecs.csus.edu

Abstract. The icon language interface is designed to provide the people with language disabilities with more smooth and convenient communication environment than the traditional keyboard-based input system. In order for that, vocabulary commanding tendencies and characteristics of proto-corpus built upon the frequently-used conversation sections will be analyzed, and the Korean language's vocabulary and their meanings applied to the icons will be retrieved by the use of morpheme, phrase and semantic analysis techniques. The icon types to be intuitively recognized and communicable by users are selected, and they are matched with the retrieved Korean vocabulary and meanings. In order to create a relevant situation to communicate from the relations between neighboring icons, the icon language is formed through the each definition of icon language's vocabulary, grammar rules, parts of speech and semantic system.

1 Introduction

We are under the technology-oriented environment where the fully usable knowledge-based information via Internet is easily brought by everyday language without any further particular education. However, most of system environments are likely to rely on a simple keyboard-based input system that is unable to implement more accurate and complicated communication; it also brings an information isolation problem to language-impaired people who have difficulty in keyboard typing. Therefore, there is an immediate need for the development of a general-purpose interface. So, this study is proposing the icon-based interface to provide the language-impaired people with the convenient system control environment with reflecting the natural language's characteristics.

The existing studies adopt the interface to use symbols in an auxiliary communication system designed for people with language disabilities, but it was only connecting a word or sentence to each of symbols. There were some cases that language process was introduced to try vocabulary prediction, but it showed many limits in dealing with various properties of natural language. Especially in domestic electronic engineering and application engineering sectors, some of studies to try to translate Korean

K.S. Candan and A. Celentano (Eds.): MIS 2005, LNCS 3665, pp. 93–101, 2005.
© Springer-Verlag Berlin Heidelberg 2005

into sign language are published, but the amount of those studies is insufficient so that there is significant difficulty in the application and realization of the system for language-impaired people[1,2].

2 Information and Expression of Icon Language

The icon interface environment provide the environment to reconfigure a series of selected icons according to natural language's properties; such icons are selected in a way to combine the contexts to be communicated and input them into the system by selecting a number of graphic based icons externally. The icon language interface in this study doesn't show any process load comparing to other voice/screen recognition systems, underway to research for the well-being of people with disabilities. And since the interface is expressed via icons to be intuitively recognized by users, it has some strong points that information input by language-impaired people can be accepted more accurately and instantaneously.

The icon language gives the vocabulary, parts of speech, meaning and properties to the user recognizable meaningful pictures, and such diverse context-information among the vocabulary properties are reconstructed to create Korean from a diversity of icon combinations selected by users. In the Figure 1, the overview of system structure is shown through the language auxiliary interface in order to create the Korean language.

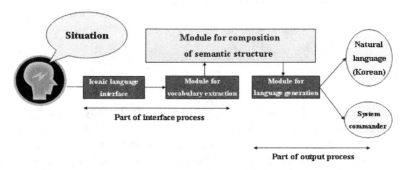

Fig. 1. Structure of Icon Language Interface System

The icon language is featured in putting the context-based meaning onto an icon picture, so users are able to communicate the proper meaning by combining relevant contexts through connecting each of icons without accurate linguistic expression. And each icon provides the consistent interface to users from external point of view, and internally, it is easy to add language features in terms of parts of speech, vocabulary, and semantic system for commanding various natural languages.

3 Icon Language Design and Vocabulary Data Construction

3.1 Design Process of Icon Language

In order to make use of icon language as the communication means, it is necessary to collect and analyze usable vocabulary for the construction of the vocabulary database used for the icons. Also the study to analyze the relationship between an icon and vocabulary is necessary. In order for that, a wide variety of factors should be taken into account, including the individual requirements and interest according to the user's language impairment degree, communication situations, and vocabulary functionalities.

Design Process of Icon Language

1) Define icon language's parts of speech and synthetic information
2) Select the application areas and construct the proto-conversation corpus
3) Construct the corpus with the parts of speech in icon: based upon the analysis of conversation contents through the corpus construction with icon parts of speech, the characteristics of vocabulary, parts of speech, and semantics applied to icons will be retrieved.
4) Connect a word and its meaning to an icon

3.2 The Grammatical Structure Definition of Icon Language

From the structural point of view, the Korean language is an agglutinative language in which each component of meaning is represented by its own morpheme to which a postposition and suffix is added. On the other hand, the sign language mostly used by people with language disabilities doesn't show any development of morpheme to represent the grammatical relations, and it is similar to an isolation language in which each of vocabularies is independently used and grammatically functions according to the word location.

When it comes to the icon language, it is important to design to express meanings by connecting a picture to the full morphemes commonly found in both the Korean language and sign language. Taking into account such contents, the parts of speech are defined based upon the following items.

Reference to Define Parts of Speech in Icon Language

1) The icon language is composed of core words such as substantives and verbs representing meaning, and modifiers like a pre-noun and adverb, and sentence pattern information; this is different from the Korean language with agglutinative and additive characteristics requiring the relation words like postpositional words and dependent forms like inflection and suffix.
2) Each icon can have more than one part of speech according to the property of the picture.
3) Each of parts of speech in the icon language is designed to match to the part of speech of the vocabulary with core meaning in the Korean language.

Table 1. Relation between Parts of Speech of the Icon Language and Korean One

Part of speech of icon language	Korean part of speech	Descriptions
Noun (N)	NG	Noun group except the numerals
	NA	Noun transformed into adverb
Numerals (NU)	NU	Numerals
Predicate (V)	VG	Common Predicate (verb, adjective)
	DV	Transformed into the pre-noun
	AV	Transformed into the adverb
Pre-noun (DT)	DT	Pure pre-noun
Adverb (AD)	AD	Pure adverb
Negative (F)	NF	Antonym of noun
	VF	Antonym of vocabulary

Table 2. Tag Sets of Ending Sentence, Tense and the Other in Icon Language

(a) Ending sentence of icon language

Ending sentence of icon language	Tag set
Declarative sentence	SD
Question sentence	SQ
Request sentence	SR
Imperative sentence	SI
Negative sentence	SF

(b) Tense of icon language

Tense of icon language	Tag set
Present sentence	TN (Time-Now)
Past sentence	TP (Time-Past)
Future sentence	TF (Time-Future)

(c) The other sentence informations of icon language

The other sentence informations of icon language	Tag set
Anticipation, Assumption (maybe, perhaps)	MM (Modal-Maybe)
Necessity, duty (have to, need to)	MH (Modal-Have to)
Possibility (can)	MC (Modal-Can)
Will, hope, wish (want to)	MW (Modal-Want to)

3.3   Icon Corpus Construction and Icon Vocabulary Selection

In order to define the user-friendly and intuitive picture and endow it with its relevant meaning within the appropriate usage areas, the applicable domain sections should be selected, and sentence data should be collected. This study set limits to the applicable target domains as traffic, shopping, school, home and hospital, which provide a definite communication purpose for people with language disabilities. As the sentence data collection method for the construction of proto utterance corpus, the developmental approach and environmental approach were applied; the former is a way of collecting general vocabulary used by the public based upon the language development of ordinary people, and in the latter approach, the vocabulary is collected by putting more emphasis on the individual utterance environment for each of language-impaired people.

The reason why corpus is constructed for the parts of speech in the icon is to analyze the frequency used for collecting icon candidate vocabulary and the core vocabulary by the categories. And it is also purposed to figure out the representative vocabulary configuration comprising the condensed vocabulary. The parts of speech in the icon are defined and processed based upon following items

■ Tagging Reference for Parts of speech in the Icon

(1)   The representative core vocabulary is extracted, which can play a role as efficient condensed vocabulary commonly found in the proto-utterance sentences. And after the possible meanings and ambiguities that might be arisen from the icon expression are considered, the parts of speech are endowed corresponding to various vocabulary types.

(2)   When the component words in the utterance sentences can be isolated into the representative single word, each of isolated words can have a part of speech.
Ex)   Traveler = i travel/N + i person/N,
Express bus = fast/V + ibus/N (*i: icon)

(3)   With respect to the words made of number and unit noun, since the number of icon-enabled vocabulary is limited, only single number is used for the expression.
Ex) a piece of, one unit = i1/NU

(4)   The situational sample sentences given in the tagging process can show even the information about sentence pattern.

(5)   When noun is transformed into verb by the suffix addition, it is endowed with the verb/adjective parts of speech.

(6)   When an auxiliary inflectional word is added to an inflectional word of an utterance   sentence, or it is a necessary component, the verb/adjective parts of speech are endowed like core vocabulary in order to make it use of the reference information in the Korean language creation.
Ex) Go to play = i go/V + i play/V

(7)   The ordinary sentence and progressive sentence, which are mostly shown in the tagging process of sentence pattern information, is set as the basic tag, and as for the questioning words like "where", questioning tag abbreviation is allowed when tags are given.

(8) The adjective/verb components that can be transformed into noun or adverb can   make an icon appear two times in a row in order to express the emphasis.
Ex) ultra high quality = i good/V + i good/V

(9) With respect to verb, the original form is applied regardless of the tense.
Ex) did = i do/V + /TP

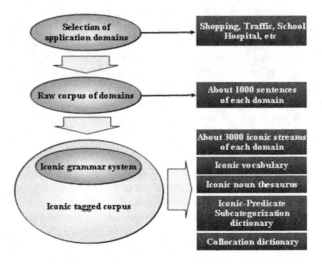

Fig. 2. Process of vocabulary information extraction in Icon Language Corpus

Table 3. Examples of Iconic Corpus where Parts of Speech is tagged

Raw Sentence	Part of speech conferred iconic row
첫 기차는 몇시에 있습니까? What time does the first train leave?	i시작(start)/N i기차(train)/N i시간(time)/N i언제(when)/N /SQ
	i처음(first)/N i기차(train)/N i시간(time)/N /SQ
최고급 호텔로 가주세요. Go to the first class hotel.	i좋다(good)/V i호텔(hotel)/N i가다(go)/V /SR
	i가장(very)/AD i좋다(good)/V i호텔(hotel)/N i가다(go)/V /SR
	i좋다(good)/V i좋다(good)/V i호텔(hotel)/N i가다(go)/V /SR
우등 버스의 요금은 얼마입니까? How much is the fare for luxury bus?	i고급(luxury)/N i버스(bus)/N i요금(fare)/N i얼마(how much)/N /SQ
	i요금(fare)/N i고급(luxury)/N i버스(bus)/N /SQ

(10) The condensed word, for example, 'if you do' is divided into two words as 'do' and 'and then'.

(11) An honorific word is changed into the ordinary form.
Ex) thou, thee = i you/N

4   Results and Evaluation

Regarding such general themes as traffic, shopping, school, home and hospital, 500 sentences are composed respectively; the number of total sentences amounts to about 2,500. Around 2.3-icon candidate vocabulary are retrieved from one sentence. It became possible that several icon candidate vocabularies were retrieved from one sentence since an operator listed a series of icon-enabled vocabulary regarding sample sentences not the sentence analysis but the context examples. From each of icon candidate vocabulary, around 2.1 of noun icon vocabulary and 1.8 of verb icon vocabulary were retrieved; the reason that such small number of nouns was extracted was because there were mostly composed of short sentences.

According to this process, 12,000 of noun icon vocabulary, and 10,300 of verb icon vocabulary were gained, and of those, 600 of noun icon vocabulary and 250 of frequently used verb icon vocabulary were used for defining, matching and constructing 700 number of icons. Per each icon, 1.3 nouns and verbs were endowed as the parts of speech, and it was designed that other parts of speech such as adverb and prenoun could be appeared through the transformation of noun and verb properties. Of lots of candidate vocabulary, there were many words difficult to be matched with the icon. Especially, when it comes to the verb property, since it was hard to select the picture representing the movements, it couldn't create more matching icons than the noun words. Targeted the icon-matched vocabulary, noun semantic dictionary and sub-categorization dictionary data were established, and it was possible to construct the idiom dictionary among neighboring icon vocabularies.

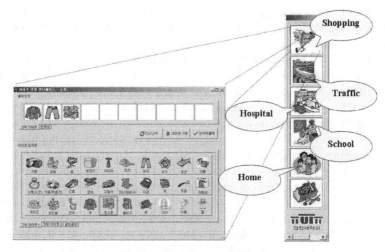

Fig. 3. Implemented Icon Language Interface System

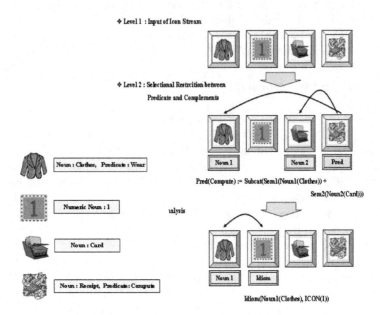

Fig. 4. Process of Sentence Generation of Icon Language

5 Conclusion

Until now, the design and construction of the icon language has been discussed. The icon language is an auxiliary language interface, more intuitive than the natural language interface to be controlled by keyboard-based input system, and designed for people with language disabilities to easily perform the communication through the composition of icons since the user-friendly picture has the vocabulary property. This study has its own significance in that it defines the composite unit by an icon picture and word, and makes it featured in the linguistic system unlike the previous studies that simply defined the picture and endowed a word on it.

When it comes to the future task to be resolved, since the current icon language is dependently designed on its utilization area, many endeavors should be subsequently exerted for the application to other areas. Therefore, it is necessary to acquire the general purpose through the broadened research on icon vocabulary and construction of vocabulary database. Since icons tend to bear the considerable ambiguities such as multiple meanings and parts of speech for the words, the grammatical system of the icon language should be strongly consolidated so as to create the efficient Korean language. And another research project is underway to define and apply the linguistic rules used in creating the Korean language system onto the core vocabulary structure model generated from the icon language discussed in this study. Therefore, it is expected for the development of the convenient auxiliary language interface system, easily accessible by people with language disabilities.

Acknowledgements

This study was supported by research fund from University of Incheon and Multimedia Research Center of the Korea Science and Engineering Foundation(KOSEF)

References

1. Kathleen F. McCoy and Patrick Demasco, "Some Applications of Natural Language Processing to the Field of Augmentative and Alternative Communication" In Proceedings of the IJCAI-95 Workshop on Developing AI Applications for People with Disabilities, Montreal, Canada, August, 1995.
2. Injeong Hwang, "Design of supplemental communication devices by the semantic symbol", paper of master's degree in Incheon university, 1998
3. Younghun Seo, "Development of Korean analyzer based on the token-establishment of Korean semantic analysis dictionary and sub-categorization dictionary", Report of Korea Electronic Telecommunication Research Institute, 1998
4. Seunghyun Yang and Yoseop Woo, "Constructing a Korean Subcategorization Dictionary with Semantic Roles using Thesaurus and Predicate Patterns", Paper of Information and Science Association, 2000. 6
5. Kyonam Choo, "Korean Lexical Sense Analysis for the Concept-Based Information Retrieval", Paper of master's degree in Incheon university, 1998

Modeling Context in Haptic Perception, Rendering and Visualization

Kanav Kahol, Priyamvada Tripathi, Troy McDaniel, and Sethuraman Panchanathan

Center for Cognitive Ubiquitous Computing,
Department of Computer Science and Engineering,
Arizona State University, Tempe, Arizona USA 85287
{kanav, pia, troy.mcdaniel, panch}@asu.edu

Abstract. Haptic perception refers to the human ability to perceive spatial properties through tactile and haptic sensations. Humans have an uncanny ability to analyze objects based only on sparse information from haptic stimuli. Contextual clues about material of an object, its overall shape, size and weight configurations perceived by individuals, lead to recognition of an object and its spatial features. In this paper, we present strategies and algorithms to model context in haptic applications that allow user to explore objects in virtual reality/augmented reality, haptically. Our methodology is based on modeling user's cognitive and motor strategy of haptic exploration. Additionally we also model physiological arrangement of tactile sensors in the human hand. These models provide the context to adapt haptic displays to a user's style of haptic perception and exploration and the present state of the user's exploration. We designed a tactile cueing paradigm to test the validity of the contextual models. Initial results show improvement in accuracy and efficiency of haptic perception when compared to the conventional approaches that do not model context in haptic rendering.

1 Introduction

The term 'haptics', derived from the word *haptikos*, means the ability to touch and it generally includes both kinesthetic and tactile modality [13]. Both sighted and blind individuals perceive spatial information through haptics. While the significance of touch as a modality is controversial topic when studying sighted individual, it is a widely accepted fact that individuals who are blind/deaf blind employ haptic perception to develop spatial representations and that haptic sensation can lead to spatial representations and forms an important part of the human sensory and perceptual apparatus [13].

The desire for natural and intuitive human machine interaction has led to the inclusion of haptics in human-computer interfaces. Such interfaces allow users to provide input to a system through hand movements, and to receive haptic feedback through vibrotactile stimulation of the hands. Haptic Joysticks, haptic mouse and haptic gloves are examples of commercially available devices that can simulate force and/or tactile feedback. While the potential for haptics in natural human machine interaction is intriguing, the realization of practical interfaces has not yet been

K.S. Candan and A. Celentano (Eds.): MIS 2005, LNCS 3665, pp. 102–114, 2005.

achieved. A primary reason for this has been the absence of systems and algorithms that systematically incorporate knowledge about haptic perception in the design stage. Although there has been research in the areas of psychophysics of haptics, and the biomechanical models of haptic perception, extensive research is still needed to link knowledge about haptic perception with haptic interfaces.

2   The Role of Context in Haptics

Research conducted in the psychology and physiology of the haptic perception system of humans clearly highlights the role of context in haptic perception. Johannson conducted seminal research on the arrangement of tactile sensors in the human hand and showed that different regions of the hand are specialized to perceive certain spatial features [5]. For example, the index finger of the hand is specialized to perceive the texture information while the tactile sensors in the palm are primarily suited to perceive the shape information. The physiological arrangement of tactile sensors and their spatial arrangements allow humans to perceive various spatial features such as shape, texture, size, weight and material in parallel through multiple sensors in the hand and assemble prototypes and templates of objects and their features. However to assemble and build these prototypes, static touch is not sufficient. The exiguity of the tactile sensory system necessitates manual exploratory movements to haptically perceive 3D environments [7].

Research in psychology of haptic perception suggests that, perception and action are closely related in the haptic modality [4]. A seminal study of haptic exploration was performed by Lederman and Klatzky [9,10]. They asked adults to use haptic exploration to classify objects, according to a given criterion. This allowed identification of specific exploratory hand movements (called "exploratory procedures") which were characterized by (1) the quantity and the nature of the information that each procedure provided, and (2) the range of properties for which each procedure was useful. Lederman and Klatzky reported that many of the exploratory procedures used by their participants were related to the object property being explored, in a one-to-one relation. For example, lateral motion was always used for perceiving texture by certain subjects. Lederman and Klatzky also noted that there are two distinct phases of the object exploration procedures in human adults. During the first phase, they employ generalized procedures that mobilize the whole hand, and gather vague haptic and tactile information about several properties. During the second phase, specific exploratory procedures are used to perceive particular object features. The regularity of hand movements utilized to perceive tactile features of large regions of space is also depicted in the order of feature perception of regions larger than the grasp of the hand. Humans tend to perceive tactile features of large regions in a serial order systematically exploring object piecewise and assembling the instantaneous stimuli into a mental representation of the object [13]. Nielsen [12] studied this ability of humans to assemble serially perceived instantaneous haptic stimuli as tactile representation of objects. She specifically studied the effect of alteration of the haptic exploration process in children who are blind to guide and teach them haptic concepts. Nielsen concluded that any deviation from the natural strategy of the visually impaired child would decrease the perceptual accuracy of tasks. She also noted that "only one strategy for tactile search which is of value for the child who is visually impaired is his own" emphasizing the importance of user-specific nature of haptic exploration. The user-specific nature of haptic exploration is manifested as stylistic differences in individual haptic exploratory procedures as well as sequence of haptic exploratory procedures employed. To a lesser degree, user's style may also be observed through differential sensitization of fingers in different individual. For example, certain individuals use thumb for fine texture perception rather than index finger. This can be attributed to mannerism of the user.

In summary, haptic perception by humans is a complex process that is influenced by primarily by three contextual variables. Figure 1 summarizes the haptic perception process from the viewpoint of modeling context.

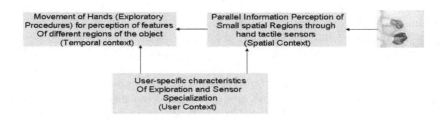

Fig. 1. The Role of Context in Haptic Perception

The static grasp of the hand over an object and the placement of fingers on the object affect the information being perceived in parallel by different regions of the hand. The spatial position of the fingers and the palm could be modeled as *spatial context* in the haptic perception process. Spatial context allows dynamic adaptation of haptic stimuli based on position of the palm and the fingers. This ensures maximal perceptual accuracy by providing perceptually consistent stimulation in different regions of the hand.

The movement of the hands or exploratory procedures employed to perceive large spatial regions and assemble sequential tactile stimuli into a complete object can be modeled as *temporal context* in the haptic perception process. Research has shown the existence of regularity and structure in the movement employed to perceive haptic features such as texture, shape, size etc [7]. This allows modeling of the temporal context of haptic perception as a sequence of discrete hand movements: herein referred to as *haptic gestures*. Modeling temporal context allows development of *active haptic interfaces* that adapt the information presentation to the current state of haptic exploration of the user. This can be accomplished by monitoring the hand movements of the user in virtual/augmented reality environment and probabilistically predicting the feature user is trying to perceive and presenting the required information to the user. This is especially useful in realistic haptic rendering bearing in mind the limitations of current haptic interface technology that cannot provide tactile and force feedback to the entire hand. This means that the information perceived in virtual environments through the grasp of the hand is severely limited and exploratory procedures assume higher importance in conveying spatial information.

Lastly, we can model the user's style of haptic perception and their mannerisms as *user context*. This allows customization of the haptic rendering and visualization schemes to the user's style of haptic exploration and their cognitive strategy to assemble piecewise information into haptic object memory.

In this paper, we present methodology to model spatial, temporal and user context in haptic perception. Modeling perceptual context can aid in creating haptic virtual reality/augmented reality environments that allow user's to perceive stimuli in a veridical manner. Section 3 describes the methodology employed to model temporal context and user context in real environments. Section 4 introduces the haptic rendering scenario wherein we further discuss modeling of spatial context. Then in order to test the validity of the temporal contextual models, spatial contextual models and user contextual models, we developed a *haptic cueing system* that presents tactile information to the user through cues. This limited simulation based on haptic cues only (no visual information is provided to the user) provides a suitable test-bed to determine the effect of contextual models on haptic rendering. We show that contextual models allow conveying complex multidimensional haptic stimuli and objects through simple cues rather than complete haptic rendering. However, these models can also be utilized in creating realistic haptic virtual reality/augmented reality simulations that are dynamic and adapt to the user's style, the current state of haptic exploration and the physiology/specialization of the hand regions.

3   Modeling Temporal Context and User Context in Real Environments

In order to model temporal and user context, there is a need to study and formalize the process by which humans haptically explore objects in real environments. One important research question is "How do humans integrate the various object properties perceived through manual exploration, (namely shape, weight, texture, and size) to form a mental representation of an object, and to recognize that object?". In order to answer this question, it would be helpful to determine whether humans use a predictable strategy to explore objects, and whether it would be possible to formalize the cognitive nature of that exploratory strategy. Secondly while psychological research has shown the existence of one-to-one relation between manual movements and spatial features perceived, experiments need to be conducted to explore if these movements can be recognized automatically through computer algorithms and formalize the motor strategy of exploration. Together the cognitive strategy and the motor strategy represent a formal model of the temporal context and user context as modeled in our approach.

3.1   Experimental Procedure

The experiment to model temporal and user context involved 6 participants who were legally blind. The data capture setup consisted of three digital video cameras, a pair of CyberTouch® data gloves, and Ascension® trackers. (The gloves captured the angle of each joint in the hand, and the trackers captured the (x,y,z) position as well as the 3D orientation of each hand in space.) Data streams were captured from the trackers and from two data gloves (right and left hand) at 120 frames/sec. In all experiments, the participants wore the gloves (augmented with the trackers) and were seated on a chair in front of a table, with no arm support. The participants were then asked to hold the palms of their hands facing upwards, and an object was placed on their hands. The participants then explored the objects with their hands in their natural manner, while data streams were captured from the gloves and the trackers. In addition to recording these data streams, the experimental apparatus also recorded the exploration process with the 3 digital video cameras – all in real time.

In order to evaluate the cognitive strategy of haptic exploration, we designed a psychophysical experiment that consisted of two phases: the *free-running phase* and the *memory phase*. During the *free-running phase*, participants explored the objects as they verbalized their strategy of exploration. This verbalization was captured with the three digital video cameras, and by an observer who took notes during the capture process. Five objects were presented to each participant during this phase. The five objects were randomly chosen from a set of 12 objects, which are shown in Figure 2. One of the goals was to, compare the exploration strategy used during free object exploration phase to that used during task-based exploration of the memory phase, to determine the degree to which the exploration strategies of each participant were consistent across both situations.

The memory phase employed task-based exploration that required users to compare pairs of objects, and then indicate the similarities and dissimilarities between those objects. Six pairs of objects were presented to each participant during the memory phase. Each pair involved a controlled variation of one parameter. The parameters chosen were: shape, texture, size, weight, state of being filled or empty, and state of being open or closed. The video data gathered from the free-running phase and the memory phase was subsequently annotated using Anvil video annotation software [3].

Fig. 2. Objects used in the experiments

(Different annotation schemes were used for the two phases.)   The 'start' and 'end' frame numbers were marked in the exploration of each object feature. Then for each object, the order of exploration was noted, in terms of shape, weight, texture, identification, and object-specific exploration patterns. For example if a participant first explored shape, then texture, and then weight, the annotation for that participant was "shape, texture, weight". For each object feature, the exact amount of time spent on exploration was noted.

Using the procedure given above, videos for each of the tasks, and each of the six participants, were annotated. For each participant, the order of exploration of the object features was recorded for each object. A standard deviation was calculated between objects' order of exploration employed for various objects.   After determining the most consistent order of exploration for each participant, we compared the orders of exploration of all the six participants in the experiment.

A separate experiment was designed to formalize the motor strategy of haptic exploration. In this experiment each participant was given five objects and requested to explore specific features such as texture, shape etc. of different regions of the objects. For each of the six participants, the objects were selected randomly from the set of 12 objects shown in Figure 2, with no repetitions. This experiment was designed to allow the capture of the exploratory hand movements used by the participant to explore particular object features, across a set of different objects. To analyze the exploratory hand movements used to perceive the object features, we selected the set of hand movements that were used to characterize each of the following features: (1) the texture of the object, (2) the size of the object, (3) the curvature of the object, (4) the rim of the object, (5) whether the object was open or closed, (6) whether the object was filled or empty, (7) the edges of the object, (8) the base of the object, and (9) to identify the object.

Since there were 6 participants, and 5 objects per participant, this experiment yielded 30 exploration sequences. Each of these sequences was then analyzed to extract nine types of exploratory hand movements – one for each of the nine types of object features listed above.   In order to develop a personal hand movement vocabulary, we trained and tested Hidden Markov Models (HMMs) for each set. HMMs are probabilistic modeling tools employed for temporal sequence analysis, and have been widely used in gesture and speech recognition. An HMM models a temporal sequence of events (called an *observation sequence*) in terms of a state machine, in which the current state of the model is probabilistically dependent on the previous states.

In the case of hand movement analysis, a movement sequence is modeled as a sequence of *poses*, each of which is represented by one state of the HMM. A library of HMMs is built, with one HMM for each class of hand movement. The probability that the hand movement sequence being tested is exploring for each type of object feature is then calculated, using the forward-backward procedure for each of the HMM's in the library. The HMM that yields the highest probability for generation of a test sequence is determined to be the type of object feature that the hand motion sequence is exploring.

During the participant's exploration of each object, the movements of both the right and left hand were captured for each of the nine types of object features. This captured data included the 3D orientation of each hand, plus the angle of each joint in each hand. The (x,y,z) position of each joint and the angle of each joint were assembled into a vector that was used as a observation symbol. Empirically determined poses were then used as states for each of the HMMs. Using these poses, nine HMM's (each representing the hand movement used to explore one type of object feature) were trained and tested for each participant, as per the procedure described above. The accuracy of recognition for each test sequence was then recorded.

3.2 Results

Table 1 shows the most consistent order of exploration for each participant. Table 2 gives the accuracy of automatic Hidden Markov Models to recognize the nine classes of gestures.

Table 1. Consistent Object Exploration Strategy for 6 participants. R,C: Rim and Curved Regions, B: Base and I: Inside.

Subject1	Subject2	Subject3	Subject4	Subject5	Subject6
Object recognition	Object recognition	Object recognition	Object recognition	Object recognition	Object recognitio n
Object specific exploration	Object specific exploration	Object specific exploration	Object specific exploration	Object specific exploration	Object specific exploratio n
Texture	Shape (R,C)	Shape (R,C)	Texture	Size	Size
Shape (R,C)	texture	Shape (B)	Material	Texture	Weight
Shape (B)	material	Shape/Text ure (I)	Shape (R,C)	Shape (R,C)	Shape/Tex ture (I)
Size	Shape (B)	Texture	Shape (B)	Shape (B)	Texture
Weight	Weight	Material	Shape/Text ure (I)	Material	Shape (R,C)
Material	Size	Weight	Weight	Shape/Text ure (I)	Shape (B)
Shape/texture (I)	Shape/textur e (I)	Size	Size	Weight	Material
Standard deviation 0.2	Standard deviation 0	Standard deviation 0	Standard deviation 0	Standard deviation 0	Standard deviation 0.2(r

The results shown in Table 1 show a pattern that is consistent across all six participants. The cognitive strategy can be summarized in terms of 3 processes:

(1)   Object class identification (2) Object-specific exploration and (3) Object characterization.

Where object class identification is the act of recognizing the class of the object. (The object class was identified almost instantaneously by all of the six participants.) Following the class identification, the participants tended to look for features of the object that distinguished it within that class – a process that we called *object specific exploration*. Following the object identification, participants tend to confirm their hypothesis about the object class. It is during the object-specific exploration that the exploration strategy starts to show signs of individuality. It is significant to note here that the temporal order of exploration for each participant was the same during free exploration of the objects and during the comparison of pairs of objects in memory phase.

Table 2. Accuracy of Hidden Markov Models to recognize haptic gestures

Spatial Feature or Task	Recognition % using personal vocabulary
texture	99.00%
size	100.00%
curvature	97.80%
rim	100.00%
open or closed	100.00%
filled or empty	100.00%
edges	99.00%
base	100.00%
recognition	100.00%

The results of these experiments suggest that the plan used for haptic exploration is consistent across various tasks. The very high accuracy in the prediction of object features based on the personal vocabularies of exploratory hand movements suggests that humans use personalized hand movements to perceive certain types of features. These results suggest a common methodology to model temporal and user context. The methodology requires a training phase, wherein users are requested to explore a certain number of objects and their features while their hand movements are captured and analyzed. The hand movements are used to train a library of hidden markov models that are subsequently used to model motor strategy. The cognitive strategy is modeled as the consistent object exploration strategy as recorded from the training phase.

4   Tactile Cueing as a Validation Scheme for Contextual Models

Section 3 described the psychophysical experiments designed to capture the user's style of exploration as well as the temporal context models. In this section we first describe design of an experimental paradigm that allows us to test spatial, temporal and user contextual models and then state how spatial context is modeled in this paradigm.

Current haptic interfaces such as the CyberTouch® gloves place haptic feedback devices on different regions of the human hand. These devices could be programmed to communicate information in parallel to the user and to *cue* a user about certain information relevant to the virtual environment the user perceives. *Haptic cueing systems* present an alternative to conventional haptic rendering of visual forms. Haptic cueing is analogous to audio-visual messaging used in conventional GUI's, where the user's attention is attracted to an event through audio-visual cues [6]. For the purposes of testing our contextual models, we propose development of haptic cueing systems that can convey information about the virtual environment by supporting or replacing conventional haptic rendering. The conceptual framework that guides this proposal is based on a) the simplicity of the haptic cueing systems and b) comparison of non-contextual cueing paradigms to contextual cueing paradigms to show the validity of contextual models. Research on visual cueing in psychology has shown that users are able to recognize contextual cues better than non-contextual cues [6]. In our research, we wanted to establish if the same results hold in the haptic modality wherein contextual cues offer better perceptual accuracy of cues rather than non-contextual cues.

We designed an experiment that involved a participant who was blind. The experiment involved the subject exploring a set of 5 objects and quantifying their texture, shape, size and material into pre-determined quantization levels for each feature. Then the participant determined a tactile code to communicate the quantization level for a particular feature. The code was designed to be a combination of three pulses of tactile analogies of 'dot' or 'dash' visual pattern in morse code. For example the participant chose 'dot' 'dot' 'dot' to represent small size, 'dot', 'dash', 'dot' to represent medium size and 'dash', 'dash', 'dash' to represent large size. A lexicon of codes representing feature, quantization level and code was created for the participant. A Software was designed to read in the lexicon for a participant and then based on the object feature values fed in, automatically send the user tactile cues.

Each of the vibrotactile motor was dedicated to presentation of quantization levels of a particular feature. The assignment of a feature to a finger motor was based on neurophysiological distribution of tactile sensors (spatial context). For example texture information was assigned to the index finger vibrotactile motor as the index finger contains Merkel receptors that are specialized to perceive texture information [5]. In a similar manner, shape information is sent to the palm, material information is sent to the ring finger, size information is sent to the thumb and so on. This encoded the spatial context in our approach.

A training phase was employed for each of the users. In the training phase, users were presented with haptic cues and were requested to recall the quantization level represented by the code. To present codes for the entire object, each object was divided into 7 regions. These regions were numbered based on the order in which the cues would be presented. Figure 3 shows the division of object into the 7 regions. The first phase of cues provided information about the overall shape, size, texture and material of the object. The second phase cues were programmed to convey information about objects base. The third, fourth and fifth phase were designed to provide information about the vertical regions of the object and the sixth phase provided information about the rim or the top of the object. The last phase presented information about the inside of the object. This phased information delivery mimicked the exploratory procedure of the participant that initially perceives the overall object characteristics and then proceeds from the base of the object to the rim of the object for our participant.

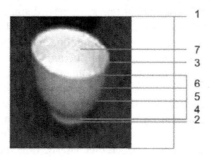

Fig. 3. Division of object into regions for presentation of tactile cues. The cues for shape, size, material, texture for the regions are presented in a serial order as depicted.

Feedback was provided to the users on their recognition accuracy and adjustments to the code were made based on the user's request. This iterative process led to development of the final haptic cues vocabulary that was used to convey spatial information. In the test phase, features of the unknown objects were presented in a pre-determined serial order and the participant's task was to recognize the object. The cues were once again presented in seven phases, consistent with the seven regions shown in Figure 3. The recognition accuracy of the objects was measured for each participant. In our experiments, users were trained with 5 objects. The software interface designed for cueing is shown in figure 4. An average training time of 0.5 hours was required for each of the user following which users were able to recognize a set of 55 objects through tactile cues only with 100% accuracy.

The results above show that contextual model based cueing paradigm ensures high perceptual accuracy and ease. We tested the perceptual accuracy and ease by removing spatial context and temporal context information separately from the system and then providing cues. In order to remove spatial context model, we changed the assignment of feature to a scheme that was inconsistent with the neurophysiological specialization of the hand. We trained and tested the system with three such schemes. With 5 Objects in the training set and training time of 0.5 hours the perceptual accuracy decreased to an average of 95%. The accuracy remained the same when training time was increased to 2 hour.

Temporal context was removed by presenting sets of cues in an order that was inconsistent with the cognitive strategy of exploration of the user. We trained and tested the system with three such schemes. With 5 objects in the training set and a training time of 0.5 hours the perceptual accuracy decreased to 75%. When the training time was increased to 2 hours the accuracy marginally increased to 77%. These results clearly indicate the validity of the temporal contextual model and highlight the fact that deviation from the model limits the rendering accuracy of the system.

A strong case for contextual models may be made by comparing results of our experiments to one of the notable attempt at design of haptic assistive devices that convey spatial environmental information called tactile vision sensory substituition system (TVSS) [1]. It converted an image captured by video camera into a low-resolution tactile image, and displayed that image using a matrix of 400 vibrotactile elements (20 rows and 20 columns of one millimeter diameter solenoids). The system however has had limited success. Lenay *et.al.* [11] argue that the real answer lies in fully understanding the term sensory substitution, and its implications. Lenay *et.al.* criticize the methodology of simply transducing a signal from one modality to another, which does not take into account contextual factors. We surmise that the poor performance of sensory substitution devices can be attributed to the fact that humans perceive the world at the *perceptual level* rather then the *sensory level*. Information at the perceptual level is influenced by many contextual variables and systems need to explicitly encode these variables for information presentation. We perceive the world in terms of surfaces and objects. In fact, much of the time the mind is not consciously aware of the sensory-level details of surfaces and objects. In sighted people, retinal images activate percepts, and these percepts are the basis for further processing, rather than the pixel-level content. However, the TVSS essentially communicates pixel-level information through the tactile modality imposing a steep learning curve on the user to tactilely interpret non-contextual pixel-level data. The effort involved in traversing this learning curve far outweighs the benefits accounting for the failure of users to embrace sensory substitution systems.

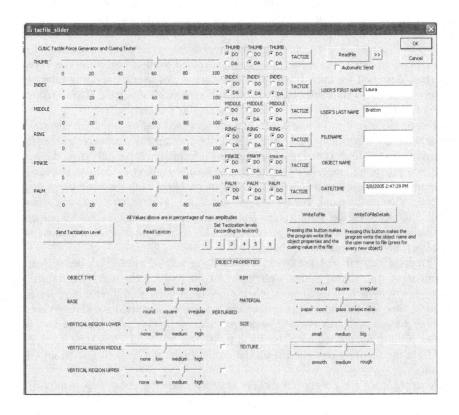

Fig. 4. Tactile Cueing Software

In a variation of the cueing experiment, we designed an experiment where we tested our hypothesis that interactive object exploration allows better haptic object recognition. We define interactive object exploration as the process of command-response interactions between the user and the system wherein a user can command the system to present information about a feature through a hand gesture. The system responds with a haptic cue that is coded to represent a specific quantization level. This experiment explicitly models the user's contextual model as it gives user the control over what information is desired. The interactive methodology provides high flexibility and dynamic adaptation that mimics the human reasoning process in real environments. People often employ contextual clues to locate objects and guess their identity. Visual clues, sensory information and memory helps in location and recognition of familiar and non-familiar stimuli. It is often tedious to model such interactions and the human reasoning process. However the interactive methodology allows users to guide the system based on what they deem necessary. This allows customization of the information flow from the system to the user based on the current state of the user, his/her style and user strategy to recognize the stimuli. The experimental results confirmed the hypothesis. In addition, the performance of the haptic object recognition task in the interactive contextual methodology was better than the performance in the non-interactive contextual methodology. It is also noteworthy that the communication between the system and the device in interactive systems is bidirectional and involved the user cognitively engaging the attentional networks in the brain. This may cause the involvement of cognitive neural circuitry and be one of the reasons for better perceptual accuracy.

5   Conclusion and Future Work

Haptic Perception in real environments is influenced by various factors. In this paper, we conducted experiments to model spatial, temporal and user context of haptic perception in the haptic rendering process. We designed a tactile cueing paradigm to test our models. Initial results show that modeling context in haptic rendering environments improves perceptual accuracy even with a simple paradigm of contextual tactile cueing. To our knowledge, this is the first attempt at modeling context in haptic rendering and the results indicate that encoding contextual information is a key to realistic haptic rendering. It ensures that users can perceive object features and its identity with piecemeal information that is only a subset of information available in the real environments. This may help overcome the current limitations of the haptic interfaces. While tested in haptic object recognition, contextual modeling can benefit other applications of haptic rendering such as telesurgery, teleoperation, motor training etc. To further test our model, we propose to incorporate them in veridical haptic rendering environments. A methodology to explicitly encode the motor strategy of haptic exploration will be designed. We will test a proactive system against the baseline haptic rendering system wherein the rendered objects and environments are static and do not adapt to a user's state of exploration, or their temporal context.

References

1. P. BachyRita, *Brain mechanisms in sensory substitution.* New York: Academic Press, 1972.
2. J. P. Fritz and K. E. Barner, "Design of a haptic data visualization system for people with visual impairments," *IEEE Transactions on Rehabilitation Engineering,* vol. 7, pp. 372-384, 1997.
3. K. S. Hale and K. M. Stanney, "Deriving haptic design guidelines from human physiological, psychophysical, and neurological foundations," vol. 24, pp. 33, 2004.
4. Y. Hatwell, A. Streri, and E. Gentaz, *Touching for Knowing. Cognitive psychology of haptic manual perception.* Philadelphia, PA, USA: John Benjamins Publishing Company, 2003.
5. R.S. Johansson, and A.B. Vallbo, , "Tactile sensory coding in the glabrous skin of the human hand," Brain Res., Vol. 6, No. 1, pp. 27-32 1983.
6. K. Kahol, P. Tripathi, and S. Panchanathan, "Haptic User Interfaces: Design, testing and evaluation of haptic cueing systems to convey shape, weight, material and texture information (submitted)," presented at Human- Computer Interaction, Las Vegas Nevada, 2005.
7. K. Kahol, P. Tripathi, S. Panchanathan, and M. Goldberg, "Formalizing Cognitive and Motor Strategy of Haptic Exploratory Movements of Individuals who are Blind," presented at IEEE International Workshop on Haptic Audio Visual Environments and their Applications, 2004.
8. M. Kipp, "Anvil - A Generic Annotation Tool for Multimodal Dialogue," presented at 7th European Conference on Speech Communication and Technology, Aalborg, 2001.
9. S. J. Lederman and R. L. Klatzky, " Hand movements: A window into haptic object recognition," *Cognitive Psychology,* vol. 19, pp. 342- 368, 1987.
10. S. J. Lederman and R. L. Klatzky, "Action for perception: Manual exploratory movements for haptically processing objects and their features," in *Hand and brain: The neurophysiology and psychology of hand movements,* A. M. Wing, P. Hagard, and J. R. Flanagan, Eds. New York: Academic Press, 1996.
11. C. Lenay, S. Canu, and P. Villon, "Technology and perception: The contribution of sensory substituition systems," presented at IEEE Second International Conference on Cognitive Technology, Aizu, Japan, 1997.
12. L. Nielsen, , How the approach of guiding the hands of the visually impaired child can disturb his opportunity to build up strategies for tactile orientation, The British Jour. of visual impairment, 14,1, 29-31, 1996.
13. G. Revesz, *Psychology and art of the blind.* London: Longmans Green, 1950.
14. D. Tzovaras, G. Nikolakis, G. Fergadis, S. Malasiotis, and M. Stavrakis, "Design and Implementation of Haptic Virtual Environments for the Training of the Visually Impaired," *IEEE Transactions on Neural Systems and Rehabilitation Engineering,* vol. 12, pp. 266-278, 2004.

Improving Image Annotations Using WordNet

Yohan Jin, Lei Wang and Latifur Khan

Department of Computer Science University of Texas at Dallas Richardson,
Texas 75083-0688, USA
yohan@student.utd.edu, lwang@utd.edu, lkhan@utd.edu

Abstract. The development of technology generates huge amounts of
non-textual information, such as images. An efficient image annotation
and retrieval system is highly desired. Clustering algorithms make it
possible to represent visual features of images with finite symbols. Based
on this, many statistical models, which analyze correspondence between
visual features and words and discover hidden semantics, have been published. These models improve the annotation and retrieval of large image
databases. However, current state of the art including our previous work
produces too many irrelevant keywords for images during annotation.
In this paper, we propose a novel approach that augments the classical model with generic knowledge-based, WordNet. Our novel approach
strives to prune irrelevant keywords by the usage of WordNet. To identify
irrelevant keywords, we investigate various semantic similarity measures
between keywords and finally fuse outcomes of all these measures together to make a final decision. We have implemented various models to
link visual tokens with keywords based on knowledge-based, WordNet
and evaluated performance using precision, and recall using benchmark
dataset. The results show that by augmenting knowledge-based with classical model we can improve annotation accuracy by removing irrelevant
keywords.

1 Introduction

Images are a major source of content on the Internet. The development of technology such as digital cameras and mobile telephones equipped with such devices
generates huge amounts of non-textual information, such as images. An efficient
image retrieval system is desirable where given a large database, we need, for
example, to find the images that have tigers, or given an unseen image, find
keywords that best describe its content [DB1]. Hence, these techniques raise the
possibility of several interesting applications such as automated image annotation, browsing support, auto-illustrate. Content-based image retrieval (CBIR)
computes relevance based on the visual similarity of low-level image features
such as color histograms, textures, shapes and spatial layout etc. However, the
problem is that visual similarity is not semantic similarity. There is a gap between low-level visual features and semantic meanings. The so-called semantic
gap is the major problem that needs to be solved for most CBIR approaches.
For example, a CBIR system may answer a query request for 'red ball' with an

K.S. Candan and A. Celentano (Eds.): MIS 2005, LNCS 3665, pp. 115–130, 2005.
© Springer-Verlag Berlin Heidelberg 2005

image of a 'red rose'. If we provide annotation of images with keywords, then typical way to publish an image data repository is to create a keyword-based query interface to an image database. Images are retrieved if they contain (some combination of the) keywords specified by the user. To achieve all these goals at this fine granularity there are several technical challenges.

1 Segment images into meaningful visual segments/tokens.
2 Determine correlation between associated keywords and visual tokens.

With regard to the first problem, we rely on normalized cut that segment images into a number of visual tokens [SM1]. Each visual token will be represented by a vector of colors, textures, shapes etc. Therefore, visual token means a segmented region or object, and it will be described by a set of low level features like color, texture, and shape. In Fig. 1, the first column corresponds images and the second column represents segmented images or a set of visual tokens. With regard to the second problem, there are several tasks one could attack. First, one could attempt to predict annotations of entire images using all information present which is annotation task. Next, one might attempt to associate particular words with particular image visual tokens which is correspondence task. Last but not least one might attempt to predict keywords for image object which is recognition task. With annotation task, most of images are not annotated. Furthermore, it is laborious, error prone, and subjective, to manually annotate a large collection of images. In addition, we would like to address correspondence problem between visual tokens and keywords that appear in images.

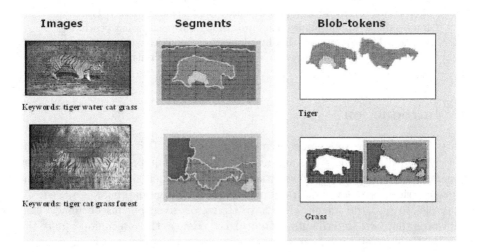

Fig. 1. Demonstration of Correspondence between Image objects and their Keywords

Therefore, given a set of images where each image is captioned with a set of keywords that describe the image content, researchers already proposed various algorithms to determine correlation between keywords and visual image features/tokens. Once we identify correlation between keywords and image visual tokens, this association can be used to annotate images that do not have captions. A couple of statistical models have been proposed in recent years [MTO1, JLM1, DB1, BD1] to determine correspondence between image objects and keywords. By analyzing the statistical relations between visual features and keywords, these methods [BJ1, LW1, KJC1] can discover hidden semantics. Each image will be represented by a set of keywords and visual tokens. It is possible that the same visual token can be shared by more than one image. Since the concept of the similarity of visual tokens is ill defined as compared to keywords, visual tokens will be clustered together and a finite set of visual tokens will be generated. Each of the final set of visual tokens will be known as blob-token (see third column in Fig. 1). The premise is that if some visual tokens are the same, they will belong to the same cluster.

To construct blob-token, current state of the art uses traditional clustering (e.g., K-means) algorithm. Since each visual token is usually high dimensional data (30 dimensions for the Corel dataset) and normal clustering algorithms (e.g., K-means) assign equal weights to all dimensions. Due to curse of dimensionality, data become sparse and distance measures become gradually meaningless as the number of dimensions increase. This will degrade the quality of the clustering result for traditional clustering algorithms. In order to solve this problem, we propose a weighted feature selection mechanism (See[WK1]for more details). In other words, some features will be more relevant than other features for a set of visual tokens. For example, for all, shape feature will be more important than color feature, and texture feature. On the other hand, for rose, visual token color feature will be dominating. To determine the correlation between keywords and blob-tokens, we need to apply statistical models to estimate the correspondence between each pair of keyword and blob-token and then construct a W×B probability matrix based on these estimates. W is the total number of keywords and B is the total number of blob-tokens. This is a difficult task because image datasets usually do not provide explicit correspondence. This matrix will be filled up based on unweighed frequency count, weighted frequency count, singular value decomposition, and expected maximization algorithm (EM). Then it will be trivial to determine correlation between words and blobs based on maximum probability or weight. However, the current annotation accuracy is quite low due to too many noisy words. Therefore, it is quite difficult to get meaningful understanding of images. We propose a novel approach that improves annotation accuracy by exploiting generic Knowledge-based, WordNet. WordNet [M1] is a lexical reference system whose design is inspired by current psycholinguistic theories of human lexical memory. English nouns, verbs, adjectives and adverbs are organized into synonym sets, each representing one underlying lexical concept. WordNet2.0 contains around 110,000 synsets, noun group has 79,689 synsets. Each synset has a gloss that describes the concept and connects to another synset through explicit semantic relations.

Here, we discard an annotated keyword from an image which does not correlate with other annotated keywords that appeared in that image. For this, we investigate various semantic similarity measures between keywords with the usage of WordNet. Each semantic similarity measure tries to find the distance between keywords using several different approaches (e.g., node-based, edge-based, gloss-based). To the best of our knowledge, this is the first attempt to improve the annotation accuracy by applying the semantic similarity between keywords with the usage of WordNet. We have evaluated the performance of our novel approach with classical one using precision, and recall using benchmark dataset. The results show that by augmenting knowledge-based with classical model we can improve annotation accuracy.

This paper is organized as follows: Section 2 presents a description of Translation Model. Section 3 explains several semantic similarity measures along with shortcomings and presents motivation behind various measures. Section 4 presents experimental setup and results of our approach. Section 5 presents related work. Section 6 presents conclusion and a comment on future work.

2   Translation Model(TM)

TM is a way to automate image annotation by addressing the following problems.

2.1   Segmentation

We segment images into a number of visual tokens using Normalized cuts [SM1]. Each visual token will be described by colors, textures, shapes, area etc. However, it does not occupy a discrete space. For example, each image segment in COREL is represented by 30 features [Corel1, CorelKDD1]. The features represent, rather roughly, major visual features/properties.

2.2   Clustering to Generate Blob-Token

We would like to quantize image object representation. For this, we will apply clustering algorithms to group similar visual tokens (i.e., image objects) into a blob token. Thus we generate a fixed set of blob tokens. The problem is that most current image clustering algorithms do not consider the relevant features, but assign the same weight to all low-level features. Yet image data are high dimensional data (e.g., say 30 dimensions in Corel image case), and many dimensions are irrelevant. These irrelevant dimensions will hide clusters in noisy data and confuse the clustering algorithms.

The objects in the same cluster are very similar with regard to dominant feature dimensions, but the distance or similarity measures may indicate dissimilarity due to the noisy value in irrelevant dimensions. The problem could become even worse when the data have different scales in different dimensions [Eccv02]. For example, all segmented 'tiger' visual tokens have the same color; the color features are relevant for all 'tiger' visual tokens. However, shape or position features are not relevant for 'tiger'. For all 'ball' visual tokens, the relevant features are shape as compared to the color feature. Thus, the set of relevant features may be different for different clusters. The relevant features or dominant features are very useful when we measure similarity between two visual tokens (i.e., clusters). Furthermore, the scales of some features are much larger than those of other features. Hence, we normalize data $< x_{i1}, x_{i2}, ...x_{im} >$ into its normal form using mean(μ_j) and variance(σ_j) for j-th low-level feature as $< (x_{i1} - \mu_1)/\sigma_1, (x_{i2} - \mu_2)/\sigma_2, .., (x_{im} - \mu_m)/\sigma_m >$.

2.3 Weighted Feature Selection

Our weighted feature election mechanism is as follows: First, we cluster visual tokens using K-means assuming equal weight. Second, we distribute visual tokens into clusters and update centroids. Third, for each cluster we identify the most important features and discard irrelevant features. Finally, the same process will be repeated until the algorithm converges. In fact at step 3 we apply weighted feature selection to determine the relevancy of a feature. In other words, we determine the weight of features. We represent m features in j-th cluster as $< f_{j1}, f_{j2}, ...f_{jm} >$, and corresponding weights of these features are $< w_{j1}, w_{j2}, ...w_{jm} >$. Let us assume that we have altogether N visual tokens and the dimension of a visual token is m. Then the i-th visual token in the dataset is represented by $< x_{i1}, x_{i2}, ...x_{im} >$. Hece, we need to determine dominating features across a set of visual tokens/cluster on the fly and assign more weight over others. Each feature in a cluster will be assigned a weight according to how relevant the feature is to the cluster. We present a method estimating this relevance based on a histogram analysis (See [WK1] for more details).

2.4 Link Between Keyword and Blob-Token

To determine a link between keywords and blob-tokens, first we construct a probability table. Let us assume that there are W keywords, B blob-tokens, and N images. Then, the dataset can be represented by a matrix . Where in M matrix, row N corresponds to the number of images and first W column corresponds to W keywords, and next B column corresponds to B blob-tokens. Next, we calculate probability table by implementing various weight calculation strategies. Finally, the relationship between keywords and blob-tokens can be determined by probability table. For example, we assign a keyword w_i to a blob-token b_j if $p(w_i|b_j)$ is the maximum in j-th column of probability table.

– Unweighted Matrix (M1) First, we generate $M_{N \times (W+B)}$ by counting the frequency of keywords and blob-tokens.

$$M_{N \times (W+B)} = [M_{N \times W} | M_{N \times B}] = [M_{W1} | M_{B1}] = M_1. \tag{1}$$

$M_{W1}[i, j]$ is the frequency of j-th keyword which appeared in i-th image. Similarly, $M_{B1}[i, j]$ is the frequency of j-th blob-token that appeared in i-th image. Based on above two matrixes, there are following different models to calculate probability table.

- Correlation Method (CRM) We use $M_W^T \times M_B$ that gives a matrix with the dimension of W x B and normalize each column to get a probability table T_{corr} based on co-occurrence. $T_{corr}[i, j]$ is an estimate of $p(w_i|b_j)$ which is a conditional probability of keyword w_i given blob b_j.
- Cosine Method (CSM)

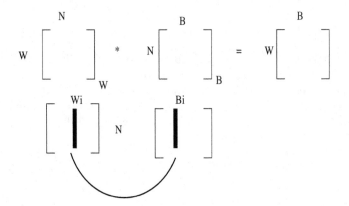

Fig. 2. Matrix Multiplication of Words and Blobs

Instead of using $M_W^T \times M_B$, we can apply cosine to calculate the matrix with the dimension of W x B in which the element of ith row and jth column is the cosine between ith column in M_W^T and jth column in M_B. Then, same as CRM, we normalize each column to get a probability table T_{corr}. In fact, correlation method takes into account the following fact: If a keyword appears across a set of images, and a blob also appears in the same set of images, then there is a chance that this blob and keyword are correlated (see Fig. 2).

2.5   Auto-annotation

To annotate the image automatically, we calculate the distance between the given image object and all centroids of blob-tokens, and represent this image object with the keyword of the closest blob-token. The annotation is generated using keywords assigned to all objects in the image.

3   Measuring Semantic Similarity

Using Semantic similarity, we would like to remove noisy keywords for an image from annotated keywords generated by translation model. However, at the same time, we would like to keep relevant keywords. To do this, first we will find relevant concepts from annotated keywords in an image. Next, we will measure similarity between these concepts. Finally, some concepts corresponding keywords will be discarded in which total similarity measure of a concept with other concept falls below a certain threshold. We will use the structure and content of WordNet for measuring semantic similarity between two concepts. Current state of the art can be classified to the three different categories such as: Node-Based Approach([Res1, JC1, Lin1]), Distance-Based Approach([Lea1]) and Gloss-Based Approach([BP2]). In this section, first, we will present various measures to determine semantic similarity between two concepts. Second, we will present drawback of each measure. Finally, we will present hybrid model by fusing these various measures.

3.1   Resnik Measure (RIK)

Resnik et al. [Res1] introduce first *Information Content (IC)* notion by relying node based approach. More higher value of IC (*Information Content*) means that the concept has specified and detailed information. For example, *cable-television* has more specific information than *television*. RIK first uses Corpus (in our case SemCor2.0) to get the probabilities of each concept and computed how many times the concept appear in the Corpus.

$$freq(c) = \sum_{n \in word(c)} count(n) \qquad (2)$$

where word (c) is the set of words subsumed by concept c. Next, the probabilities of each concepts are calculated by the following relative frequency.

$$Prob(c) = \frac{freq(c)}{\tilde{N}} \qquad (3)$$

If only one root node is selected, the probability of that node will be 1. This is because root node concept subsumes every concept in WordNet. Second, RIK calculates IC of a concept by taking the negative logarithm of above mentioned probability. Finally, semantic similarity between two concepts will be calculated in the following way. First, RIK determines lowest common subsumer (lcs) between two concepts and then for that lcs concept IC will be determined.

$$IC(concept) = -\log Prob(concept) \qquad (4)$$

$$sim(w1, w2) = max_{c1,c2}[sim(c1, c2)] \qquad (5)$$

Note that a keyword may be associated with more than one concepts in WordNet. However, the keyword will be associated with a single concept. For example, keywords *w1* and *w2* are associated with concept set, *c1* and *c2* respectively. Based on that, pair wise similarity between concepts from set *c1* and set *c2* are calculated and we keep pairwise similarity which yields maximum value. Therefore, word similarity takes into account the maximal information content over all concepts of which both words could be an instance. RIK measure does neither consider the IC value of two concepts/keywords, nor the distance between concepts/keywords in the WordNet. If we consider the similarity between sand and rock in Fig. 3, the *lcs* will be the material and its IC value will be 4.82. However, this value will be the same as the value between soil and rock. This is the weakness of RIK measure.

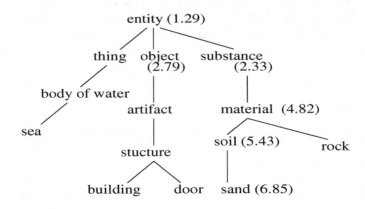

Fig. 3. An Example of Information Content in the WordNet

3.2   Jiang and Conrath Measure (JNC)

Jiang et al. [JC1] use the same notion of the Information Content and takes into account the distance between selected concepts. In regard to this, JNC combines node-based and edge-base approach. Let us consider the above example. Hence, the two different pair of keywords (*sea* and *door*, *sea* and *sand*) have the same semantic similarity based on RIK measure. There is no way to discern the semantic similarity between them. However, with regard to semantic similarity between two concepts, JNC uses the IC values of these concepts along with the IC value of lcs of these two concepts. Therefore, the similarity will be different since the IC value of house and apartment are not the same.

$$similarity(c_1, c_2) = \frac{1}{IC(c_1) + IC(c_2) - 2 * IC(lcs(c_1, c_2))} \tag{6}$$

3.3   Lin Measure (LIN)

Lin et al. [Lin1] follows the similarity theorem, use the ratio of the commonality and information amounts essential for describing each concept. Commonality between two concepts is the Information Content of lcs. In reality, Lin measure has the close relation of JNC.

$$similarity(c_1, c_2) = \frac{2 * IC(lcs(c_1, c_2))}{IC(c_1) + IC(c_2)} \tag{7}$$

3.4   Leacock and Chodorow Measure (LNC)

Leacock et al. [Lea1] measure only between noun concepts by following IS-A relations in the WordNet1.7 hierarchy. LNC computes the shortest number of intermediate nodes from one noun to reach the other noun concept. This is a measurement that human can think intuitively about the semantic distance between two nouns. Unfortunately, WordNet1.7 has a different root node. Therefore, no common ancestor between two keywords can happen. To avoid that, LNC measure introduces the hypothetical root node which can merge multiple-root tree into one-root tree.

$$similarity(c_1, c_2) = max[-\log(ShortestLength(c_1, c_2)/(2 * D))] \qquad (8)$$

Shortest Length means the shortest path between two concepts. D is the overall depth of WordNet1.7 and a constant value of 16.

3.5   Banerjee and Pedersen Measure(BNP)

Banerjee et al.[BP2] use the gloss-overlap to compute the similarity. Originally, Gloss-overlaps were first used by [Les1] to perform word sense disambiguation. The more share their glosses, the more relate two words. BNP not only considers the gloss of target word but also augments with the shared glosses by looking over all relations including hypernym, hyponym, meronym, holonym, troponym. Based on that, BNP measures proliferate their gloss vocabulary. By gathering all glosses between A and B through all relations in WordNet, BNP calculates the similarity between two concepts. If the relations between two concepts are gloss, hyponym, and hypernym,
related-pairs = {(gloss,gloss),(hype,hype),(hypo,hypo),(hype,gloss),(gloss,hype)}

$$similarity(A, B) = \sum_{\alpha \in related-pairs, \beta \in related-pairs} score(\alpha(A) + \beta(B)) \qquad (9)$$

Here, BNP computes the *score* by counting the number of sharing word and especially if same words appeared consecutively, and assign the score of n^2 where n is the shared consecutive words.

3.6   Comparison of Various Methods

Every measures has some shortcomings. On the one hand, RIK measure cannot differentiate the two keywords which have the same lcs. On the other hand, JNC and LIN address this problem. Their measures give the different similarity value of a pair of keywords having a same ancestor by considering its IC. However, JNC and LIN are sensitive to the Corpus. Based on Corpus, JNC and LIN may end up with different values. Furthermore, LNC measure has additional limitation. For some keywords, SL(ShortestLength)value does not reflect true similarity. For example, furniture will be more closely related with door as compared to sky.

However, with LNC, SL for furniture and door and SL for furniture and sky will be 8 in both cases. Due to the structural property of WordNet, it is quite difficult to discriminate between such keywords with LNC. BNP measure relies heavily on shared glosses. If there exists no common word in the augmented glosses by considering every possible relation in WordNet, then this approach will fail to get semantic distance. For example, there is no shared word between glosses of sky and jet , which causes the score between sky and jet is 0. From the above discussion, it is obvious that we cannot solely rely on a single method. We need to fuse all these measures together to get rid of noisy keywords.

3.7 Applying Semantic Measures for Improving Annotations Using Hybrid Measure (TMH Model)

Here, we propose how we can apply similarity measure to remove unrelated keywords. For this, we rely on the annotated keywords of each image. To remove noisy keywords from each image, we determine correlation between keywords produced by TM model. Intuitively, highly correlated keywords will be kept and non-correlated keywords will be thrown away. For example, annotation for an image by TM model is: *sky, sun, water, people, window, mare, scotland*. Since *scotland* is not correlated with other keywords, it will be treated as noisy keyword. Hence, our strategy will be as follows: First, in an image for each annotated keyword, we determine the similarity score with other annotated keywords appeared in that image based on various methods (JNC, LIN, BNP) discussed in Section 3.1 -3.5. Second, we sum these scores for each keyword. This summation score for each keyword will demonstrate how correlated this keyword with other annotated keywords in that image. Therefore, non correlated keywords will get lower score. Finally, scores of keywords that fall below a certain threshold will be discarded by treating as noisy words. These steps are presented in Fig. 4.

λ_i : test images
$\lambda_i = \{\lambda_1, ...\lambda_n\}$
χ_j : annotated keywords of λ_i
$\chi_j = \{\chi_1, ...\chi_m\}$
$SSDT$: Semantic Similarity Distance Table
/*– Detect the unlated keywords in each images –*/
    i → 1 to Num.images
/*– Compute similarity values for every pairs –*/
    j → 1 to Num.annotate words
        k → 1 to Num.annotate words
            $similarity_j = \sum_{j \neq k}$ find_similarity(χ_j, χ_k) in $SSDT$
            $sum_i = sum_i + similarity_j$
        $\frac{similarity_j}{sum_i} < Threshold \Rightarrow$ remove χ_j from ith image

Fig. 4. Pseudo Code for removing the noisy keywords

4   Experiment and Results

The dataset used in this paper is downloaded from [Eccv02] which is same as [DB1]. There are 5000 images from 50 Stock Photo Cds in this dataset. Each Cd contains 100 images on the same topic. We use 4,500 images as training set and the remaining 500 images as testing set. The image segmentation algorithm is normalized cut [SM1]. Each image is represented as a 30 dimensional vector, which corresponds to 30 low-level features. The vocabulary contains 374 different keywords. First, we cluster a total of 42,379 image objects from 4,500 training images into 500 blobs using K-means algorithm and weighted selection method. Second, we apply EM algorithm to annotate keywords for each images automatically. This will be known as TM model. Finally, we applied hybrid measures (TMH) to get rid of some noisy annotated keywords. In Fig. 5 we demonstrate the power of approach, TMH over our previous approach, TM. For example, in Fig. 5 let us consider the image with identifier 147066 (the last image). This image has a set of noisy keywords (*beach, coral, crab, nest*). We can see TM generates these noisy keywords and TMH discards all noisy irrelevant keywords and keep only relevant one. However, if we consider the second image in Fig. 5 (identifier 17017), TMH discards irrelevant keywords snow along with relevant keywords, sky and tree. Therefore, this TMH not only discards irrelevant keywords but also discards occasionally some relevant keywords. Furthermore, it is obvious that if TM model generates all noisy keywords along with zero relevant keyword for an image, TMH will not be able to generate correct keywords at all.

Table 1. Performance of Most Frequently Used Keywords for TM and TMH

Keywords	TM		TMH	
	precision	recall	precision	recall
water	0.2482	0.8965	0.5000	0.0431
window	0.1111	0.1250	0.1111	0.1256
plane	0.1428	0.1600	0.1481	0.1600
tiger	0.1428	0.3000	0.5000	0.1000
stone	0.1666	0.3809	0.1702	0.3809
garden	0.0952	0.2000	0.1666	0.1
nest	0.1250	0.1428	1.000	0.1428

4.1   Comparison of Various Measures

Here we would like to demonstrate the power of TMH over various measures. We report two sets of results based on two accuracy levels (50% and 33%). To make these dataset, initially we select 500 images along with 6 manually annotated correct keywords.

First, we prepare dataset with 50% accuracy in keyword annotation, which means that the ratio of correct and incorrect keywords of an image is 1:1. To get this, we remove three correct keywords from an image and insert three noisy

Table 2. With a 50% accuracy test data set

Measure	Num.correct remained	Num.incorrect remained	Accuracy
JNC	994	452	67.4%
LIN	855	372	63.6%
LNC	805	562	57.4%
RIK	756	1030	38.7%
BNP	880	700	61.2%

Table 3. With a 33% accuracy test data set

Measure	Num.correct remained	Num.incorrect remained	Accuracy
JNC	655	930	58.6%
LIN	778	978	55.6%
LNC	604	990	36.2%
RIK	705	487	40.8%
BNP	650	746	53.4%

1055
TM:sky sun water people
window mare soctland
TMH:sky sun water window

17017
TM:sky water tree buildings
snow
TMH:water buildings

101050
TM:sun clouds beach people
light soctland
TMH:sun clouds light

101058
TM:sky water tree sunset
TMH:sky water tree

118083
TM:tree people flowers coral
cat garden
TMH:people flowers garden

118086
TM:sky water people
buildings sunset
TMH:water people buildings

119045
TM:sky water people buildings
street
TMH:buildings street

131014
TM: tree people grass snow
flowers pillar
TMH:tree people grass flowers

147066
TM:beach people leaf
flowers plants coral crab nest
TMH:people flowers plants

Fig. 5. Examples of removing unrelated keywords by Hybrid Measure

keywords randomly. Similarly, the second dataset has been constructed with 33% accuracy. In Table 1, given the first daatset with 50% accuracy, JNC improves the accuracy to 67.4%. Here, JNC measure chooses 994 correct keywords out of 1,500 keywords and remove 1,058 incorrect keywords from 1,500 keywords. Furthermore, JNC,LIN and BNP measures outperform RIK and LNC measures. In Table 2, with dataset 2 (accuracy 33%), accuracy of JNC, LIN, BNP measures are still greater than 50% even with 67% noisy keywords in images. This demonstrates the power of semantic similarity measure. From these two tables, JNC, LIN and BNP are the best measures regardless of distribution of noisy data. Therefore, in TMH, we fuse all these three: JNC, LIN and BNP and ignore the other two.

Table 4. Performance of Most Frequently Used Keywords for TM and TMH

Keywords	TM		TMH	
	precision	recall	precision	recall
water	0.2482	0.8965	0.5000	0.0431
window	0.1111	0.1250	0.1111	0.1256
plane	0.1428	0.1600	0.1481	0.1600
tiger	0.1428	0.3000	0.5000	0.1000
stone	0.1666	0.3809	0.1702	0.3809
garden	0.0952	0.2000	0.1666	0.1
nest	0.1250	0.1428	1.000	0.1428

4.2   Comparison of TMH with TM

Here we report results based on most frequently used keywords for TMH and TM. Recall that TMH considers hybrid measures. For keyword nest, we observe that precision of TMH (100%) is substantially higher than precision of TM (12.5%), on the other hand, recall is the same in both cases. This happens due to the removal of only noisy keywords and as no relevant keywords will discarded (i.e., recall is the same). For all these keywords, precision of TMH has increased as compared to TM at some extent. Note that with the increasing precision recall will be dropped. However, here we observe that except keywords, water, tiger and garden, recall will be the same in both models. On average, precision values of TM and TMH are 14.21%, and 33.11% respectively. This number demonstrates that TMH is 56.87% better than TM.

As we know, JNC,LIN,BNP measures generated better results than others. We hybrid these measures(TMH) by taking the average value of them. We used the same annotation result of TM. In Fig. 5, we can see the improvement by removing noisy keywords. If an image is not annotated by any relevant keyword, we cannot improve the accuracy since all of annotation in the image are noisy. To check the accuracy of detecting noisy keywords in an efficient way, we introduce Valid Accuracy (VAccuracy). We define an image as a τ(valid image) if it is annotated with at least one relevant keyword. Note that we do not calculate the accuracy of an image which is associated with all irrelevant keywords. In

Table 5, VAccuracy of TMH is increased substantially as compared to TM only, TM along with LIN, LNC, RIK and BNP. This demonstrates power of TMH over individual measures.

$$\lambda = \text{Number of Correct Keywords}$$
$$\chi = \text{Number of InCorrect Keywords}$$
$$\tau = \text{valid image(has at least one correct keyword)}$$

$$VAccuracy = (\lambda \cap \tau)/(\lambda + \chi) \cap \tau \qquad (10)$$

Table 5. With a TM data-set, the results of TM and TMH

Measure	Precision	Recall	VAccuracy
TM	0.2001	0.3501	0.2858
TMH(JNC+LIN+BNP)	0.2948	0.2001	0.6495
TM+JNC	0.2214	0.1427	0.3718
TM+LIN	0.2007	0.1606	0.3356
TM+LNC	0.2201	0.1408	0.3343
TM+RIK	0.1983	0.1466	0.3340
TM+BNP	0.2230	0.1402	0.3577

5   Related Work

Many statistical models have been published for image retrieval and annotation. Mori et al. [MTO1] used a co-occurrence model, which estimates the correct probability by counting the co-occurrence of words with image objects. [DB1] strived to map keywords to individual image objects. Both treated keywords as one language and blob-tokens as another language, allowing the image annotation problem to be viewed as translation between two languages. Using some classic machine translation models, they annotated a test set of images based on a large number of annotated training images. Based on translation model, Pan et al. [PYRD1] propose various methods to discover correlations between image features and keywords. They apply correlation and cosine methods and introduce SVD as well, but the idea is still based on translation model with the assumption that all features are equally important and no knowledge (KB) based has been used. The problem of translation model is that frequent keywords are associated with too many different image segments but infrequent keywords have little chance. To solve this problem, F. Kang et al. propose two modified translation models for automatic image annotation and achieve better results [KJC1]. Jeon et al. [JLM1] introduce cross-media relevance models (CMRM) where the joint distribution of blobs and words is learned from a training set of annotated images. Unlike translation model, CMRM assumes there is a many to many correlation between keywords and blob tokens rather than one to one.

Therefore, CMRM naturally takes into account context information. However, almost all of these proposed models treat all features are equally important and their annotation contains so many noisy keywords. On the other hand, in our case, we apply weighted feature selection and using knowledge based we strive to improve annotation accuracy.

6   Conclusions and Future Works

Our experimental results show, our proposed translation model along with knowledge based would get better annotation performance and correspondence accuracy than other traditional translation model. Since traditional translation model annotates too many irrelevant keywords, our model strives to prune irrelevant keywords by exploiting knowledge-based (here WordNet). During pruning we keep relevant keywords. To identify irrelevant keywords, we investigate various measures to determine semantic similarity between keywords/concepts. In our model, we fuse outcomes of all these methods together to make a final decision.

In future, we would like to extend the work in following directions. First, we will do more experiments based on different grid analysis, image features, clustering algorithms and statistical models. Next, we would like to extend the work in video domain.

References

[BD1]   K. Barnard, P. Duygulu, N. de Freitas, D. Forsyth, D. Blei, M. Jordan. "Matching words and pictures", *Journal of Machine Learning Research* **3** (2003) 1107–1135.

[BJ1]   D. Blei, M. Jordan. "Modeling annotated data", *26th Annual Int. ACM SIGIR Conf.*, Toronto, Canada, (2003).

[BP1]   S.Banerjee and T.Pedersen. "An adpated Lesk algorithm for word sense disambiguation using WordNet", *In Proceedings of the Third International Conference on Intelligent Text Processing and Computational Linguistics*, Pittsburgh (2001)

[BP2]   S. Banerjee and T. Pedersen. "Extended gloss overlaps as a measure of semantic relatedness", *In Proceedings of the Eighteenth International Joint Conference on Artificial Intelligence*,(2003) 805–810.

[Corel1]   http://corel.digitalriver.com/

[CorelKDD1]   http://kdd.ics.uci.edu/databases/CorelFeatures/
              CorelFeatures.data.html

[DB1]   P. Duygulu, K. Barnard, N. de Freitas, D. Forsyth. "Object recognition as machine translation: learning a lexicon for a fixed image vocabulary", *In Seventh European Conference on Computer Vision (ECCV)* **4** (2002) 97–112

[Eccv02]   "http://www.cs.arizona.edu/people/kobus/research/data/eccv_2002"

[JLM1]   J. Jeon, V. Lavrenko, R. Manmatha. "Automatic Image Annotation and Retrieval using Cross-Media Relevance Models", *26th Annual Int. ACM SIGIR Conference*, Toronto, Canada, (2003).

[JC1]   J.Jiang and D.Conrath. "Semantic similarity based on corpus statis-
           tics and lexical taxonomy", *In Procedeeings on International Confer-
           ence on Research in Computational Linguistics*, Taiwan, (1997).
[KJC1]   F. Kang, R. Jin and J. Y. Chai. "Regularizing Translation Models for
           Better Automatic Image Annotation", *CIKM'04*, (2004) 350–359.
[LW1]   J. Li and J. Z. Wang. "Automatic linguistic indexing of pictures by a
           statistical modeling approach", *IEEE Trans. on Pattern Analysis and
           Machine Intelligence*, **25(10)**, (2003)
[Lea1]   Leacock, C., and Chodorow, M. "Combining Local Context and Word-
           Net Similarity for Word Sense Identification", In C. Fellbaum, Editor
           , *WordNet:An electronic lexical database*, MIT Press (1998) 265–283.
[Les1]   M.Lesk. "Automatic sense disambiguation machine readable dictio-
           naries: How to tell a pine cone from an ice cream cone.", *In Proceedings
           of SIGDOC '86*, (1986).
[Lin1]   D.Lin. "Using syntatic dependency as a local context to reslove word
           sense ambiguity", *In Proceedings of the 35th Annual Meeting of the
           Association for Computational Linguistics*, Madrid (1997) 64–71.
[MTO1]   Y. Mori, H. Takahashi, and R. Oka. "Image-to-word transforma-
           tion based on dividing and vector quantizing images with words", *In
           MISRM'99 Frist International Workshop on Multimedia Intellegent
           Storage and Retrieval Management*,(1999).
[M1]   George Miller. "WordNet: An on-line lexical database", *International
           Journal of Lexicography*, **3(4)**(1990) (Special Issue)
[PYRD1]   J. Y. Pan, H. J. Yang, C. Faloutsos and P. Duygulu. "Automatic
           Multimedia Cross-modal Correlation Discovery", *KDD 2004*, Seattle,
           WA, Aug (2004).
[PBT1]   S. Patwardhan, S. Banerjee, and T. Pedersen. "Using measures of
           semantic relatedness for word sense disambiguation", *In Proceedings
           of the Fourth International Conference on Intelligent Text Processing
           and Computational Linguistics* (2003)
[Res1]   P. Resnik. "Using information content to evaluate semantic similar-
           ity in a taxonomy", *In Proceedings of the 14th International Joint
           Conference on Artificial Intelligence*, (1995).
[SM1]   Jianbo Shi and Jitendra Malik. "Normalized Cuts and Image Seg-
           mentation", *IEEE Conf. Computer Vision and Pattern Recogni-
           tion(CVPR)*, Puerto Rico (1997)
[WK1]   Lei Wang and Latifur Khan. "Automatic Image Annotation and Re-
           trieval using Weighted Feature Selection", *To appear in a special issue
           in Multimedia Tools and Applications*, Kulwer Publisher (2005).
[YCBF1]   Yang, Y. Carbonell, J. G., Brown, R. D., Frederking, R. E. "Translin-
           gual Information Retrieval: Learning from Bilingual Corpora", *Artifi-
           cial Intelligence* **103(1-2)** (2003) 323–345.
[ZG1]   R. Zhao and W. Grosky. "Narrowing the semantic gap - improved text-
           based web document retrieval using visual features", *IEEE Trans. on
           Multimedia.*, **4(2)** (2002) 189–200.

Intelligent Delivery of Multimedia Content in a Device Aware Ubiquitous Environment

Conor Muldoon[1], Gregory O' Hare[2], Rem Collier[1], Donnacha Phelan[1],
and Robin Strahan[1]

[1] Department of Computer Science, University College Dublin (UCD),
Belfield, Dublin 4, Ireland
{Conor.Muldoon, Rem.Collier, Donnacha.Phelan,
Robin.Strahan}@ucd.ie
[2] Adaptive Information Cluster (AIC), Department of Computer Science,
University College Dublin (UCD), Belfield, Dublin 4, Ireland
Gregory.OHare@ucd.ie

Abstract. This paper introduces a Generic Language for Interface DEvelopment (GLIDE) that supports the rapid prototyping of Graphical User Interfaces for the Agents Channeling ContExt Sensitive Services (ACCESS) architecture. ACCESS is an open agent-based framework that enables the fabrication and deployment of context aware applications. GUIs developed for ACCESS are contained within dynamic composite objects that are composed of a number of interacting components. Scripts written in GLIDE define the structure of the GUI's composite object and abstract out inter-component dependencies, thus ensuring that the GUI constituents remain modular, extensible and reusable. The GLIDE framework acts as a semantic model of the interface and enables the system to dynamically reconfigure and reorganize itself at run-time so as to adapt to user interaction. Additionally, GLIDE provides a mechanism to ensure that the abstract composition of the interface remains consistent across a range of ubiquitous devices.

1 Introduction

With improvements in the processing capabilities and the screen resolution of mobile devices multimedia applications will increasingly be developed for, and operate within, context-aware ubiquitous environments. To reduce the development costs of such applications and increase the quality of service to the user the Generic Language for Interface DEvelopment (GLIDE) has been created. GLIDE is used in the development of interfaces for the Agents Channelling Context Sensitive Services (ACCESS) [1][2] architecture, an open agent-based framework for the rapid proto-typing and deployment of ubiquitous computing applications. ACCESS provides a common core of functionality that developers of context-aware services may extend to provide service specific functionality thus enabling developers to focus on the business logic of their application rather than on the core infrastructure required to deliver it.

GLIDE has been designed to enforce a coding structure on the implementation of interface components that promotes reuse and extensibility. The GLIDE framework

K.S. Candan and A. Celentano (Eds.): MIS 2005, LNCS 3665, pp. 131–145, 2005.
© Springer-Verlag Berlin Heidelberg 2005

enables GUIs to be created that provide independence (1) among interface components, and (2) between interface components and agents, allowing these entities to interact without requiring them to directly reference one another. Rather than sending messages through object references, the components pass first order structures through an object in shared memory. This removes dependencies between the various entities and enables agents to dynamically reorganize and restructure the GUI.

Agents use the abstract information provided by GLIDE in the retrieval of content and in deciding on the most appropriate form of multimedia to obtain. If for example an agent is operating on a low specification device it may be more appropriate to obtain information content as text rather than a video clip. Because GLIDE provides an abstract representation of the components within the interface agents need only specify the type of device they are operating on in addition to the name of the abstract component that requires the data. Using this information server side agents send the most appropriate form of multimedia content.

The GLIDE framework distinguishes itself from other systems developed for the construction of mobile context-sensitive interfaces in several ways. It prevents dependencies being encoded into interface components by abstracting out the requisite information necessary for the interface components to communicate with, and view, each other. This leads to the creation of a semantic model of the interface that agents may alter so as to adapt to user interaction with the system. Additionally, it ensures that components are agnostic as to whether they are communicating with agents or other components. Thus allowing components to be replaced with agents and vice versa without making coding-level alterations.

2   Related Research

Considerable research has been invested into the development of adaptive interfaces that operate across a range of devices. The Wireless Markup Language (WML) is an XML based language that was developed to operate on top of the Wireless Application Protocol (WAP) stack. WML and WAP were specifically targeted at the cellular phone market. When combined with Java Server Pages, Servlets, PHP or other application server technology WML may be used to deliver dynamic web interfaces to the mobile citizen. The system described in [3] produces digital talking books from digital copies of text and audio narration that may be presented within a web browser. The authors identify variables governing the adaptation of the generated books and how these variables may be used to alter the behavior of particular interface components. The objective of the system is to enable the creation of books tailored to a predetermined group of users and usage situations. The Personal Universal Controller (PUC) [4] system automatically generates an intermediary interface for an appliance to allow the user to control the device from a Personal Digital Assistant (PDA) or cellular phone. The system is capable of generating a single combined user interface for multiple connected devices such as a home theatre. A device is required to have an abstract description of its functions, which is used within the code generation process. In [5] a system is described that provides support for the construction of cooperative user interfaces. The goal of this research is to produce collaboration aware applications that present a number of alternative interfaces to a community of users.

The work presented in this paper differs from pre-existing systems in that the GLIDE framework coerces the developer to adopt a structure within their code, which promotes the reuse of interface constituents and prevents inter-component dependencies. This leads to a greater level of decoupling within the system than a standard object-oriented approach and enables the interface to be dynamically restructured. Thus allowing intelligent agents to rearrange the GUI so as to adapt to the user's context and perceived behavior.

3   The ACCESS Architecture

The ACCESS architecture has been realized as an extension of a pre-existing framework for agent development, known as *Agent Factory* [6], [7], [8]. Agent Factory supports the fabrication of a type of software agent that is: autonomous, situated, socially able, intentional, rational, and mobile [7]. Practically, this has been achieved through the design and implementation of an agent programming language and associated interpreter. Together, the language and interpreter facilitate the expression of the current behaviour of each agent through the mentalistic notions of belief and commitment. These are augmented with a set of commitment rules that describe the dynamics of the agents' behaviour through the definition of the conditions under which the agent should adopt commitments. This approach is consistent with the well-documented BDI-agent model [7,9]. Additionally, Agent Factory provides FIPA-compliance through an Agent Management System (AMS) agent and a Directory Facilitator (DF) agent. Agent-oriented applications built using Agent Factory use these prefabricated agents to gain access to the infrastructure services provided by the run-time environment (i.e. yellow and white pages services, migration services).

Conversely, ACCESS augments the basic infrastructure delivered by Agent Factory through the implementation of additional agents, which deliver infrastructure services that are relevant to many context-sensitive applications. These agents form a cohesive management layer into which multiple heterogeneous context-sensitive services may be plugged. This facilitates service developers by enabling them to focus on the implementation of their service, and not the infrastructure required to deliver it.

The ACCESS Management agents provide the generic core functionality of the ACCESS architecture through a number of key functional areas, which include user profiling, context management, map generation, location sensing, service brokerage and content delivery. A detailed description of how these functional areas have been implemented is given in [2].

A key requirement with the development of a generic framework is that the design of the core system components cannot be polluted by the idiosyncrasies of concrete instances of that framework. If this is not enforced the framework could no longer be considered a generalization, as it would be coupled to specific implementations. Thus generic systems must be developed to the lowest common denominator. To overcome this problem for the development of agents ACCESS defines a *Service Provider Contract*, which outlines how service specific agents may interact with the core [2]. Providing agents adhere to this contract they should have no problem communicating with the generic agent community. A similar problem exists for the development of the graphical interfaces required by ACCESS services and has been solved through the use of the GLIDE scripting language.

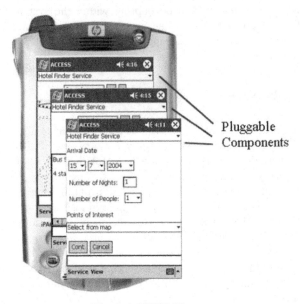

Fig. 1. ACCESS Viewer

Declaring a component within a GLIDE script leads to the construction of a screen for the component within the ACCESS Viewer (Fig. 1). The ACCESS Viewer provides the generic GUI functionality of ACCESS. The use of GLIDE extends the functionality of the viewer with service specific components. The Viewer acts as a multi-user and multi-service environment. It provides functionality to enable the user to log in to the system and maintains a separate information space for user data. When an ACCESS compliant interface is created within the Viewer its components are loaded in accordance with the order in which they are declared within the GLIDE script.

4 Hardware / Software Technology Set

The initial version of ACCESS has been designed to operate on lightweight PDAs and cellular phones. The PDA we are currently using is a Bluetooth-enabled Hewlett Packard iPaq H5450. A Navman GPS receiver is used as the position sensing technology. Our wireless GPRS network connection is realised through a Bluetooth-enabled Nokia 6310 phone. Client side software for the PDA includes the Java 2 Micro Edition (J2ME) Connected Device Configuration (CDC) environment augmented with the Foundation and Personal profiles whereas the cellular phone uses the Connection Limited Device Configuration (CLDC) and the Mobile Information Device

Profile (MIDP). ACCESS gateway technologies include the standard java software development kit (jsdk1.4.1), Apache, Tomcat, Struts and MySQL.

5 The GLIDE Framework

The GLIDE framework offers the core functionality responsible for the creation of ACCESS compliant GUIs. The framework is centered on the notions of *factories* and *interactions*. A factory is a class that returns an instance of a particular interface component. The inclusion of the name of a factory class within the GLIDE script causes an instance of its interface component to be created within a composite object, which forms part of the GUI. When a component is created in this manner a handle is associated with the component so as to enable it to be identified within an interaction. An interaction defines within the script a dependency that a component has on another component or on an agent. The rationale for interactions is to prevent components having direct object references to other components and to ensure that they are agnostic as to the entity they are interacting with. In order for a component to communicate with another component or agent a message is passed to the composite object in which it was created specifying the interaction that is to be used. The composite object maps the specified interaction on to a handle that was defined within the GLIDE script. The handle is then resolved to the name of a factory class or agent. If a component to be communicated with exists within the same composite object, a direct object reference is used to pass the message. Otherwise the message is recorded and subsequently perceived by an agent who informs the recipient.

The abstract information provided by GLIDE ensures that the interface's conceptual structure remains consistent across range of ubiquitous devices. The reason that one interface cannot be developed that will operate on all java enabled devices is that Sun no longer supports the concept of one size fits all and has divided up the platform at the micro-level into a number of different profiles and configurations. The decomposition of the platform in this manner improves the efficiency of the system and prevents lowest common denominator problems whereby low specification devices effectively limit the capabilities of the JVMs and the APIs developed for higher specification devices. This allows developers to tailor their algorithms, design patterns and general coding style to maximize the performance and efficiency of the particular configuration and profile they are working with.

The impact this has on GLIDE however is that now there may be a number of different interfaces each with their own profile and configuration idiosyncrasies. To reduce interoperability and maintainability problems the GLIDE framework ensures that the abstract composition of interfaces and the way in which they communicate with the core architecture and services remains consistent across the board. GLIDE provides a semantic model of the interface so we are assured that a particular interface component exists even though it may be implemented differently for different devices. Conversely the system will be aware that the interface does not contain any additional interface components   not   defined   within the script. Since an agent

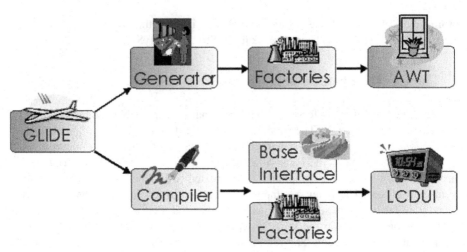

Fig. 2. GLIDE development process

perceives the interface and informs external entities of messages the type of device that component is operating on is transparent to the recipient.

Fig. 2 illustrates the GLIDE development process for the Connected Device Configuration (CDC) augmented with the Foundation and Personal profiles, and the Connection Limited Device Configuration (CLDC) augmented with the Mobile Information Device Profile (MIDP). These configurations are used within the GLIDE development process to create interfaces for PDAs and cellular phones respectively. It is not possible to implement a single interface for both profiles since they do not support the same APIs. A single GLIDE script however may be used to bootstrap the interface development process for both CDC/Personal Profile and CLDC/MIDP.

When developing for a PDA, a stub generator creates stub factory classes for the interface. By implementing the stub factories the developer may add an Abstract Windowing Toolkit (AWT) component to the CDC version of the interface. The generator only needs to be invoked when a new component is added to the script. Within CDC a composite object dynamically loads the script through the use of Java Introspection therefore changes to interactions do not necessitate recompilation.

An alternative approach is necessary when using GLIDE for a cellular phone since CLDC does not support introspection. Rather than a composite object dynamically loading a script at run-time a compiler is used to generate a base interface. When the developer makes an alteration to the script this base interface must be regenerated to reflect the change.

6   GLIDE Grammar

GLIDE is composed of a set of components identified by keywords namely *factory*, *interacts*, *agent*, *view*, *subfactory*, *nest*, and *composite*. These keywords are used to give a scripting level description of the GUI's structure. The following outlines the grammar of how these keywords are used within GLIDE in context-free Backus-Naur Form[1].

```
<glide-syntax>        ::= [<glide-component>]
<glide-component>     ::= <factory>|<function>|<function-call>|<nest>|
                          <composite> [<glide-component>]
<factory>             ::= <basic-factory>|<extended-factory>
<basic-factory>       ::= "factory " <word> " " <word> ";"
<word>                ::= any_character [<word>]
<extended-factory>    ::= "factory " <word>" " <word> "{" [<dependency>]
                          [<sub-component>] "}"
<dependency>          ::= <interaction>|<view>
<interaction>         ::= "interacts " ["agent "] <word> ";" [<depend-
                          ency>]
<view>                ::= "view " <word> ";" [<dependency>]
<sub-component>       ::= <basic-sub>|<extended-sub> [sub-component]
<basic-sub>           ::= "subfactory " <word> ";"
<extended-sub>        ::= "subfactory " <word> "{" [<dependency>] "}"
<function>            ::= <word> "(" [<argument>] "){" [<function-body>]
                          "}"
<function-body>       ::= <factory>|<nest>| <composite> [<function-
                          body>]
<argument>            ::= <word> [ ","<argument>]
<function-call>       ::= <word> "("[<argument>] ");"
<nest>                ::= "nest " <word> " " <word> ";"
<composite>           ::= "composite " <word> " " <word> ";"
```

Fig. 3. GLIDE Grammar

As stated in section 4 the concepts of factories and interactions are the main workhorses of the GLIDE infrastructure, these notions are represented by the *factory* and *interacts* keywords respectively. The *factory* keyword is used to inform the composite object which Java classes it should load to create service specific interface components. The *interacts* keyword is used to define how the composite object maps interactions to entities where entities may be either components or agents. If components wish to communicate or to influence each other's behaviour they must do so through the GLIDE framework. Consequently this removes inter-component dependencies from the Java code ensuring components are agnostic thus forcing developers to structure their code in a manner that promotes reuse.

The *agent* keyword has been developed in order to create interactions that are associated with agents. To enable an interface component to communicate with an agent, handles defined within the interaction must be resolved to agent names. The requisite names are communicated to an agent on the device by a service provider agent once a request has been made for a service initiation. The agent that receives this information subsequently perceives events that occur within the component and then informs the specified agents of the events accordingly. Both agents and interface components communicate through the use of first order structures, which are handled generically

---

[1] It should be noted that whitespace has been neglected within this description and also that the any_character reference within <word> refers to any ASCII character excluding brackets, semi colons and spaces.

by the components. This enables the knowledge of whether an agent or interface component is being communicated with to remain hidden. In this manner an interface component may be used to communicate with an agent in one service and then used to communicate with a component in a different service and vice-versa. The alteration is reflected within the GLIDE script, not within the Java code for the components.

The *view* keyword allows interface components to switch the current screen viewed within the service. The rationale for the inclusion of the *view* keyword is again to prevent inter-component dependencies. When interfaces are loaded in the ACCESS Viewer they are added in the order in which they are defined within the GLIDE script. Functionality is provided to view the next or previous screen however if an interface component wishes to view a component contrary to this ordering the *view* keyword must be used.

To further enhance the rapid development process the GLIDE framework supports the augmentation of interface components with sub-components that provide additional functionality. Consider a situation in which two similar service specific components are required. An abstract base class could be used to capture common functionality however extensions of the base class would be tightly coupled to their ancestors. Conversely within the GLIDE framework dynamic plug-ins are used instead of inheritance. In this situation the common functionality of the two similar classes would be captured as an interface component and the extended functionality as sub components. Using this approach the necessary functionality is realized through a combination of the interface component together with its specified plug-ins. The advantage of using this approach is that now a third component could be created that contains the functionality of both the plug-ins without making any structural alterations. This functionality is facilitated through the use of the *subfactory* keyword. Subcomponents assume the identity of their parent components therefore handles for subcomponents are not required.

In order to enable the reuse of entire GLIDE scripts the *nest* and *composite* keywords have been created. These keywords are used to specify the name of a script that the developer wishes to include. A developer may do this in situations whereby they want to combine the interfaces of two pre-existing services. Within the construction process once the framework encounters a *nest* or *composite* it recursively adds all interface components within the script to a composite object within the ACCESS Viewer. In this way an interface developed for one service may be incorporated as a component of another service. A handle is required for the ACCESS recursive naming policy to prevent naming collisions. The recursive naming policy works by augmenting names defined in embedded scripts with the name of the handle therefore if the top-level handle for an embedded script is unique all lower-level handles will be unique since they also follow the naming policy. The *nest* and *composite* keyword differ from one another in terms of the structure of the composite object that they produce. The *composite* keyword produces a new composite object that maintains its own state whereas the *nest* keyword causes interface components to be added to the parent scripts pre-existing composite object.

GLIDE supports the creation of functions to further minimize redundancy and promote reuse within scripts. Functions are composed of a prototype and body. Within the prototype the names of arguments are identified but not the type. The declaration of a function creates a reusable structural construct within the interface.

7   Dynamically Restructuring the Interface

Because GLIDE interface components do not use direct object references to communicate with or to view each other, agents can adapt the structure of the interface to match user interaction patterns. The interface's layout is viewed as an abstract concept within the system that agents may systematically alter. Agents continuously monitor and record the user's behavior and how they interact with the system through the use of the interface. Based on this information agents adopt beliefs and if an agent infers that the user could benefit with an alternative interface structure a commitment will be adopted to reorganize and rearrange the GUI. This is useful if the user never uses a particular component, as the agent can remove it from the interface freeing up resources and screen real estate. Additionally, agents may change the order in which the user views components to better suit the way in which the user typically interacts with the system. Had a standard object-oriented approach been used for the development of the GUI this behavior would not have been possible because objects contain direct object references and are therefore more tightly coupled and represent a single static structure.

The recorded data used by an agent to adopt beliefs about the users behavior is periodically transferred to a server side database thus enabling the adapted interface structure to be recreated across an array of devices. So, if a the user who frequently uses a PDA begins to use a mobile phone as an alternative, the evolved structure from user interaction with the PDA will be reflected within the phone interface. To enable information transfer across devices the system needs some mechanism to identify the user. It is for this reason that the user must log in to an ACCESS application specifying a universally unique name for identification purposes. Once the user logs in to the system the current user interaction patterns are downloaded from the database.

Because this type of adaptive behavior is dependent on user interaction with the system, how the interface will evolve cannot be predicted. It may be the case that the user does not like how an agent has altered the structure or layout. This is why the ACCESS Viewer provides an option for the user to reverse the process. If the user chooses to avail of this option the agent that is adapting the interface will use this data as feedback and be less likely to structure the interface in a similar manner in the future.

8   Delivering Multimedia Content with GLIDE

Since GLIDE interfaces may operate across a range of ubiquitous devices there is a need to adapt the type of multimedia content delivered to a particular interface. The approach adopted by ACCESS is to have an agent that monitors user interaction with the system and any processor intensive tasks being performed on the device. When an agent wishes to obtain multimedia content this information is sent to a content delivery agent together with the abstract name of the component that requires the data. The content delivery agent uses the name of the component to search its database to obtain a list of alternative forms content available. Using the information sent from the interface the agent makes a decision as to the most appropriate type of information to be sent to the device. If the agent is operating on a low specification device or if the device already has a high computational load it may be more appropriate for the user to receive content in a text format rather than audio or video.

On receiving the appropriate data an agent on the device must construct the correct type of interface for the content type received. For example if the content delivery agent sent a video clip to a mobile phone an agent on the device would construct a video player based on MIDP's mobile media API or had text been received a simple text box would have been created. The manner in which GLIDE handles multimedia content forms part of the core interface API. The developer need only be aware that the content will be placed in a particular location within the interface and that the data may be displayed in a number of different forms.

9 GLIDE Security

The tracking of user interaction and processor intensive tasks on the device introduces privacy issues in to the system. At present the user is simply given the option to enable or disable the transmission of personal data. If the transmission of personal data is disabled the system still adapts locally to user interaction however the evolved interface structure is not transferred across devices. Additionally, content is still tailored to the device type but processor intensive tasks are not taken into account. We are currently working on the development of another option that would enable the user to encrypt their personal data and transmit it to trusted services over SSL (Secure Socket Layer). This adds an additional computational overhead to the process of transmitting user data but ensures that a third party cannot intercept the information.

10 Case Study

To illustrate the usefulness and appropriateness of GLIDE we will use Sos[2][10] as a case study. Sos is a location aware and context-sensitive accommodation finding service for mobile citizens who require help finding somewhere to stay when they arrive at their chosen destination. Specifically, Sos helps users to find and book hotel accommodation that is most appropriate to their current context. This context combines the users current location, personal preferences, hotel availability, and agenda (e.g. business meeting, tour of city).

When the user loads the Sos interface they are initially presented with a welcome screen to the service followed by a component that allows the user to select the room preferences that they wish to avail of. At this point the user has two options, they may select the area that the hotel is to be located in by drawing a bounding circle on a map, or they may choose a location in accordance with their diary context. Their diary context reflects information the system is aware of in relation as to why the user is in a particular location. For example if the system is aware that the user is in a city for a

---

[2] Our application takes its name from the Irish word for rest – Sos.

conference, the diary context may recommend that the user request a hotel in close proximity to the conference centre. In order to achieve this the service must be aware of additional information regarding travel plans, conference location etc. It is for this reason that Sos interacts with another autonomous meeting service that handles the users diary.

When an area has been selected, be it through the diary context or an explicit map selection a request is made to the service provider agents for hotels within that region. The service provider agents adopt a Collaborative Filtering approach [1][11] in searching for and returning a list of hotels in accordance with user preferences. The user then has an option to view hotel information such as location on a map, facilities, star rating and so forth. Once the user has found a hotel that they wish to book they may request an offer from the service provider. When the user accepts the offer a credit transaction takes place and the user is finally presented with a screen tracking their location on the map.

As the user interacts with the system an agent on the device records how the various interface components are being used. If the user always chooses to view the location of the least expensive hotel as soon as the list of hotels arrives on the device, an agent on the device will preempt the user and restructure the interface to reflect this behavior. This will lead to a screen automatically being displayed centered on the location of the appropriate hotel. The user will still have the option to view the entire list of hotels if they wish to do so.

The interface screens presented in Fig. 4 illustrate the use of GLIDE within the Sos service. The primary map based component within the interface as with all other components is defined through the use of the *factory* keyword. This keyword causes the components to be created within the interface and is used to associate a handle with a component so that it may be used within an interaction. The map controller class provides the generic functionality for interacting with maps. The default functionality of the map controller is to track the users position and to update the map displayed when the user icon approaches the edge of the screen. Pluggable extensions to the map controller may be developed to provide additional functionality. Within the select area instance of the map controller (Fig. 4) an extension for selecting a region on the map and an extension to cancel the selected region have been developed. Following the use of the *factory* keyword and associated handle two interactions are set up. One to allow the component to communicate with a component whose handle is roomPanel the other to allow the component to communicate with an agent whose name is associated with the locDelAgent handle. Next a *subfactory* is used to define an extension for canceling a selected region. Finally the extension to enable the user to select a region is defined again with the use of the *subfactory* keyword. This extension contains interactions to enable communication with a component and an agent that are identified by the hotelList and hotelDelAgent handles respectively.

Within the hotelView instance of the map controller (right screen in Fig. 4) the extended functionality is different. This component provides a means by which the user may view the location of a specified hotel and augments the map with a hotel icon. Once the user clicks on the icon another screen is displayed with further information related to the specified hotel. Within the factory there is *view* set up to enable the component to display the component identified by the hotelList handle, the extended functionality is contained within the HotelViewFactory.

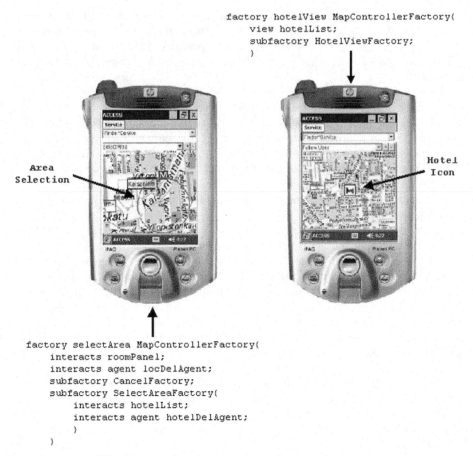

```
factory hotelView MapControllerFactory{
     view hotelList;
     subfactory HotelViewFactory;
     }
```

```
factory selectArea MapControllerFactory{
     interacts roomPanel;
     interacts agent locDelAgent;
     subfactory CancelFactory;
     subfactory SelectAreaFactory{
          interacts hotelList;
          interacts agent hotelDelAgent;
          }
     }
```

Fig. 4. Screens for selecting room preference and map area

Fig. 5 illustrates the use of functions within GLIDE. Functions were included within the language to reduce the incidental complexity of the scripts. This is achieved by removing redundant information. The two screens presented in Fig. 5 have identical scripting level semantics and therefore have a similar structure within the interface. The use of functions abstracts out this information and allows the developer to pass arguments when they want to create an interface component of this type. In this instance the function is named TwoViewInter.

The screen on the left was created to enable the user to select specific details such as arrival date in relation to their hotel booking. Through the use of the function an interaction is set up with a hotel service agent that will handle the users details. Within this screen the user has the option to select the area in which they want the hotel to be located from a map or they may use their diary context to automatically select an appropriate location. The screen on the right presents the user with a list of hotels that best suit their context and explicit requirements for hotel booking. Within this screen the function sets up an interaction with a hotel service delivery agent,

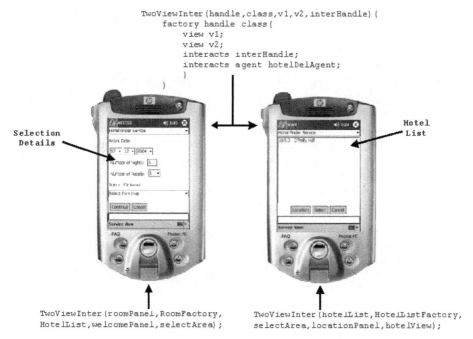

```
TwoViewInter(handle,class,v1,v2,interHandle){
    factory handle class{
        view v1;
        view v2;
        interacts interHandle;
        interacts agent hotelDelAgent;
    }
}
```

Selection
Details

Hotel
List

```
TwoViewInter(roomPanel,RoomFactory,        TwoViewInter(hotelList,HotelListFactory,
HotelList,welcomePanel,selectArea);        selectArea,locationPanel,hotelView);
```

Fig. 5. Screens for selecting an appropriate room and for selecting a hotel

which will allow the hotel service to know which hotel the user has selected. In this screen the user has the option to view where the hotel is located or to select a hotel. Selecting a hotel causes the interface to display a default map controller screen that tracks the users location.

These two components have similarities in terms of how they interact with agents and other components, and in terms of how they use views. Through the use of functions the developer only needs to define this information once. The factory handle, name of the factory class and the handle names of interactions and views are passed to the function as arguments.

10 Conclusion

This paper introduced GLIDE, a language developed to enable the extension of a common core of GUI functionality for mobile and context sensitive services. It is our belief that GLIDE is the first language to be developed for this purpose. The GLIDE framework distinguishes itself from other systems developed within the mobile computing arena in several ways.

- It provides a generic infrastructure for the development and deployment of GUI's for multiple heterogeneous context sensitive services.
- It solves the lowest common denominator problem of the infrastructure by enabling its functionality to be extended through the use of either introspection or code generation.

- It prevents dependencies being encoded into the extensions by abstracting out this information in to a script.
- It further promotes the reuse of interface components by allowing them to be extended with plug-ins.
- It ensures that components are agnostic as to whether they are communicating with agents or other components. This allows components to be replaced with agents and vice versa without making coding-level alterations.
- It provides a means for an entire GLIDE script to be reused through the use of nesting and the construction of new shared composite objects.
- It ensures that scripts are maintainable and reduces scripting level redundancy with functions.
- It provides a mechanism to enable the interface to dynamically reorganize itself at run-time so as to adapt to user interaction.

A fully functional prototype has been developed and demonstrated at [2]. Work on the GLIDE framework is ongoing. Specifically, efforts are currently directed at the fabrication of an array of u-commerce service demonstrators, and at the refinement and improvement of the existing language and infrastructure.

Acknowledgments

We gratefully acknowledge the kind support of Enterprise Ireland through their grant ATRP/01/209 to the E=mC^2: Empowering the mobile Citizen Creatively project. Gregory O'Hare gratefully acknowledges the support of Science Foundation Ireland (SFI) under grant no. 03/IN.3/1361.

References

1. Strahan, R., O'Hare, G.M.P., Phelan, D., Muldoon, C., Collier, R. W.: ACCESS: An Agent based Architecture for the Rapid Prototyping of Location Aware Services. In: Proceedings of the 5th International Conference on Computational Science, Atlanta (2005)
2. Muldoon, C., O'Hare, G.M.P., Phelan, D., Strahan, R., Collier, R.W.: ACCESS: An Agent Architecture for Ubiquitous Service Delivery. In: Proceedings of Seventh International Workshop on Cooperative Information Agents (CIA), Helsinki (2003)
3. Duarte, C., Carrico, L: Identifying adaptation dimensions in digital talking books. In: Proceedings of the 9th international conference on Intelligent User Interfaces (IUI), Madeira (2004)
4. Nichols, J.: Automatically generating user interfaces for appliances. In: Proceedings of Second International Conference on Pervasive Computing, Vienna (2004)
5. Smith, G., Rodden, T.: Access as a means of configuring cooperative interfaces. In: Proceedings of Conference On Organisational Computing Systems (COOCS), California (1993)
6. Collier, R.W., O'Hare, G.M.P., Lowen, T., Rooney, C.F.B.: Beyond Prototyping in the Factory of the Agents. In: Proceedings of 3rd Central and Eastern European Conference on Multi-Agent Systems, Prague (2003)

7. O'Hare, G.M.P.: Agent Factory: An Environment for the Fabrication of Distributed Artificial Systems. In: O'Hare, G.M.P., Jennings, N.R. (eds.), Foundations of Distributed Artificial Intelligence: Sixth Generation Computer Series, Wiley Interscience (1996)

8. Collier, R.: Agent Factory: A Framework for the Engineering of Agent-Oriented Applications. Ph.D. Thesis, Department of Computer Science, University College Dublin, Ireland (2001)

9. Rao, A.S., Georgeff, M.P.: BDI Agents: From Theory to Practice. In: Proceedings of the First International Conference on Multi-Agent Systems, San Francisco (1996) 312-319

10. Phelan, D., Strahan, R., Collier, R., Muldoon, C., O'Hare, G.M.P.: Sos: Accommodation on the fly with ACCESS, In: Proceedings The 17th International FLAIRS Conference, Miami (2004)

11. Breese J.S., Heckerman, D., Kadie, C.: Empirical Analysis of Predictive Algorithms for Collaborative Filtering. In: Proceedings of the Fourteenth Annual Conference on Uncertainty in Artificial Intelligence, pp 43--52, Madison (1998)

Context-Based Management of Multimedia Documents in 3D Navigational Environments

Fabio Pittarello

Università Ca' Foscari di Venezia - Dipartimento di Informatica,
Via Torino 155, 30123 Mestre (VE) Italy
pitt@dsi.unive.it

Abstract. This work proposes an approach for managing multimedia information associated to 3D environments navigated by the user. The influence of context (location, user profile, user history, time, device and network) on such management is considered in different stages of the multimedia information lifecycle, with a particular reference to the authoring and presentation phases. The different types of contexts will be modeled (i.e., with a particular emphasis on location and user history) and analyzed in relation to content creation, leading both to the definition of a hierarchy of contexts and to a data structure modeled on authoring needs. Such formalizations will be then used as key components of an implementation architecture for controlling and proactively managing multimedia information in the presentation phase. Application examples related to cultural heritage are presented, showing how such architecture can manage complex user experiences on the basis of changes of context.

1 Introduction

This work proposes an approach for managing context-based multimedia information on the basis of different typologies of context.

Such approach is relevant for all the situations where the authoring and the presentation of content is done with a direct reference to location: art exhibitions, urban information systems, multimedia systems for orientation inside complex buildings, annotation systems related to context (e.g., researches writing notes on a PDA while working in an archeological area). The approach takes advantage of previous research related to the formalization of the structure of 3D environments [19] belonging to the realm of mixed reality [12] (i.e., paradigms with different mixtures of real and virtual elements, ranging from immersive virtual reality to real environments enhanced with different devices) and to the definition of an agent-based architecture [4] for managing proactively user interaction inside explorative environments. Such architecture is extended for managing presentation of information, adapting content to different typologies of context (location, user profile, user history, time, device and network).

2 Related Work

The notion of context has been exploited by a number of authors [5] [11] that consider different types of it, including location, user, device, network and time.

K.S. Candan and A. Celentano (Eds.): MIS 2005, LNCS 3665, pp. 146–162, 2005.

Context-aware applications customize user's experience in relation to context and to its modifications, influencing both interaction and information fruition.

Nack et al. propose a sophisticated architecture [15] for adaptive information spaces; the *dynamic presentation environment* [14], a key component of such architecture, enables easy access to data without requiring to the user any knowledge of the underlying information organization. The presentation of content is dynamically driven by queries generated by the user model, the browsing history and device constrains. The authors address also the issue of information generation, supporting the need for a collective set of information growing over time, created by multiple authors. Such attention towards authoring characterizes also this work, although the main focus is on examining the influence of different types of context in relation to content creation.

Studies on context and adaptation have been particularly developed in the hypermedia and web realms [1] [18], leading to the development of different applications. One of the first examples is an architecture [13] for automatically transcoding multimedia content into a multiresolution representation hierarchy and serving the appropriate version on the web, on the basis of the client capabilities (i.e., screen size, color, network bandwidth, etc.). Other forms of context considered in our paper, that typically require a direct involvement of the author for producing distinct versions of content, are not modeled.

For what concerns the domain of navigational 3D real and virtual environments, location has been considered at first as the only relevant form of context influencing information fruition and interaction opportunities. One of the first examples of location-aware applications is the *Active Badge* system [20], that provides a means of locating individuals within a building by determining the location of a wearable active badge. The system has been used for several services, from re-direction of incoming phone calls to rerouting of personal X-Windows sessions at any suitable display near to the user position.

Later on, other typologies of context have been considered, including the user profile and the user history. In some works adaptation is focused on content presented to the user; for example in [6] the presentation of objects in a 3D virtual store varies as a consequence of the choices made by users in previous sessions. Other works customize interaction, focusing on navigation [10] or other types of activities [4].

Thanks to the availability of a new range of devices that combine access to web information and mobility in a real environment, some works propose customization of web content on the basis of different contexts, including the location of the user inside the environment. Physical hypermedia builds relationships among physical, real world objects and virtual ones: *Hycon*, a framework for context-aware applications [9], supports authoring in the field and automatic collection of related context information that will be used in the information browsing phase; other examples include museum guides [8] that augment physical objects with digital information and provide links to other digital or physical objects. All such works don't consider the context user history, that is modeled and discussed in detail in our paper as a significant trigger for content presentation.

A recent work uses context-awareness to support tourism during the vacation through a web portal cultural called *Medina* [7]; different kinds of context (device, user profile, network, location and time) trigger the presentation of hypertextual information. The context relevant for retrieving information is defined as a vector of context property values over time (i.e., not only the current context but also previous variations over time are considered as an input for multimedia information retrieval). While our work shares with this approach such attention for variations of context over time, it introduces other contexts (e.g., the context user history) that are not considered in the *Medina* proposal.

The modeling of the context user history proposed in this work is partially based on [4], where the interaction done by the user was logged to the so-called *interaction process*. Although useful, such modeling was unable to capture the most complex experiences (e.g., education, e-learning, etc.) where also the content browsed by the user influences the evolution of the experience itself.

Besides, in [4] the user history was used by a set of distributed cooperating agents to discover the recurring behaviors and proactively adapt the following interaction sequences. In this work agents control the presentation of multimedia documents on the basis of the changes of a wider number of contexts; concerning user history, they take advantage of a more complete logging that enables them to perform a larger number of control and adaptation activities.

Finally, a preliminary approach to the problem of presenting information for the different segments of mixed reality focused on the authoring of different versions of the same document and on the integration for the presentation by an architectural component named *integration engine* [19]; the approach of creating different versions of the same document in relation to specific devices can be found also in [3] that introduces the concept of *virtual document* and *virtual component*.

3   Modeling Contexts

This work considers a variety of contexts for managing multimedia documents: location, user profile, user history, time, device and network. Some of them are modeled as simple numeric strings (e.g., *time*) or a set of alphanumeric pairs (e.g., *user profile*, *device* and *network*); the other contexts (e.g., *location* and *user history*) have a more complex formalization that will be described in this section.

3.1   Location

This work takes advantage of the *Interaction Locus* model (from now on: IL) for defining the context location; such model, described in [19], aims to identify in the 3D scene the zones that are perceived by the users as morphologic and functional units (e.g., the main hall of a public library, the pavilions of a fair, the rooms of an art exhibition, etc.). Explicit identification of zones that are semantically relevant for the user in terms of perception and use of space is followed by the association of labels and sound loops enhancing the user's perception of such locations, lists of actions allowed/inhibited in such zones and complex multimedia content for augmenting the user knowledge.

The locations of a 3D environment are modelled as a set of ILs organized in hierarchy. For example the locations of an art exhibition environment are modeled as a set of ILs corresponding to the exhibition rooms, containing nested ILs corresponding to the locations of the works of art; multimedia content related to the rooms is distributed and associated to the first level ILs; additional multimedia content containing detailed information about the works of art is associated to the second level ILs.

The IL concept permits to model the context location as a set of places rather than as a set of space positions; as a consequence, content authoring and presentation, rather than being associated to raw Cartesian triples identifying the user position in space, are done in relation to zones semantically relevant for the user.

3.2 User History

A sophisticated logging of the user activity is proposed: the *experience process*, summa of the interaction done by the user and of the multimedia information browsed by him/her during the navigation in the 3D environment.

In more formal terms all the possible states of the interactive 3D environment (e.g., *user inside IL 1.1*) are mapped to a control finite state machine (CFSM).

The *experience process* is defined as a sequence of tuples $<s_t, a_t, s_{t+1}, content_{t+1}>$, where s_t is the state of the CFSM mapping the 3D environment at the time t, a_t is the action performed by the user at the time t, s_{t+1} is the state of the CFSM at the time t+1 determined by the action a_t, $content_{t+1}$ is an indexed version of the multimedia content presented to the user as a consequence of his/her activity a_t; this work proposes for the latter component an implementation based on an array of the most relevant words used in such content. The *experience pattern* is defined as a sub-sequence of the experience process that identifies a recurring behavior. Section 5 will show how such concepts, introduced in this work, represent a fundamental contribution to the definition of a context-based architecture for presenting multimedia information.

4   Modeling Multimedia Documents for the Authoring Needs

The role of the content author is fundamental for building complex and interesting experiences for users. Therefore this work considers the author's habits as the starting point for modeling the structure of multimedia documents, whose fruition is a fundamental part of the user's experience in media-rich navigational environments. The influence of the different contexts on the author's work is examined, pointing out how the definition of new context conditions can be managed or not by automatic procedures that don't require additional direct intervention by the author.
In particular the following observations can be done:

– authors produce content in relation to a specific audience (e.g., children, students, experts of a specific discipline); changing type of audience (i.e., an important component of the context *user profile*) typically requires a strong revision of the content authored for adapting it to the skills and background of the new one; such revision can hardly be realized by an automatic procedure;

– authors that create content for a navigational 3D environment associate their production to different locations that must be reached (physically or virtually) by the
user; while a book's reader simply can go back through the previous pages for retrieving a concept that s/he can't recall, a 3D environment's user must navigate
through the scene for doing the same operation; therefore creators of distributed
content, unlike books' authors, tend to organize content as self-contained or redundant units, in a way that doesn't require the user to spend a lot of time for additional unwanted navigation. Besides, a rearrangement of the zones of the 3D scene
typically requires a strong revision of the author's work in order to re-elaborate and
assign different chunks of content to the new set of zones;

– content creators can guide the evolution of a certain experience as a result of sense-
d user interaction with objects belonging to the scene or content browsed (i.e., the
user history); deciding different relations between the accumulated user history and
the prosecution of the experience or taking into account the role of different objects
and information requires a direct intervention of the author. While such changes
can lead to a very different experience, often such modifications can be decided
without affecting the structure of places (e.g., an interactive thriller may be
changed by the author without modifying the structure of the 3D environment and
the basic information associated to the different locations that compose it); on the
contrary altering the structure of places typically has more dramatic effects and requires also a redesign of the interaction with objects associated with locations and
derived content presentation; concluding, we may say that modifications of the
conditions influencing the context user history can have a significant impact on the
author's work, although less important if compared with modifications related to
the context location;

– authors can consider time as an additional variable determining the range of validity of content inside information nodes, inhibiting access or presenting alternative
information; again modifications to the conditions related to the context time can
have a significant impact on the author's work, although less important if compared to modifications due to a revision of the set of places that characterize the
context location.

– the device owned by the user can influence the author's work requiring him/her to
produce separate versions for different devices (e.g., the desktop computer or the
PDA); in spite of that, as will be explained in the Section 4.2, the introduction of a
new device at some extent can be managed automatically, avoiding additional author's work;

– also the influence of the network (in terms of bandwidth and availability) on the
author's work may be minimized with automatic techniques.

4.1 A Hierarchy of Contexts

Such observations lead to a conclusion that represents one of the novelties of this
work: not all the contexts are equal in relation to the production of content and to the
additional effort for revising it, but a hierarchy can be designed; in such hierarchy,
shown in Table 1, the highest levels are occupied by contexts where the definition of
new conditions (e.g. a new user profile or a new set of locations) requires a consistent
revision of multimedia content by the author, while the lower levels are occupied by

contexts where the definition of new conditions can be automatically (or semi-automatically) managed for producing an appropriate content presentation.

While it is possible to design an appropriate hierarchy for different categories of multimedia information systems, the choice of considering distributed multimedia information systems for navigable environments as a target of this work produces as a result the peculiar hierarchy shown in Table 1, where the context location occupies a relevant position and conditions strongly the content production.

Table 1. The Hierarchy of Contexts

Context	Author's intervention in relation to modification of context conditions
User profile	High
Location	High
User history	High/Medium
Time	High/Medium
Device	Low
Network	Low

4.2 Data Structures for Storing Experiences

The data structures deriving from such hierarchy use as primary organizational principle the higher level contexts (i.e., the primary organization principles for the author): user profile and location.

A data structure is defined and associated to each location (i.e., the IL) of the 3D environment; a set of such data structures, defined for a specific user profile, is called *experience layer* (see Figure 1). More precisely:

Experience layer. The multimedia content of such data structure is coherently authored by one author or by a set of coordinated authors for a certain user profile. Specific experience layers associated to distinct user profiles can be authored for the same environment; for example four different experience layers for the user profiles *primary school student, casual visitor* and *art expert* can be authored for a building hosting an art exhibition. More details about the experience layers can be found in [4].

Data structure associated to the IL. Its detailed definition represents a novelty of this work; in particular such structure includes the following components:

- XHTML [23] multimedia content organized in a hierarchical structure (different navigation modalities of such content, including transversal navigation, are possible but they are not shown in Figure 1 for the sake of simplicity);
- a set of CSS [2] rules for presenting content with a variety of devices;
- an X3D[22] description o the 3D volume that defines the limits of the associated IL and the geometry of other interactive 3D elements associated to that IL;
- other data, including also a description of the conditions for accessing 3D objects and multimedia data of the IL.

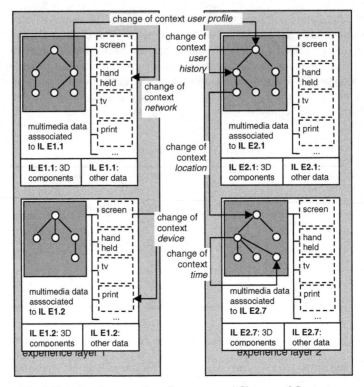

Fig. 1. Relations between Data Structures and Changes of Contexts

Multimedia content nodes are created using XHTML, denoting the structural properties of their elements (e.g., paragraphs, headings, etc.). According to the guidelines
suggested by the WAI group [21] of the W3C Consortium content is created once and
complemented with *textual equivalents* that offer the same information (or at least a
summarization of it) of the multimedia components associated to content itself. Then
a set of rules specified in associated style sheets [2] enables content presentation on a
variety of devices, from visual browsers to Braille keyboards.

The introduction of the separation of structure from presentation rationalizes the
authoring effort, reducing greatly the direct intervention of the content creator for
producing new versions for different browsers and avoiding potential problems of
content coherence related to updates realized in different times.

Such separation is used also for managing at some extent variations of network bandwidth, changing the presentation from text-only to full multimedia (e.g., low bandwidth is treated as a communication of the same content to a small screen device).

Figure 1 evidences how, in the presentation phase, context changes produce very
different shifts of the pointers to multimedia data presented to the user.

In particular changes to the context user profile have the most dramatic effect; a
new experience layer related to the new user profile must be available and takes the

place of the current data structure; the pointer shifts to the default node of the multi-media data associated to one of the ILs of the new experience layer.

Modifications of the context location leading to a new IL cause a jump of the pointer from the current node to the default content node associated to the new IL.

Changes of the contexts user history and time typically cause a jump to a different node of the same hierarchy of content associated to the current IL.

The context device doesn't cause any modification of the pointer to multimedia data; instead a different set of presentation rules for the new device is selected (e.g., Figure 1 shows the shift from the device *screen* to the device *print*). Modifications in the context network related to bandwidth are modeled as changes of device (e.g., Figure 1 shows how a reduction of the bandwidth is modeled shifting the presentation rules from *screen* to *handheld*).

5   An Architecture for Context-Based Presentation of Multimedia Information

While the previous section gave a vision of the relations between the defined data structures and contexts decoupled from implementation details, this section will explain in detail a component based architecture (see Figure 2) controlling the evolution of the multimedia presentation in relation to context changes. Such architecture applies to different segments of the mixed reality domain, including desktop virtual reality and augmented reality with mobile devices.

A set of distributed cooperating agents take care of the changes of context; concerning the context user history, their action is based on an accurate logging of the user experience, namely the experience process described in Section 3.2.

An agent named *genius loci* is associated to each IL and accesses the data structures defined in Section 4.2; therefore the genius loci knows the IL topology, its interaction opportunities, the multimedia content associated and the set of conditions for interaction and content fruition. The genii loci are implemented as a hierarchical structure of coordinated components modeled on the hierarchy of ILs.

An agent named *numen* (i.e., a kind of *guardian angel*) is associated to the user; it maintains the knowledge about the previous user activity. Such agents monitor and manage the user experience; a communication protocol between the *numen* and a *genius loci* is activated anytime the user enters or exits an IL or whenever necessary for their coordination, enabling a distributed computation.

At the start of the user experience, the *experience selector and integrator* component aggregates the *3D base world* and the *3D components of the data structure experience layer* on the basis of the current context *user profile*. The *enhanced 3D world* contains a variety of elements ranging from the definition of ILs and associated multimedia content to active components such as the *IL experience handlers* (i.e., from now on the *genii loci*).

Such aggregation can take different forms in relation to the different segments of the mixed reality domain: in a virtual environment for desktop computer or in immer

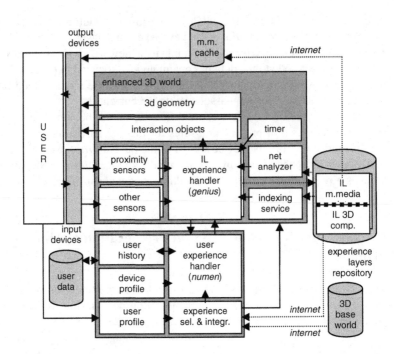

Fig. 2. An Architecture for Presenting Multimedia Content in a 3D Navigational Environment

sive vr different virtual components are put together to create a new enhanced virtu-
alworld, while in augmented reality the active components are loaded and synchronized with the underlying real world. The experience selector and integrator takes
care also of unloading the current experience layer and of loading a new one if the
user profile changes during the interactive session (e.g., a user may change his/her
profile from *business man* to *tourist* while navigating in an urban landscape).

Information about the contexts user profile, device and user history (if available
from a previous session) are passed to the *user experience handler* (i.e., from now on
the *numen*) for initialization.

The input and output devices are initialized for enabling users to send input and receive presentation of multimedia data and output generated by the 3D objects of the
navigational experience; the specific devices used depend on the segment of mixed
reality and on the constraints fixed for communication between the user and the system (e.g., monomodal or multimodal interfaces).

Changes of the context location are perceived by a set of *proximity sensors* (i.e.
sensors specialized for perceiving the presence of the user inside the volume controlled by them) associated to the ILs. Such sensors receive data from different input
devices (i.e., a mice for desktop virtual reality, gps data filtered for correcting errors
that characterize such technology for augmented reality) and pass them to the genii
loci. When a relation of inclusion is found, comparing such values with the ILs spatial

limits, the appropriate genius loci acts for managing access to multimedia data or 3D interactive objects under its influence. In particular the genius loci points at the *multimedia data* associated to the IL under its control, which reside on the *experience layer repository*. Such data are sent to the output devices for presentation to the user.

All the user interaction data, including those ones monitored by *other sensors* (e.g., *touch sensors* for monitoring the user touching specific 3D objects, *visibility sensors* for monitoring the user viewpoint on specific locations of the scene, etc.) are logged by the genii loci as fundamental components of the context user history.

Also the other complementary component of the user history, the content browsed, is managed by the genii loci, taking advantage of the *indexing service* component.

In the current proposal each genius loci, using the indexing service, generates a set of *local arrays of keywords* (*laks*) associated to multimedia information (i.e., an array for each information node); when the genius loci accesses the experience layer repository for sending multimedia data to the user, it logs in parallel the appropriate *lak* to the experience process (more details will be given in Section 6).

The genii loci are both loggers of user history data (i.e., the *experience process*) and active managers that use them for managing content presentation. In general their action is mediated by the numen that receives such data, performs some elaboration activities and passes the results back to the current genius loci (i.e., the genius associated to the IL currently navigated by the user) as an input for its action.

Changes of the context *time* are controlled by the *timer* component that passes such values to the genii loci, which use also such data for modifying access to multimedia data or 3D interactive objects (e.g., they may inhibit access to certain data if the current time is out of a fixed interval).

The context *device* is passed by the numen to the genii loci at the beginning of the user experience for enabling them to request the appropriate presentation rules associated to multimedia content. Changes of the context device can happen also inside a specific experience (e.g., the user may request to print the current multimedia content; in such case the presentation rules related to the media print will be requested by the current genius loci in order to format the content appropriately).

A *net analyzer* component is available to check periodically changes of the context *network*, in terms of speed and availability, and to inform the genii loci of the relevant changes. In the current implementation architecture, speed modifications are managed as changes of device, varying accordingly the presentation from text-only to full multimedia. Preliminary caching of content on a local *multimedia cache* (a technique that can be found in a range of web browsers for optimizing network bandwidth) faces with momentary network failures. Of course, in case of persistent network unavailability (e.g., a PDA with a very bulky connection to the network), the multimedia data structures should be local to the device.

6 Application Examples Related to Cultural Heritage

This section will discuss three application examples of the concepts described above, related to the cultural heritage domain, with a particular reference to the influence of the context user history. In the examples proposed such context affects the evolution of such experience in several ways; multimedia information are selected and presented on the basis of the following factors:

- recurring classes of multimedia information that the user has shown to be more interested in during previous content browsing;
- comparison between multimedia information available in the current IL and most relevant multimedia information indexed during previous content browsing;
- answers given in educational tests associated to previous navigation and browsing.

In the first and in the second case the behavior of the system is proactive (i.e., the system suggests a content on the basis of previous browsing); in such cases the user, in accordance to usability heuristics [16], is enabled to make a different choice; for example s/he may choose to shift to the default content. In the third case the action of the system is a constrain that, for educational purposes, prevents the user from making different choices.

While in all the three cases listed above agents base their action on the logging and analysis of the experience process, there are important differences to consider.

Recurring classes of multimedia content. Such proactive system behavior has already been discussed in [4], but it is reported in this work with a specific example related to content fruition for giving a complete vision of the potentialities of the architecture proposed for managing content presentation.

In this case, agents base their action on the classification of 3D objects and nodes of multimedia content in classes (e.g., the class *technical information for a work of art*, the class *artist's biographical notes*, etc.); class information is associated to the states of the CFSM that maps the experience; when such states are reached as a consequence of user interaction, information related to the class is logged by the set of genii loci to the tuples that describe the single steps of the experience process.

The numen receives the experience process from the genii loci and seeks it in order to find recurring sequences of tuples; in this case the numen takes in exam only the first three components of each tuple (i.e., states and actions triggering the change of state); the fourth component (i.e., indexed content) is not considered.

Fragment of the Experience Process Logged by a Set of Genii Loci

```
<IL1.1corridor(connection),enters,IL1.7bauhaus(exhib_room),content1>
<IL1.7bauhaus(exhib_room),approaches,IL1.7.1klee2(work_art),content2>
<IL1.7.1klee2(work_art),clicks,IL1.7.1.2klee2tech(work_tech),content3>
...
<IL1.4corridor(connection),enters,IL1.5blauereit(exhib_room),content5>
<IL1.5blauereit(exhib_room),approaches,IL1.5.3marc4(work_art),content32>
<IL1.5.3marc4(work_art),clicks,IL1.5.3.2marc4tech(work_tech),content7>
```

For example the numen, analyzing the experience process shown above (only the relevant fragments, including class information between brackets, are shown), will identify the following recurring sequence of classes: *connection, exhib_room, work_art* and *work_tech* and the associated actions: *enters, approaches* and *clicks*. In other words the numen will recognize the following repeated activity: the user enters a room from the corridor, gets near to a work of art and clicks for having technical information about it. The numen will pass information related to such recurring sequence (i.e., the experience pattern) to the genii loci.

When the user will enter the room *cabaret_voltaire*, approaching an artwork of the artist *Hugo Ball*, the genius loci logging the user activity will recognize the first part of the recurring sequence of states and actions and will proactively conclude the interaction performing the action *clicks* on behalf of the user and presenting (if available) multimedia information belonging to the class *work_tech*.

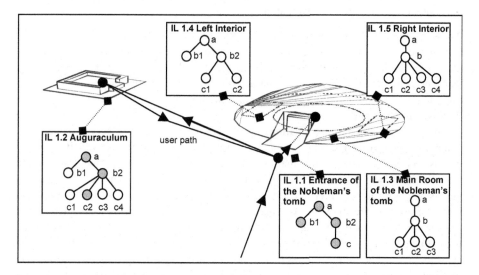

Fig. 3. An Example of 3D Environment Mapped with a Set of ILs and Associated Hierarchies of Multimedia Information; the Gray Nodes Represent Visited Content

Indexed multimedia content. The second and third agents' behaviors represent a novelty of this work that has been made possible by the enhancements in the logging of the user history. In particular, in this second example agents base their action on the indexing of multimedia information previously browsed.

As stated in Section 5, each genius loci generates a set of local arrays of keywords (*laks*) corresponding to the nodes of multimedia content associated to the IL; when the user browses a specific content node the associated array is logged as fourth component of the current tuple of the experience process and sent to the numen.

The numen progressively parses the fourth component of the tuples of the experience process and generates a *global array of the most relevant keywords (gak)* for all the content browsed by the user; such array is updated each time a genius loci sends its data to the numen.

When a user enters a given IL, the associated genius loci requests the *gak* and compares it with its set of *laks*. As a result of such comparison the genius loci will choose from its hierarchy of multimedia content the node that best match the *gak* and will present it to the user.

For example agents monitoring the user experience in an art exhibition may have collaboratively generated the *gak* containing the keywords *klee(4.5)*, *itten(4.2)*, *bauhaus(3.5)*, *van der rohe(3.2)*, *weimar(3.1)* and *angel(3.0)* (i.e., the number in brackets represents the relevance of the keyword), extracted from the content browsed by the user in the visited exhibition rooms; when the user enters a new room such array will be compared with the arrays of keywords extracted from local multimedia data; on the basis of such comparison the current genius loci will proactively select and present the content node whose *lak* best matches the *gak*.

Answers given to tests. In an e-learning experience at least one IL is organized for testing the knowledge acquired by the user through previous browsing; correct answers to a set of questions formulated in such ILs let the user to proceed along his/her learning path, entering other ILs characterized by conditional access. Again such important part of the user experience is controlled by the coordinated set of agents on the basis of the experience process.

The genii loci of the test locations are programmed for giving access to different content in relation to the answers given by the users (e.g., if the answer is right the genius loci will present an information node telling the user that s/he has resolved the test and that s/he may proceed to the following IL, while if the answer is wrong the genius will present an alternate information node inviting the user to retry). Such nodes of content are mapped, as usual, to the states of the CFSM associated to the experience; when such states are reached as a consequence of user interaction they are logged as part of the experience process, implicitly saving information related to the answers given. The numen parses the experience process to progressively build a map of all the states visited by the user (including correct and wrong answers); such map is then queried by genii loci controlling ILs with conditional access.

We'll consider a practical example related to the web site owned by Palazzo Grassi [17], the well known institution organizing cultural exhibitions in Venice. The visitor of the site navigating the 3D experience associated to the exhibition *The Etruscans* held in Venice is invited to follow a suggested path in order to acquire knowledge about the Etruscan civilization; access to information contained inside certain areas is conditioned to giving a correct answer to a set of questions associated to other zones. In particular the user arriving for the first time in front of the *Nobleman's tomb* (see Figure 3) browses a default content explaining that to gain access s/he has to reach a location called the *Auguraculum*; in such place the user is invited to answer to a question related to Etruscans' habits; the correct answer will be the key for accessing multimedia information contained inside the Nobleman's tomb and other interior locations. Modeling such experience with our approach requires to define an IL and an associated genius loci for each location involved (the Nobleman's tomb, the Auguraculum and the other locations) and a numen for coordinating their action. The mapping of the environment with a set of ILs and associated multimedia information is shown in Figure 3.

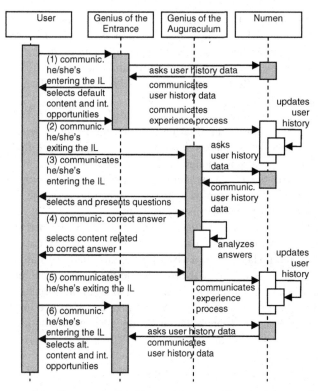

Fig. 4. A Fragment of the Communication Protocol between User and Agents for Regulating Access to Multimedia Information on the Basis of Answers Given in Test ILs

Figure 4 illustrates, according to UML notation, a fragment of the communication protocol activated to manage the selection and presentation of information.

1. The user enters the IL *Entrance of the Nobleman's tomb*; the event is perceived by the associated *genius loci* that asks to the *numen* data related to the context user history in order to select the appropriate content. Data sent by the numen include the map of the visited states of the CFSM (i.e., data include also the recurring patterns and the global array of indexed content, but they are not used in this example as input for the activity of the genii loci). Such map is sought by the genius loci to find information about visited locations and answers given. At this time no element in the map allows the genius loci to give full access to the tomb and to its multimedia content; therefore the default nodes of multimedia content associated to the IL Entrance are presented to the user (nodes *IL1.1(a)* and *IL1.1(b1)*, Figure 3); the content of such multimedia node invite him/her to go to the IL *Auguraculum*.

2. The user exits the IL Entrance and the genius loci communicates to the numen the logged tuples of the experience process; the numen elaborates such data, updating the user history accordingly.

3. The user enters the IL Auguraculum; the event is perceived by the associated *genius loci* that asks to the *numen* the user history data. Currently such data don't contain any element about previous navigations in that IL; therefore the *genius loci* presents to the user the information nodes describing the test (nodes *IL1.2(a)* and *IL1.2(b2)*, containing a question related to the religious habits of Etruscans).

4. The user gives a correct answer to the question clicking over a 3D interactive object contained inside the IL Auguraculum; the action is sensed and passed to the genius loci, which presents to the user the appropriate multimedia content node, *IL1.2(c2)*, chosen among the four available ones.

5. The user exits the IL Auguraculum and the genius loci communicates to the numen the new logged tuples of the experience process; the numen elaborates such data, updating the user history accordingly.

6. Finally the user enters again the IL Entrance; the event is perceived by the associate genius loci that asks to the numen the user history data. The genius loci then seeks the updated map of visited states and finds the state corresponding to the correct answer given by the user inside the IL Auguraculum. Such finding, compared with the constrains fixed for the IL Entrance, enables the genius loci to activate the opening of the portal that give access to the interior of the tomb and the selection and presentation of the multimedia nodes *IL1.1(b2)* and *IL1.1(c)* that contain an invitation to enter.

7 Conclusion

The work presents an approach for modeling multimedia information in relation to different kinds of context. The focus is that of the so-called mixed reality domain, where users browse multimedia content while navigating 3D environments, both real and virtual. A hierarchy of contexts was modelled in relation to the content creators habits, leading to the detailed definition of a data structure for storing experiences in rich-media navigational environments.

Such work and the detailed definition of the different contexts (i.e., in particular the context location through the IL concept and the context user history through the experience process concept) are important elements for the definition of an implementation architecture that gives different opportunities to control the presentation of multimedia content on the basis of context changes.

Future work will include a complete implementation of the architecture and a detailed validation phase for analyzing how users react to proactive presentation of content (we have encouraging results obtained in an ongoing pilot validation phase, but we need to extend the tests to the full set of opportunities offered by the new architecture).

Besides, the adoption of the experience layer data structure and of a set of distributed agents supporting distributed storage and processing, encourage the development of a system for managing multi-authored experiences where different content creators contribute to the definition of a media-rich navigational environment. We plan to explore such scenario as a part of our future work, with particular reference to the cultural heritage and e-learning realms.

References

1. Brusilovsky, P.: Adaptive hypermedia, User Modeling and User Adapted Interaction, 11(1-2) (2001) 87-110
2. Cascading Style Sheets, http://www.w3.org/Style/CSS/
3. Celentano, A., Gaggi., O.: Context-aware Design of Adaptable Multimodal Documents. Multimedia Tools and Applications, Springer Verlag 2005 (in press). Preliminary version in Proc. of MWD '04, at IEEE MSE '04, Miami, Florida, USA, December 13-15, 2004
4. Celentano, A., Pittarello, F.: Observing and Adapting User Behavior in Navigational 3D Interfaces. Proc. of AVI 2004, Gallipoli, Italia, May 25-28, 2004
5. Chen, G., Kotz, D.: A Survey of Context-Aware Mobile Computing, Technical Report TR2000-381, Dartmouth College, Department of Computer Science, 2000
6. Chittaro, L., Ranon, R.: Dynamic Generation of Personalized VRML Content: a General Approach and its application to 3D E-commerce. Proc. of the 7th International Conference on 3D Web Technology, Tempe, Arizona, 2002, pp. 145-154
7. Garzotto, F., Paolini, P., Speroni, M., Pröll, B., Retschitzegger, W., Schwinger, W.: Ubiquitous Access to Cultural Tourism Portals. Proc. of DEXA'04, Zaragoza, Spain, September 2004, pp. 67-72
8. Gordillo, S., Rossi, G., Lyardet, F.: Modeling Physical Hypermedia Applications. Proc. of SAINT-W'05, Trento, Italy, January 2005, pp. 410-413
9. Hansen, F., Bouvin, N., Christensen, B., Gronbaek, K., Pedersen, T., Gagach, J.: Integrating the Web and the World: Contextual Trails on the Move. Proc. Hypertext 2004, Santa Cruz, California, USA, August 2004, pp. 98-107
10. Hughes, S., Brusilovsky, P., Lewis, M.: Adaptive navigation support in 3D e-commerce activities. Proc. of Workshop on Recommendation and Personalization in eCommerce at AH'2002, Malaga, Spain, 2002, pp. 132-139
11. Kappel, G., Retschitzegger, W., Kimmerstorfer, E., Schwinger, W., Hofer, Th., Pröll, B.: Towards a Generic Customisation Model for Ubiquitous Web Applications. Proc. of the 2nd Int. Workshop on Web Oriented Software Technology (IWWOST), Spain, June, 2002
12. Milgram, P., Kishino, F.: A Taxonomy of Mixed Reality Visual Displays. IEICE Transactions on Information Systems, Vol. E77-D No. 12 (1994) 1321-1329.
13. Mohan, R., Smith J. R., Li, Chung-Sheng Li: Adapting Multimedia Content for Universal Access. IEEE Transactions on Multimedia, 1(1) (1999) 104-114
14. Nack, F.: From Ontology-based Semiosis to Computational Intelligence - The Future of Media Computing. In: Dorai, C., Venkatesh, S. (eds.): Media Computing Computational Media Aesthetics. Kluwer Academic Publishers (2002) 159 – 196
15. Nack, F., Hardman, L.: Denotative and Connotative Semantics in Hypermedia: Proposal for a Semiotic-Aware Architecture. Technical Report INS-R0202, CWI, Amsterdam, 2001
16. Nielsen, J.,: Usability Engineering, Academic Press, Boston, MA (1993)
17. Palazzo Grassi, http://www.palazzograssi.it
18. Perkowitz, M., Etzioni O.: Adaptive Web Sites. Communications of the ACM, 43(8) (2000) 152-158

19. Pittarello, F.: Accessing Information Through Multimodal 3D Environments: Towards Universal Access. Universal Access in the Information Society Journal, 2(2) (2003) 189-204
20. Want, R., Hopper, A., Falcao, V., Gibbons, J.: The Active Badges Location System. Tech. Rep., Olivetti Research Ltd, 1992. http://www.uk.research.att.com/pub/docs/att/tr.92.1.pdf
21. Web Accessibility Initiative, http://www.w3.org/WAI/
22. X3D Specification, http://www.web3d.org/x3d/specifications/x3d_specification.html
23. XHTML 1.0 Specification, http://www.w3.org/markup/

A Database Model for Querying Visual Surveillance Videos by Integrating Semantic and Low-Level Features*

Ediz Şaykol, Uğur Güdükbay, and Özgür Ulusoy

Department of Computer Engineering, Bilkent University,
06800 Bilkent, Ankara, Turkey
{ediz, gudukbay, oulusoy}@cs.bilkent.edu.tr

Abstract. Automated visual surveillance has emerged as a trendy application domain in recent years. Many approaches have been developed on video processing and understanding. Content-based access to surveillance video has become a challenging research area. The results of a considerable amount of work dealing with automated access to visual surveillance have appeared in the literature. However, the event models and the content-based querying and retrieval components have significant gaps remaining unfilled. To narrow these gaps, we propose a database model for querying surveillance videos by integrating semantic and low-level features. In this paper, the initial design of the database model, the query types, and the specifications of its query language are presented.

1 Introduction

In a traditional surveillance system, human operators monitor multiple guarded environments simultaneously to detect, and possibly prevent, a dangerous situation. As a matter of fact, human perception and reasoning are limited to process the amount of spatial data perceived by human senses. These limits may vary depending on the complexity of the events and their time instants. The acceleration in communication capabilities and automatic video processing techniques, and the reasonable cost of the technical devices have increased the interest in visual surveillance applications in the recent years. Many approaches related with content-based retrieval and automatic video processing and understanding (e.g., automatic video shot detection, event classification, low-level feature based querying, etc.) have been developed in the mean time with the advances in visual surveillance technology. These advances have led to the integration of automatic video processing and content-based retrieval with visual surveillance systems. Due to the highly variable nature of visual surveillance videos, a need has arisen for robust scene processing and event recognition.

* This work is supported in part by Turkish State Planning Organization (DPT) under grant number 2004K120720, and European Commission 6th Framework Program MUSCLE Network of Excellence Project with grant number FP6-507752.

K.S. Candan and A. Celentano (Eds.): MIS 2005, LNCS 3665, pp. 163–176, 2005.

In our work, the main focus is on *indoor monitoring*, and a framework for querying surveillance videos by integrating semantic and low-level features is developed. Regarding this issue, some powerful systems (e.g., [1,2,3,4]) exist in the literature. Besides system-level integration, some methods have been proposed for smaller units (e.g., detecting scene changes [5,6], moving object detection and tracking [7]). As far as the database indexing and retrieval parts are concerned, the researchers generally designed simple database structures for events. The event descriptors stored in a database generally contain the start and finish times, and the salient object labels. Indexing at the object feature level is not as frequent as the event level. In [8], the authors proposed an approach for traffic surveillance and stored object motion in the database. There are also some approaches that deal with the color information of the video objects (e.g., [2,4]). However, their use is either to keep track of the video objects or to classify the video objects.

The main contribution of the proposed framework is the querying capability by integrating semantic features (i.e., events, sub-events, and salient objects) and low-level object features (i.e., color, shape, and texture) for surveillance videos. To the best of our knowledge, no systems exist that are embedding object-based low-level features (e.g., color, shape, and texture) to the indexing and retrieval module in visual surveillance domain. Moreover, the framework provides support for effective query specification (e.g., query-by-example, query-by-sketch) and retrieval as opposed to keyword-based database searches. In the following, we describe our motivations and the basic assumptions we made in our work.

– Enriching the querying module with low-level object features (color, shape, texture) is more meaningful for indoor surveillance. We might need to query an event to detect an intruder in a supermarket by specifying the color of his coat, texture on his shirt, etc. This low-level feature enrichment would possibly decrease the rate of false alarms. For the intruder detection example, it is possible that there exist many innocent people making the same type of actions (events) in the supermarket at that time, causing a significant post-processing for the retrieved persons to find the intruder, or generate false alarms.

– Static camera and constant light source are assumed for the sake of simplicity in terms of database modeling. These assumptions fit most to indoor environments than the other categories. Although there are some recent approaches assuming inputs from two fixed cameras for indoor environments [9], the way of processing object motions is very different and sophisticated (e.g., contour matching and tracking in 3D) for multi-camera surveillance approaches.

– The pre-processing steps for event/object indexing into the database for querying are more straightforward in indoor monitoring.Complex background scenes are rare and the object motions (e.g., motions of humans) are generally expectable. This is basically because of the fact that indoor environments are generally simpler than others.

The rest of this paper is organized as follows: Section 2 summarizes some related studies. The proposed database model is presented in Section 3. Finally, Section 4 concludes the paper.

2 Related Work

Video Surveillance and Monitoring (VSAM) system presented in [3] is one of the complete prototypes for object detection, object tracking and classification, as well as calibrating a network of sensors for a surveillance environment. In that work, a hybrid algorithm was developed, which is based on an adaptive background subtraction by three-frame differencing. The background update scheme is based on a classification of pixels (either moving or non-moving) performed by a simple threshold test. A model is provided on temporal layers for pixels and pixel regions in order to be robust for detection of stop-and-go type of object motions. The background maintenance scheme we employ is similar to that of VSAM. However, in our framework, the extracted background is also used for both event annotation and object tracking.

Stringa and Regazzoni [1,10,11] proposed a real-time surveillance system employing semantic video-shot detection and indexing. Lost objects are detected by the help of temporal rank order filtering. The *interesting* video shots are detected by a hybrid approach based on low-level (color) and semantic features. The authors have adapted a change-detection module that processes the background image and the current image to detect the stationary object regions. Retrieving all the clips related to an alarm is the basic way of querying the system. The authors also mention about more complex query types including color and/or shape properties of the dangerous object. However, no details are provided for the storage of these low-level object features and their indexing and usage within complex queries. In our framework, we extract object-based low-level features, and provide a scenario-based querying scheme for complex querying including color and shape descriptors of the objects.

In [12,13], an object-based video abstraction model was proposed. The authors employed a moving-edge detection scheme for video frames. The edge map of a frame is extracted first by using Canny edge-detector [14]. The extracted edge map is compared with the background edge map and the moving edges and regions are detected at the end of this process. They employed a semantic shot detection scheme to select object-based keyframes. When a change occurs in the number of moving regions, the current frame is declared as a keyframe indicating that an important event has occurred. This scheme also facilitates the detection of important events. If the number of moving objects remains the same for the next frame, then a shape-based change detector is applied to the consecutive frames. A frame-based similarity metric is also defined to detect the distance between two frames. Our framework employs the strategy of moving object counting mentioned in [12] with rule-based extensions to help the event annotation process.

In [8], Jung et al. proposed a content-based event retrieval framework for traffic surveillance videos using semantic scene interpretation techniques. They employed an adaptive background subtraction and update mechanism, where the background image eventually contains the temporal median values of pixels. One of the important aspects of the work is that they designed the database indexing and retrieval in an object-based manner. However, since their primary concern is traffic surveillance, the object trajectories and motion descriptors are stored in the database. Their query interface supports query-by-example, query-by-sketch, and query-by-weighting on the trajectory descriptors. The database is searched exhaustively to find the best matches for a given query. Our framework also includes object-based querying by providing examples or sketches. However, our querying module also enables specification of more complex queries including low-level and directional descriptors.

Lyons et al. [15] developed video content analyzer (VCA), the main components of which are background subtraction, object tracking, event reasoning, graphical user interface, indexing, and retrieval. They adapted a non-parametric background subtraction approach based on [16]. A finite state model was designed for object tracking. VCA discriminates people from objects and the main events recognized are as follows: *entering scene, leaving scene, splitting, merging,* and *depositing/picking-up.* The retrieval component was designed to retrieve video sequences based on event queries. The event categories are very similar to those we use in our framework. However, as an additional feature, our framework also enables object-based querying that can be refined by providing low-level and/or directional descriptors.

Brodsky et al. [4] designed a system for indoor visual surveillance especially in the retail stores and in the houses. They assumed a stationary camera and used background subtraction technique described in [15]. The pixels detected as foreground are grouped into connected components and tracked throughout the scene. Object tracking module handles merging and splitting of moving objects by making use of a color model extracted for each moving object. A list of events that the object is participated are stored for each object, where the events are simply *entering, leaving, merging,* and *splitting.* The system also includes a classification module to distinguish people, pets, and other objects. One of the distinctions of this system and our framework is the use of color feature. In this system, the color feature of the objects is mainly used for reassigning labels for moving connected components, whereas, as an extension, we also provide object-based querying based on color and/or shape features.

Haritaoğlu et al. [17] proposed a real-time analysis of people activities. Their model uses a stationary camera and background subtraction to detect the regions corresponding to person(s). Their system, called W^4, uses shape information to locate people and their body parts (head, hands, feet, and torso). The system operates on monocular gray-scale video data, and no color cues are used. The creation of models of the appearance of person(s) helps the tracking process through people interaction (e.g., occlusions), and simultaneous activities of multiple people. The system uses a statistical background model holding bimodal distribution of intensity at each pixel to locate people. The system is capable of detecting single person, multiple persons, and multiple person groups in various postures.

In the literature, most of the systems have focused on (unattended) object detection and tracking moving object. Extracted event information, based on the object tracking and shot detection modules, is generally stored in a database and exhaustively searched when a query is submitted based on event information (e.g., [15]). From another perspective, retrieving the video sequences related to a generated alarm is the basic way of querying the system (e.g., [1]). In [1], the authors also mentioned more complex query types including color and/or shape properties of the salient objects. The querying module of [8] supports query-by-example, query-by-sketch, and query-by-weighting on the trajectory descriptors of moving objects.

3   A Database Framework for an Integrated Querying of Visual Surveillance

We propose a framework which provides an integrated environment for querying indoor surveillance videos by semantic (event-based) and low-level (object-based) features. The overall architecture of the framework is shown in Figure 1. The queries are handled by *query processing module*, which communicates with both the *feature database* and the *content-based retrieval module*. The database contains event and object features extracted by automated tools. The *visual query interface* is used to submit queries to the system and to visualize the query results. The users should be able to specify event queries enriched with low-level features for objects and directional descriptors for events.

3.1   Object Extraction and Tracking Module

A fully-automatic object detection and tracking module is designed and implemented, which employs an adaptive background maintenance scheme, similar to the one proposed in [3]. At the pixel-level, the algorithm tries to identify the moving object pixels. The adaptive background subtraction technique is combined with a three-frame differencing technique to determine the moving object pixels as a region and also to detect stop-and-go type of object motions. According to the three-frame differencing algorithm, an object is assumed to be moving if the intensities of the object have changed between current and previous frames, and between current and next-to-previous frames.

Video data can be considered as a sequence of frames. Let $I_f(x, y)$ denote the intensity value of a pixel at (x, y) at frame f. Hence, $M_f(x, y) = 1$ if (x, y) is moving at frame f, where $M_f(x, y)$ is a vector holding moving pixels. A threshold vector $T_f(x, y)$ for a frame f is needed for detecting pixel motions. The basic test condition to detect moving pixels with respect to $T_f(x, y)$ can be formulated as follows: $M_f(x, y) = 1$ if $(|I_f(x, y) - I_{f-1}(x, y)| > T_f(x, y))$ and $(|I_f(x, y) - I_{f-2}(x, y)| > T_f(x, y))$.

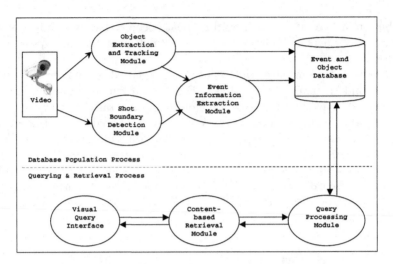

Fig. 1. The overall architecture of the framework

The (moving) pixel intensities that are larger than the background intensities $(B_f(x,y))$ are used to fill the region of a moving object. This step requires a background maintenance task based on the previous intensity values of the pixels. Similarly, the threshold is to be updated based on the observed moving pixel information at the current frame. A statistical background and threshold maintenance scheme is employed in the module as follows:

$$B_0(x,y) = 0, \tag{1}$$

$$B_f(x,y) = \begin{cases} \alpha B_{f-1}(x,y) + (1-\alpha)I_{f-1}(x,y), & M_f(x,y) = 0, \\ B_{f-1}(x,y), & M_f(x,y) = 1, \end{cases} \tag{2}$$

$$T_0(x,y) = 1, \tag{3}$$

$$T_f(x,y) = \begin{cases} \alpha T_{f-1}(x,y) + (1-\alpha)(k \times |I_{f-1}(x,y) - B_{f-1}(x,y)|), & M_f(x,y) = 0, \\ T_{f-1}(x,y), & M_f(x,y) = 1, \end{cases} \tag{4}$$

where k is set to 5 in Eq. 4. As argued in [3], $B_f(x,y)$ is analogous to local temporal average of pixel intensities, and $T_f(x,y)$ is analogous to k times the local temporal standard deviation of pixel intensities computed with an infinite impulse (IIR) filter. A snapshot of object extraction and tracking module is shown in Figure 2.

3.2   Shot Boundary Detection Module

Object tracking and event classification tasks directly benefit from the extracted video *shots*. Moving objects generally enter or leave the scene at shot boundaries. Hence, the shot boundary detection module is particularly designed for detecting

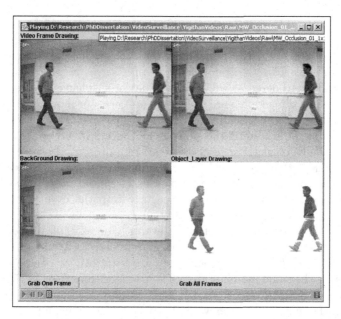

Fig. 2. Object extraction and tracking module user interface. Top-left image is the original image, top-right is the intensity layer image, bottom-left is the background layer image, and bottom-right is the object layer image where moving object pixel region can be seen.

video shot boundaries, hence *cuts*. The shot boundary detection algorithm employed can be summarized as follows: Let f_i and f_{i-1} denote two consecutive frames in a video clip. Let I_f denote the intensity histogram of a frame f. For a consecutive frame pair (f_{i-1}, f_i), let d_i denote the histogram intersection [18] distance between $I_{f_{i-1}}$ and I_{f_i}. By using histogram intersection technique, d_i can be found by

$$d_i = 1 - S_{I_{f_i}, I_{f_{i-1}}} = 1 - \frac{\sum_i^n \min(I_{f_i}[i], I_{f_{i-1}}[i])}{\min(|I_{f_i}|, |I_{f_{i-1}}|)}, \qquad (5)$$

where $|I_{f_i}|$ denotes the L_1-norm (i.e., length) of an histogram I_{f_i}. If $d_i \geq t_1$, then i is introduced as a shot boundary, or a cut. The value for t_1 is estimated by trial-error technique and it is found that 0.3763 gives best results for the video clips tested so far. A further improvement is made on the algorithm to increase the success rate. The algorithm starts with a lower t_1 value and extracts shot boundary candidates first. Then, it computes pixel-wise distance d_i^p between f_{i-1} and f_i, where i is a shot boundary candidate. If $d_i^p \geq t_2$, then i is introduced as a shot boundary. The experiments show that $t_1 = 0.3$ and $t_2 = 0.13$ give promising results.

3.3   Event Information Extraction Module

This module is intended to 'annotate' video frame intervals based on event labels, objects appearing within the interval, and low-level feature descriptions for the event objects. There are some specific types of events, which are important for indoor visual surveillance to detect suspicious events. *A person depositing or picking up an object* and *two people crossing over* are examples for two important events. *People/object entering or leaving the scene, people/object joining or splitting* can be considered as sub-events to detect suspicious events [15].

The inputs to this module are the moving objects (or moving object groups) at a frame. Our object tracking module identifies a moving object group as a single moving object until the objects in the group are separated, as described in [7]. Counting the number of moving objects also gives an important clue for detecting the events, since the number of moving objects changes at the time of the events. We also keep track of spatial (directional and topological) relations among the moving objects within the event detection algorithm.

Figure 3 illustrates the detection of events. For example, *deposit* event is detected as follows: The object tracking module detects A and B as a moving object group first at time T1. Then, they are identified as two separate moving objects by the same module through some algorithms used in [7]. Hence, at time T2, the objects A and B are detected as they are moving separately. At time T2+1, the only detected moving object is A. Therefore, a potential *deposit* event is detected at frame T2. The spatial relations among the moving objects are determined in addition to the tracking of the moving objects, which increases the accuracy of the event detection process. The detection process for the other types of events is similar to that of the deposit event. Refinements on this event detection algorithm have been carried out continuously to end up with a better scheme.

The event information extraction module can be summarized as follows: based on the above depositing event example, the event is detected at time T2. Hence, the event information is stored based on the status at time T2. This type of information storage is reasonable because the status at the time of the suspicious event is of interest while querying. For each frame that an event is identified, the objects appearing on that frame (A and B in this example) are stored in *Event and Object Database* along with their low-level features and the spatial relations among them. The low-level object features stored are *color vector* and *shape vector*, which is a composition of *angular span* and *distance span* [19].

3.4   Query Processing Module

One of the most important tasks in automated visual surveillance is the query processing module. Basically textual searches for event queries are supported in the existing systems. Some systems support object queries as well to some extent. It is observed that there might be a need for enhancing object queries with color and/or shape descriptions. In addition to this enhancement, allowing directional relation specifications among objects within suspicious events might be helpful in some domains.

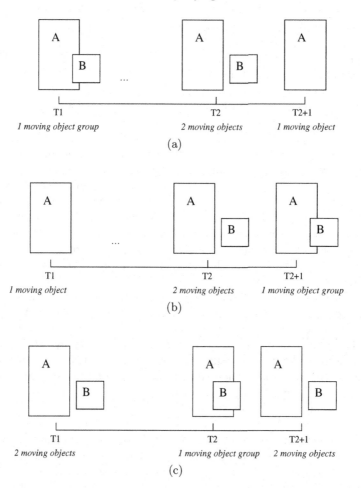

Fig. 3. Detection of Events. (a) Deposit, (b) Pick Up, and (c) Crossover.

Query Types: The main contribution of the querying module in our system is providing support to a wide range of event and object queries. A classification of the types of queries handled can be listed as follows:

- Single Object Queries,
  - Object Entering/Leaving Scene,
- Multi-Object Queries,
  - Object Depositing/Object Picking Up,
  - Objects Crossing Over.

We plan to extend the framework to support queries based on suspicious events in surveillance videos. By adding low-level and/or spatial sub-queries, more complex queries can be submitted to the system. Spatial sub-queries are more meaningful for queries involving multiple objects. However, low-level sub-queries can be supplied for each object. In real-life applications, low-level sub-query specification with high-level descriptors might be sufficient (e.g., a man with a black coat entering scene).

Query Language: An SQL-based querying language, which we call Visual Surveillance Query Language (VSQL), is designed to provide support for inte-grated querying of indoor visual surveillance videos by spatial, semantic, and low-level features. The query processing module extends the querying capability by allowing low-level object feature specifications as well as spatial relationships among the objects. In short, VSQL provides support for semantic (suspicious event), spatial (relationships among objects), and low-level (object features at a specific suspicious event) sub-queries for visual surveillance domain. Seman-tic sub-queries can be coupled with either spatial or low-level, or both, to form complex queries. A grammar for VSQL is presented in Appendix A.

VSQL identifies two single-object event conditions (*enter*, *leave*), and three multi-object event conditions (*deposit*, *pickup*, and *crossover*) in a scenario. The moving objects, detected by the system, are assigned semantic labels, namely *person*, *object*, *pet*, *other*, from a pre-defined set of labels based on the similarity of the contour polygons of the objects as described in [20]. The query processor counts the number of moving objects specified in a query by tracing the *enter* event conditions. A timegap value can be specified between event conditions. The order of the events is considered to be unimportant if a timegap value is not specified for an event condition pair of the same type (i.e., pair of single-object conditions or pair of multi-object event conditions).

Query Processing: The event and object information stored in the database is based on the frames at which an event is detected. This information includes the low-level features of the objects appearing on that frame and the spatial relations among them. By maintaining the directional relations among the objects, event querying can be refined by specifying directional predicates in the query. For example, while querying an event of *'a person depositing an object'*, the query can be enriched by directional predicates so that *'a person depositing an object to his west'* can also be queried. Moreover, since the low-level features of moving objects are also stored, more detailed queries can be submitted to the system effectively.

Based on the observation that rule-based model is effective for querying video databases [21,22], a rule-based model has been designed for querying vi-sual surveillance videos. Our framework is to provide support for scenario-based queries which are very difficult to handle in real-time systems. The submitted queries are sent to Prolog, which processes the extracted event, and object in-formation is stored in the database (i.e., knowledge-base) based on a set of rules. Prior to the processing by Prolog, the query string is passed through lexical an-alyzer and a parse tree is created. We are planning to embed a similarity-based metric in this querying process, which will be used as a confidence value for the user.

3.5   Content-Based Retrieval Module

In this section, some real-life querying scenarios are provided. We assumed a lobby of a hotel as our indoor environment for these scenarios. Since our system focuses on database querying and retrieval issues, it is assumed that there is a need to query the suspicious situation given in the scenarios. A real-time visual surveillance system has to detect such cases and inform the human operator for more security. It is also possible that the human operator does not see any danger in the situation at the time of the event. However, he may be informed later on that a dangerous situation has happened in one of the events triggered by the system. Based on this argument, the assumption of the need to query suspicious situations is not superficial.

Scenario 1: *A person with a black coat enters a lobby.*

```
select objectA from 1 where
    objectA = objdata(class = person, color = black) and enter(objectA)
```

The event is a simple object appearance type of query. It is assumed that the dominant color of the person is black, which is the color of his coat.

Scenario 2: *A person enters a lobby with a bag, deposits his bag, and leaves the lobby.*

```
select segment from 1 where
    objectA = objdata(class = person), objectB = objdata(class = object)
    and enter(objectA) enter(objectB) deposit(objectA,objectB) leave(objectA)
```

The event described in this scenario is very crucial because unattended bags are one of the primary sources of suspicious situations in indoor environments. Additional descriptors for both person and bag improve the quality of the retrieval. Directional descriptors can be added as well since the directional relations are stored. Hence, the query phrase 'deposits his bag' can be refined by 'deposits his bag to his west', which might give better results. Then, the deposit condition will be as follows:

```
deposit(objectA,objectB,west)
```

Scenario 3: *A person enters a lobby with a bag, after 3 seconds another person enters the lobby, two persons meet and exchange the bag, then they leave the lobby.*

```
select segment from 1 where
    objectA = objdata(class = person), objectB = objdata(class = object),
    objectC = objdata(class = person) and
    enter(objectA) enter(objectB) 3 enter(objectC)
    crossover(objectA,objectC) deposit(objectA,objectB)
    pickup(objectC,objectB) leave(objectA) leave(objectC)
```

This scenario is an example of a 'cross-over', and generally real-time systems detect such events and inform human operators. If we consider a quite crowded lobby, the number of crossovers is relatively large. Hence, providing additional descriptors for persons and/or bag (both low-level and directional) decreases the number of possible results of querying. This directly shortens the time and helps the security persons to catch the intruders.

Scenario 4: *A person with a black coat enters a lobby with a yellow bag, deposits the bag, another person with a white coat enters the lobby, picks up the bag.*

```
select segment from 1 where
    objectA = objdata(class = person, color = black),
    objectB = objdata(class = object, color = yellow),
    objectC = objdata(class = person, color = white) and
    enter(objectA) enter(objectB) deposit(objectA,objectB)
    enter(objectC) pickup(objectC,objectB)
```

This scenario describes a sequence of deposit and pickup events without crossover. Color descriptors are added for all of the objects acting in the scenario. The leaving times of the persons are not of interest for the querying of the event.

As mentioned in the scenarios, the suspicious events can be queried by adding low-level features to (moving) objects and/or directional relations for the event. This type of querying improves the retrieval quality and decreases the search space. These gains are more meaningful when the number of events to be searched in the database is relatively large.

4   Conclusion

In this paper, we propose a database model for an integrated querying of visual surveillance videos by semantic and low-level features. The application domain chosen is indoor monitoring environment video, which fits most into our assumptions and which is simpler than other complex environments. The system has a database population process that extracts necessary event and object information for effective querying. An SQL-based querying language is designed to express the query types. A wide range of event and object queries including semantic, spatial, and low-level is supported.

As the database modeling process is evolving, improvements will be made both in terms of database population and querying-and-retrieval processes. The design and implementation of the query processing module is an ongoing project, hence the above improvements will be employed accordingly to handle a wide range of query set effectively.

References

1. Stringa, E., Regazzoni, C.: Real-time video-shot detection for scene surveillance applications. IEEE Trans. on Image Processing **9** (2000) 69–79
2. Foresti, G., Marcenaro, L., Regazzoni, C.: Automatic detection and indexing of video-event shots for surveillance applications. IEEE Trans. on Multimedia **4** (2002) 459–471

3. Collins, R., Lipton, A., Kanade, T., Fujiyoshi, H., Duggins, D., Tsin, Y., Tolliver, D., Enomoto, N., Hasegawa, O., Burt, P., Wixson, L.: A system for video surveillance and monitoring. Technical Report CMU-RI-TR-00-12, Carnegie Mellon University, The Robotics Institute (2000)
4. Brodsky, T., Cohen, R., Cohen-Solal, E., Gutta, S., Lyons, D., Philomin, V., Trajkovic, M.: Visual surveillance in retail stores and in the home. In: Video-Based Surveillance Systems: Computer Vision and Distributed Processing, Kluwer Academic Pub. (2001) 51–65
5. Latecki, L., Wen, X., Ghubade, N.: Detection of changes in surveillance videos. In: IEEE Conf. on Adv. Video and Signal Based Surv. (AVSS'03). (2003) 237–242
6. Stefano, L.D., Mattoccia, S., Mola, M.: A change-detection algorithm based on structure and colour. In: IEEE Conf. on Adv. Video and Signal Based Surv. (AVSS'03). (2003) 252–259
7. Töreyin, B., Çetin, A., Aksay, A., Akhan, M.: Moving object detection in wavelet compressed video. Signal Processing: Image Communication 20 (2005) 255–264
8. Jung, Y., Lee, K., Ho, Y.: Content-based event retrieval using semantic scene interpretation for automated traffic surveillance. IEEE Trans. on Intelligent Transportation Systems 2 (2001) 151–163
9. Eaton, R., Scassellati, B.: ViSIT: Visual surveillance and interaction tracking. In: http://zoo.cs.yale.edu/classes/cs490/02-03a/ross.eaton/. (Social Robotics Laboratory, Yale University, accessed at February 27, 2005)
10. Stringa, E., Regazzoni, C.: Content-based retrieval and real time detection from video sequences acquired by surveillance systems. In: Int. Conf. on Image Processing. (1998) 138–142
11. Regazzoni, C., Sacchi, C., Stringa, E.: Remote detection of abandoned objects in unattended railway stations by using a DS/CDMA video surveillance system. In Regazzoni, C., Fabri, G., Vernezza, G., eds.: Advanced Video-Based Surveillance System, Boston, MA: Kluwer (1998) 165–178
12. Kim, C., Hwang, J.: Fast and automatic video object segmentation and tracking for content-based applications. IEEE Trans. on Circuits and Systems for Video Technology 12 (2002) 122–129
13. Kim, C., Hwang, J.: Object-based video abstraction for video surveillance systems. IEEE Trans. on Circuits and Systems for Video Technology 12 (2002) 1128–1138
14. Canny, J.: A computational approach to edge detection. IEEE Trans. on Pattern Analysis and Machine Intelligence 8 (1986) 679–698
15. Lyons, D., Brodsky, T., Cohen-Solal, E., Elgammal, A.: Video content analysis for surveillance applications. In: Philips Digital Video Technologies Workshop. (2000)
16. Elgammal, A., Harwood, D., Davis, L.: Non-parametric model for background subtraction. In: Int. Conf. on Computer Vision and Pattern Recognition, Workshop on Motion. (1999)
17. Haritaoğlu, İ., Harwood, D., Davis, L.: W4: Real-time surveillance of people and their activities. IEEE Trans. on Pattern Analysis and Machine Intelligence 22 (2000) 809–830
18. Swain, M., Ballard, D.: Color indexing. Int. J. of Comp. Vis. 7 (1991) 11–32
19. Şaykol, E., Sinop, A., Güdükbay, U., Ulusoy, Ö., Çetin, E.: Content-based retrieval of historical Ottoman documents stored as textual images. IEEE Trans. on Image Processing 13 (2004) 314–325
20. Dedeoğlu, Y.: Moving object detection, tracking and classification for smart video surveillance. Technical Report BU-CE-0412, Bilkent University, Dept. of Computer Eng., http://www.cs.bilkent.edu.tr/~tech-reports/2004/BU-CE-0412.pdf (2004)

21. Dönderler, M., Şaykol, E., Arslan, U., Ulusoy, Ö., Güdükbay, U.: BilVideo: Design and implementation of a video database management system. Multimedia Tools and Applications (accepted for publication) (2005)
22. Dönderler, M., Ö.Ulusoy, Güdükbay, U.: Rule-based spatio-temporal query processing for video databases. The VLDB Journal **13** (2004) 86–103

A   Grammar for Visual Surveillance Querying Language(VSQL)

Visual Surveillance Query Language (VSQL) is designed to provide support for integrated querying of indoor visual surveillance videos by spatial, semantic, and low-level features.

```
/* main query string */
<query> := select <target> from <range> [where <querycondition>] ';'

/* main query string components */
<target> := event | <objectlist> | segment
<objectlist> := [<objectlist> ','] <objlabel>
<range> := all | <videolist>
<videolist> := [<videolist> ','] <vid>
<querycondition> := <objectassignmentlist> and <scenario>
<objectassignmentlist> := [<objectassignmentlist> ','] <objectassignment>
<scenario> := [<scenario> <timegap>] <eventcondition>
<eventcondition> := <entercondition> | <leavecondition>
   | <depositcondition> | <pickupcondition> | <crossovercondition>
<objectassignment> := <objlabel> <objoperator> <objcondition>

/* single object query conditions */
<entercondition> := enter '(' <objlabel> ')'
<leavecondition> := leave '(' <objlabel> ')'

/* multi object query conditions */
<depositcondition> := deposit '(' <multiobjcondition> ')'
<pickupcondition> := deposit '(' <multiobjcondition> ')'
<crossovercondition> := crossover '(' <multiobjcondition> ')'
<multiobjcondition> := <objlabel> ',' <objlabel> [',' <directional>]
<directional> := west | east | north | south | northeast | southeast
   | northwest | southwest

/* object condition */
<objcondition> := objdata '(' <objdesclist> ')'
<objdesclist> := [<objdesclist> ','] <objdesc>
<objdesc> := class '=' <classvalue> | <colordesc> | <shapedesc> | <texturedesc>
<colordesc> := color '=' <colorlabel> | <colorvector>
<shapedesc> := [<shapedesc> ','] <shapepair>
<texturedesc> := texture '=' <textureid>
<colorvector> := [<colorvector> ','] <colorpair>
<colorpair> := '(' <intvalue> ',' <doublevalue> ')'
<shapepair> := '(' <intvalue> ',' <doublevalue> ')'

/* primitive types */
<vid> := (1-9)(0-9)*
<timegap> := null | <intvalue>
<objlabel> := (a-z)(A-Za-z0-9)*
<objoperator> := '=' | ''!=''
<classvalue> := person | object | pet | other
<intvalue> := (1-9)(0-9)*
<doublevalue> := <intvalue> '.' <intvalue>
<colorlabel> := red | green | blue | yellow | white | black | orange | violet
<textureid> := (1-9)(0-9)*  /* enumerated set of texture patterns */
```

An Effective Overlay H.263+ Video Multicast System over the Internet*

Hwangjun Song[1] and Hojong Kang[2]

[1] Dept. of Computer Science and Engineering,
POSTECH, Korea. 790-784
hwangjun@postech.ac.kr
[2] School of Electronic and Electrical Engineering,
Hongik University, Seoul, Korea 121-791

Abstract. This paper presents an effective overlay H.263+ video multicast system over the Internet. The proposed system consists of overlay multicast tree construction, target bandwidth determining process, and H.263+ rate control. Overlay multicast tree construction algorithm and target bandwidth determining process work alternatively to satisfy the average delay constraint, and H.263+ rate control is implemented to enhance the human visual perceptual quality over the multicast tree. Finally, experimental results are provided to show the performance of the proposed system.

1 Introduction

In recent years, Internet plays an important role in multimedia communication area. The number of end-systems connected to the Internet has been exponentially increasing, and the demand of multimedia services through the Internet has been increasing very fast. Generally speaking, QoS (quality of service) and multicast are the most important features that should be added to provide various multimedia services and increase network utilization [1]. Multicast has gained a large amount of interests since IP multicast was proposed. Routers play a key role in IP multicast, that is, routers classify incoming multicast packets and send them to other routers and end-systems only one time. Consequently, duplicate traffics can be significantly reduced. However, IP multicast has not been widely employed so far because of practical problems such as control overhead, computational complexity, and pricing mechanism, etc. It is unlikely that IP multicast will be widely employed in the near future.

As an alternative of IP multicast, overlay multicast has recently proposed to implement the multicast functionality in the application layer instead of the IP layer. That is, some of end-systems participating in the multicast replace the multicast routers. Overlay multicast can be directly applicable to the current Internet since it does not need any new additional modifications at routers. So far, many effective algorithms have been proposed to realize the overlay multicast for different applica-

---

* This work was supported by Grant No. R08-2004-000-10084-0 from the Basic Research Program of the Korea Science & Engineering Foundation.

tions. In general, they can be classified into three approaches: mesh-first approach, tree-first approach, and implicit approach [2]. In the mesh-first approach, a mesh is constructed randomly based on the member information and then a tree is built up by selecting a number of paths along the meshes. Due to the relatively high control overhead, it is more efficient for small multicast group. Narada [1] and Scattercast [4] are examples of the mesh-first approach. In the tree-first approach, a tree is in advance constructed by randomly selecting the potential parent node based on the list of members, and then the member in a tree searches for other members and establish control links, which is called a mesh. Yoid [5], ALMI [6] and HMTP [7] are included in the tree-first approach. In these two approaches, tree and mesh are generally constructed iteratively and progressively. While, tree and mesh are set up simultaneously in the implicit approach. This approach is more suitable when the number of multicast members is very large. NICE [8], CAN [9], and Scribe [10] are included in the implicit approach. Furthermore, other effective algorithms that make them appropriate for different applications have been proposed in [11, 12, 13, 14, 15, 16, 17, 18]. Mathy and et al [11] studied a method to build a hierarchy of nodes, based on the notion of proximity, in a distributed and scalable way, and Park and et al proposed a realistic scheme that is based on the unicast transport from a remote sender to a local subnet and the multicast forwarding to receivers within the subnet in [12]. Liebeherr and et al [15] proposed application-layer multicast with delaunay triangulations that each application locally derive next hop routing information without the need for a routing protocol in the overlay, and effective multicast tree constructing algorithms considering the delay for time-constraint media delivery have been proposed in [16, 17].

While overlay multicast has many advantages as mentioned earlier, there are still several problems to be solved. One of the serious problems is the delay, i.e. the delay may be increased compared with IP multicast because traffics must traverse several end-systems until it arrives at the final destination. The increased delay is a big obstacle for the real-time media delivery including video and audio. In this paper, we present overlay H.263+ video multicast system, which consists of two components: overlay multicast tree suitable for real-time video traffic delivery and H.263+ rate control adaptive to overlay multicast tree and delay constraint. Actually, H.263+ is adopted since its computational complexity is relatively low enough to run in real time at the computer with Pentium-4 CPU when implemented fully in software.

2 The Proposed Overlay Video Multicast System

In general, the delay of overlay multicast tree is associated with tree structure, which depends on the number of streams handled by each end system. Actually, the number is greatly related to the output bit rate of video encoder. The delay decreases but the video quality degrades when output bit rate becomes smaller, vice versa. Hence we need to control the amount of output bit rate to satisfy the given delay constraint. Under the assumption that the maximum bandwidth of each member is fixed and the target bandwidth is CBR (constant-bit-rate), the number of streams is determined by controlling the output bit rate of encoder. Now, we can formulate the problem as follows.

Problem Formulation: Determine overlay multicast tree and quantization parameters q_i, $i = 1,2,\cdots,m$ to minimize

$$\sum_{i=1}^{m} D_i(q_i),$$

subject to $\dfrac{1}{N}\sum_{i=1}^{N} RTT_i(BW_{enc}) \leq RTT_{\max}$ satisfying $\sum_{i=1}^{m} R_i(q_i)\Big/T_m \leq BW_{enc}$,

where m is the number of frames encoded in the basic unit time interval, $D_i(\cdot)$ and $R_i(\cdot)$ are the distortion and bit rate of the i_{th} frame respectively, BW_{enc} is the target bandwidth, N is the number of multicast members, $RTT_i(\cdot)$ is the round trip time of the i_{th} members, $RTT_{\max}$ is the tolerable maximum average delay, and T_m is the interval of m frames. We obtain an effective solution by dividing the problem into two sub-problems.

Problem 1: (Determination of Target Bandwidth and Overlay Multicast Tree): Determine the maximum target bandwidth BW_{enc} to satisfy

$$\frac{1}{N}\sum_{i=1}^{N} RTT_i(BW_{enc}) \leq RTT_{\max}.$$

Problem 2: (H.263+ Rate Control with Target Bandwidth) Determine the quantization parameters q_i, $i = 1,2,\cdots m$ to minimize

$$\sum_{i=1}^{m} D_i(q_i), \text{ subject to } \sum_{i=1}^{m} R_i(q_i) \leq BW_{enc} \cdot T_m.$$

2.1 Determination of Constant-Bit-Rate Target Bandwidth and Overlay Multicast Tree

Generally, the higher target bandwidth can improve the video quality at the cost of the larger delay over the Internet. We need an effective trade-off between video quality and delay. First, we consider how to construct the overlay multicast tree minimizing average delay under the assumption that numbers of streams are given. Then, we control the number of streams by changing target bandwidth of video encoder under the above assumption. To satisfy the delay constraint, two processes work iteratively. Now, we introduce the modified Dijkstra's algorithm to minimize average delay, and study how to determine the target bandwidth by using this algorithm.

A. Modified Dijkstra's Algorithm
In this scenario, end-systems are divided into clusters based on RTT values, and then one of end-systems in each cluster is selected as a proxy-sender. The other end-systems in the cluster receive data from the proxy-sender. In this case, we can formulate the given problem as follows.

Problem Formulation: Determine the number of clusters and trees to minimize

$$\frac{1}{N}\sum_{i=1}^{n_p} m_i \cdot RTT_{p_i}^{s} + \frac{1}{N}\sum_{i=1}^{n_p}\sum_{j=1}^{m_i-1} RTT_{j}^{p_i} ,$$

$$\text{subject to } s_s \le ST_s \text{ and } s_i \le ST_i,$$

where s_s and s_i are the numbers of streams handled by the sender and the i_{th} end-system respectively, and ST_s and ST_i are the maximum numbers of streams that can be supported by the sender and the i_{th} end-system, respectively. In our previous work [20], we proposed the modified Dijkstra's algorithm to obtain an effective solution of the above optimization problem with constraints. It is summarized in Figure 1 (see [20] for the detail.). In this paper, this algorithm is employed as a component.

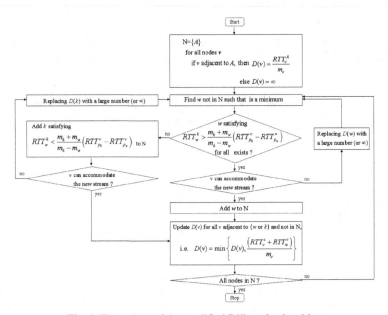

Fig. 1. Flow chart of the modified Dijkstra's algorithm

B. Determination of Target Bandwidth

A control parameter of the modified Dijkstra's algorithm is the number of streams that each end-system can accommodate. The number of streams is determined by the target bandwidth. The target bandwidth determining process is summarized in the following, which is based on the bisection method.

Step 1: Set the initial target bandwidth (BW_{int}) to the minimum bandwidth of members, i.e.

$$BW_{int} = \min_{1 \le i \le N}(BW_i),$$

where BW_i is the bandwidth of the i_{th} member.

Step 2: Set BW_{lower} and BW_{upper} to 0 and BW_{int}, respectively.

Step 3: Set $BW_{new} = \left(BW_{upper} + BW_{lower}\right) \Big/ 2$.

Step 4: Calculate the number of streams as follows.

$$ST_s = \left\lceil \frac{BW_s}{BW_{new}} \right\rceil , \text{ and } ST_i = \left\lceil \frac{BW_i}{BW_{new}} \right\rceil - 1 ,$$

where $\lceil x \rceil$ means the greatest integer smaller than x .

Step 5: Construct the overlay multicast three using the modified Dijkstra's algorithm with the above number of streams.

Step 6: If $\left| RTT_{avg} - RTT_{max} \right| < \varepsilon$, then set $BW_{enc} = BW_{new}$ and stop,

where ε is a constant and RTT_{avg} is the average delay value.

Otherwise, if $RTT_{avg} > RTT_{max}$, then go to Step 3 with $BW_{upper} = BW_{new}$,

else go to Step 3 with $BW_{lower} = BW_{new}$.

2.2 H.263+ Rate Control Algorithm Under CBR Bandwidth

After determining the target bandwidth, rate control aims at enhancing human visual perceptual quality at end systems. Since it is difficult to support both high spatial quality and motion smoothness under CBR channel, a control of encoding frame rate is adopted for a tradeoff of spatial/temporal quality based on the motion in video and the available bandwidth. This scheme aims at the reduction of temporal degradation in terms of motion jerkiness perceived by human beings [22]. In the case of video conferencing, m is set to a very small integer for the low latency. In the followings, we describe a real-time encoding frame rate control to improve video quality under CBR channel.

A. Frame-layer R-D Modeling

The R-D modeling techniques are essential for developing fast rate control algorithms. In this work, we employ an empirical databased frame-layer R-D model using quadratic rate model [24] and affine distortion model with respect to the average QP (quantization parameter) in a frame, which is given by

$$\ddot{R}(\overline{q}_i) = (a\overline{q}_i^{-1} + b\overline{q}_i^{-2}) \cdot MAD(\ddot{f}_{ref}, f_{cur}),$$
$$\ddot{D}(\overline{q}_i) = a'\overline{q}_i + b',$$

where a, b, a' and b' are the model coefficients, $\hat{f}_{ref}$ is the reconstructed reference frame at the previous time instant, f_{cur} is the uncompressed image at the current time instant, $MAD(\cdot,\cdot)$ is the mean of absolute difference between two frames and $\overline{q}_i$ is the average QP of all macroblocks in the i_{th} frame respectively. The model coefficients are determined by minimizing the MSE errors between the estimated values and observed data [22]. And then in order to increase the accuracy of the R-D model, an outlier-removing algorithm is also adopted: If the difference between the estimated value by the models and a datum of the rate-distortion table is greater than a threshold, the datum is discarded, and then based on the refined data, the coefficients are recalculated by the same method.

B. Real-time Encoding Frame Rate Control

Step 1: Calculate the estimated distortion by

$$\hat{D} = a' \frac{a \cdot MAD(f_{i-1}, f_i) + \sqrt{(a \cdot MAD(f_{i-1}, f_i))^2 + 4b \cdot R(F_{i-1}) \cdot MAD(f_{i-1}, f_i)}}{2R(F_{i-1})} + b',$$

$$R(F_{i-1}) = \frac{F_{i-1}}{G} \cdot BW_{enc},$$

where f_{i-1} and f_i are the reconstructed reference frame at the previous time instant and the uncompressed image at the current time instant, respectively, and F_i is the current encoding frame interval under the assumption the camera captures frames at a rate of G fps, BW_{enc} is the current available channel bandwidth, and a and b are the coefficients of quadratic rate model, a' and b' are the coefficients of affine distortion model, and $MAD(\cdot,\cdot)$ is the mean of absolute difference between two frames [22].

Step 2: To determine the encoding frame interval, first calculate the threshold values by

$$TH_{d1} = (1+c) \cdot D_{avg},$$

$$TH_{d2} = (1-c/2) \cdot D_{avg},$$

where D_{avg} is the average distortion of previous 5 encoded frames and c is a constant. Then, the encoding frame interval is adjusted by $\Delta F_{i-1} = \lceil 0.3 \cdot F_{i-1} \rceil$, and the target bit rate is updated by

$$\tilde{R}_i = \begin{cases} (F_{i-1} + \Delta F_{i-1}) \cdot BW_{enc} / G & \text{if } \hat{D} > TH_{d1}, \\ (F_{i-1} - \Delta F_{i-1}) \cdot BW_{enc} / G & \text{if } \hat{D} < TH_{d2}, \\ F_{i-1} \cdot BW_{enc} / G & \text{otherwise}, \end{cases}$$

Step 3: Call macroblock level rate control TMN8 with the target bit rate $\tilde{R}_i$, which will return q_i, R_i and D_i.

Step 4: Update the database and the coefficients of rate-distortion models. Go to Step 1.

3 Experimental Results

The overview of the proposed overlay video multicast system is shown in Figure 2. Due to the practical difficulties such as firewall and security problem, the experiment is performed in the laboratory, that is, 12 computers in the laboratory are used. RTT values between two end systems and maximum bandwidth of each end system are set as shown in Table 1 and Table 2, respectively. Actually, delay manager in the Figure 2 controls the delay by adjusting packet transmission time. Basically, H.263+ coder

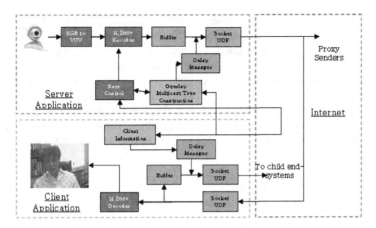

Fig. 2. Overview of the proposed overlay video multicast system

Table 1. RTT values among end-systems

	Sender	1	2	...	10	11
Sender		91	101	...	67	70
1	91		57	...	158	124
2	101	57		...	159	158
...	...	...	...		...	...
10	67	158	159	...		91
11	70	124	158	...	91	

Table 2. Bandwidth of end-systems and number of streams

Host	BW (bps)	No. of Streams		
		128K	190K	160K
sender	512K	4	2	3
1	1M	6	4	5
2	1M	6	4	5
....	....	....	....	....
10	1M	7	5	6
11	512K	4	5	3

[23] is employed as the video encoder with the above rate control algorithm. The tolerable maximum delay is set to 90ms.

A. Performance of Modified Dijkstra Algorithm

Some examples are presented to show the performance of modified Dijkstra's algorithm. It is compared with extended ring algorithm [16] and MSN algorithm [17] since they also consider the delay problem for real-time media delivery and they show very good performance. The performance comparison with extended ring algorithm is shown in Figure 3. In spite of member dispersion, extended ring algorithm builds up same structure tree. While, the modified Dijkstra's algorithm sends a stream from sender is given to end-system 4 instead of end-system 1 as shown in (b) of Figure 3. As a result, the obtained average delay values of modified Dijkstra's algorithm and extended ring algorithm are 423.0ms and 428.5 ms respectively. Compared with MSN that shows one of the best performances with respect to delay, it is observed that the performance depends on member dispersion. Figure 4 shows one of examples that modified Dijkstra's algorithm works better than MSN. The resulting average delay of the modified Dijkstra's algorithm is 180.4 ms and that of MSN is 188.1 ms.

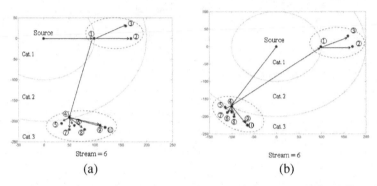

(a)   (b)

Fig. 3. Performance comparison between extended ring algorithm and modified Dijkstra's algorithm: (a) extended ring algorithm and (b) modified Dijkstra's algorithm

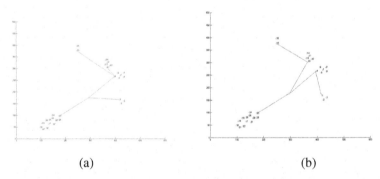

(a)   (b)

Fig. 4. Performance comparison between MSN algorithm and modified Dijkstra's algorithm: (a) MSN algorithm and (b) modified Dijkstra's algorithm.

B. Overlay Multicast Tree Construction and Target Bandwidth Determination

End-systems are clustered into 4 groups: (1, 5, 6), (2, 7, 8), (3, 9, 10), and (4, 11) as shown in Figure 5. The first entry of each parenthesis is the proxy sender in each cluster. The target bandwidth satisfying the given delay constraint is determined by the following three iterations.

Iteration 1: The initial target bandwidth is set to 128 Kbps, and the number of streams at each end-system is given the third column of Table 2. Now, the modified

Dijkstra table among proxy senders is shown in Table 3. Thus, the resulting average RTT value is 78 ms, which is too small although the delay constraint is satisfied. It means that we can not sufficiently support video quality.

Table 3. Modified Dijkstra Table at 128Kbps

Step	N	D(1)p(1)	D(2)p(2)	D(3)p(3)	D(4)p(4)
0	S	30,S	34,S	**21,S**	33,S
1	S-3	**30,S**	34,S		33,S
2	S-3-1		34,S		**33,S**
3	S-3-1-4		**34,S**		
4	S-3-1-4-2				

Iteration 2: The target bandwidth is increased to 192Kbps, and the number of streams at each end-system is given in the fourth column of Table 2. Hence, the corresponding modified Dijkstra table is shown in Table 4. In this case, the resulting average delay is 102.92 ms. Although we can improve the video quality, the resulting delay is much larger than the maximum value.

Table 4. Modified Dijkstra Table at 192Kbps

Step	N	D(1)p(1)	D(2)p(2)	D(3)p(3)	D(4)p(4)
0	S	30,S	[34,S]	**21,S**	[33,S]
1	S-3	**30,S**	73,3		72,3
2	S-3-1		**49,1**		72,3
3	S-3-1-2				**72,3**
4	S-3-1-2-4				

Iteration 3: Now, the target bandwidth is adjusted to 160Kbps of the middle value of 128Kbps and 192Kbps. The number of streams at each end-system is given in the fifth column of Table 2, and the results are given in Table 5 and Figure 5. In Figure 5, the achieved delay is 89.75ms, which very close to the tolerable maximum delay. Therefore, target bandwidth is finally set to 160Kbps. Now, video is compressed at this target bandwidth.

In summary, the above iterating processes are summarized in Table 6. We obtain an effective multicast tree and the largest target bandwidth in three steps to satisfy the time constraint.

Table 5. Modified Dijkstra Table at 160Kbps

Step	N	D(1)p(1)	D(2)p(2)	D(3)p(3)	D(4)p(4)
0	S	30,S	[34,S]	**21,S**	33,S
1	S-3	**30,S**	73,3		33,S
2	S-3-1		49,1		**33,S**
3	S-3-1-4		**49,1**		
4	S-3-1-4-2				

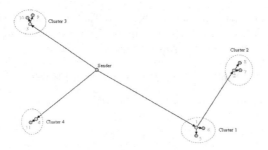

Fig. 5. The multicast tree when the target bandwidth is 160Kbps

Table 6. Summary of target bandwidth determination

	Step 1	Step 2	Step 3
Target bandwidth (bps)	128K	192K	**160K**
Delay (ms)	78	102.92	**89.75**

C. Performance of Adaptive Encoding Frame Rate Control

"Salesman (QCIF)", "Silent Voice (QCIF)", and "Foreman (QCIF)" videos are employed for the test, whose average target rates are 24 kbps (for Salesman and Silent Voice) and, 48 kbps (for Foreman) respectively. The predetermined PSNR range is set to 29 dB to 32 dB for Foreman, and 30 dB to 31 dB for Salesman and Silent Voice. c is set to 0.03 for Salesman and Silent Voice and 0.05 for Foreman, respectively. The objective performance is summarized in Table 7. It is observed that PSNR is improved at the cost of number of encoded frames. In this case, the subjective quality comparison is more important than objective quality comparison. For the subjective spatial quality comparison, some figures are given in Figure 6. The face and hand parts of Silent Voice is obviously improved as shown in (a) and (b) of Figure 6. And the improvement is much more obvious in Foreman sequence as shown in (c) and (d) of Figure 6. Regarding to temporal quality, the obvious temporal quality degradation caused by the time-varying encoding frame rate is not observed.

Table 7. Objective video quality comparison between TMN8 and adaptive encoding frame rate control

Rate Control	Sequence QCIF)	Avg. PSNR	No. of encoded frames
TMN8	Salesman	31.0255	137
	Silent Voice	30.0892	139
	Foreman	30.8537	97
Adaptive Control	Salesman	31.2966	130
	Silent Voice	30.3594	127
	Foreman	31.6028	84

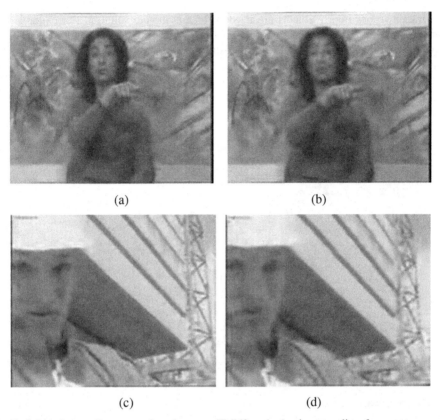

$$(a) \qquad\qquad (b)$$

$$(c) \qquad\qquad (d)$$

Fig. 6. Subjective quality comparison between TMN8 and adaptive encoding frame rate control: (a) and (c) show adaptive encoding frame rate control, and (b) and (d) show results of TMN8

D. Implementation of Overlay Real-time Video Multicast System

Finally, all components are implemented in overlay video multicast system. Now, the graphic user interfaces (GUI) of server side and client side are presented in Figure 7. As shown in (a), three end systems, node 1 (IP: 203.249.80.37), node 3 (IP: 203.249.80.40), and node 4 (IP: 203.249.80.41), are selected as proxy senders. (b) is the GUI of node 2. We can see that node 2 receive a stream from proxy sender node 1 (IP: 203.249.80.45) and then sends streams to node 7 (IP:203.249.80.45), and node 8 (IP:203.249.80.46). Actually, this tree topology is exactly same as Figure 6.

4   Conclusions

In this paper, we have presented an overlay H.263+ video multicast system over the Internet not to support IP multicast functionality. It includes overlay multicast tree minimizing average delay, target bandwidth determining process, and H.263+ rate control adaptive to overlay multicast tree. The whole video multicast system is implemented and tested over the real Internet, which has shown a good performance.

However, more improvements are needed for a complete solution. For example, the maximum delay is also very important factor for real-time media communication, the overlay multicast system must work in distributed way for receiver scalability, and the system must be tested over the real Internet environment (i.e. Planetlab). Furthermore, dynamic tree maintenance is required when member change occurs or conditions over the Internet are changing. These issues are under our current investigation.

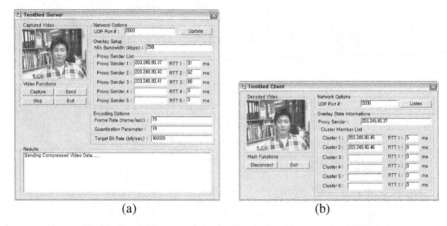

(a)   (b)

Fig. 7. Graphic user interfaces: (a) sender side and (b) node 2

References

1. Y. Chu, S. Rao, S. Seshan and H. Zhang, "A case for end-system multicast," ACM SIGMETRICS, Santa Clara, June 2000.
2. S. Deering, "Host Extensions for IP Multicasting," RFC1112, August 1989.
3. S. Banerjee and B. Bhattacharjee, "A comparative study of application layer multicast protocol," available at http://www.cs.wisc.edu/~suman/pubs.html.
4. Y. Chawathe, "Scattercast: An architecture for Internet Broadcast distribution as an Infrastructure service," Ph. D. dissertation, University of California, Berkeley, Dec. 2000.
5. P. Francis, "Yoid: Extending the multicast Internet architecture," available at http://www.aciri.org/yoid, 1999.
6. D. Pendarakis, S. Shi, D. Verma and M. Waldvogel, "ALMI: An Application level multicast infrastructure," Proceedings of 3rd Usenix Symposium on Internet Technologies & Systefeeder (USITS 2001), San Francisco, Mar. 2001.
7. B. Zhang, S. Jamin, and L. Zhang, "host multicast: A framework for delivering multicast to end users," Proceedings of IEEE Infocomm, June 2002.
8. S. Banerjee, B. Bhattacharjee, and C. Kommareddy, "Scalable application layer multicast," Proceedings of ACM SIGCOMM, Aug. 2002.
9. S. Ratnasamy, P. Francis, M. Handley, R. Karp, and S. Shenker, "A scalable content-addressable network," Proceedings of ACM SIGCOMM, Aug. 2001.
10. M. Castro, P. Druschel, A. Kermarrec, and A. Rowstron, "Scribe: A large scale and decentralized application-level multicast infrastructure," IEEE Journal on Selected Areas in Communications, Vol. 20, No. 8, pp. 1489-1499, Oct. 2002.

11. L. Mathy, R. Canonico, S. Simpson, and D. Hutchison, "Scalable adaptive hierarchical clustering," IEEE Communication Letter, Vol. 6, No. 3, pp. 117-119, March 2002.
12. J. Park, S. J. Koh, S. G. Kang, D. Y. Kim, "Multicast Delivery Based on Unicast and Subnet Multicast," IEEE Communications Letters, Vol. 5 No. 4. pp. 181-183, April 2001.
13. S. Y. Shi and J. S. Turner, "Multicast routing and bandwidth dimensioning in overlay network," IEEE Journal on Selected Areas in Communications, Vol. 20, No. 8, pp. 1444-1455, Oct. 2002.
14. S. Banerjee and B. Bhattacharjee, "Scalable secure group multicast over IP multicast," IEEE Journal on Selected Areas in Communications, Vol. 20, No. 8, pp. 1511-1527, Oct. 2002.
15. J. Liebeherr and M. Nahas, "Application-layer Multicast with Delaunay Triangulations," IEEE GLOBECOM, 2001.
16. C. K. Yeo, B. S. Lee and M. H. Er, "A framework for multicast video streaming over IP networks," Journal of Network and Computer Applications, pp. 273-289, Vol. 26, 2003.
17. S. Banerjee, C. Kommareddy, K. Kar, B. Bhattacharjee, and S. Khuller, "Construction of an efficient overlay multicast infrastructure for real-time applications," Proceedings of IEEE Infocomm, June 2003.
18. M. Casro, M. B. Jones, A. Kermarrec, A. Rowstron, M. Theimer, H. Wang, and A. Wolman, "An evaluation of scalable application-level multicast built using peer-to-peer overlays," Proceedings of IEEE Infocomm, June 2003
19. J. F. Kurose and K. W. Ross, Computer Networking: A Top-down approach featuring the Internet, 2nd ed., Addison Wesley, 2002.
20. Hwangjun Song and Dong Sup Lee, "Overlay multicast tree minimizing average time delay," LNCS (Networking 2004), Vol. 3042, April 2004.
21. M. Sun and A. R. Reibman, Compressed video over Networks, Marcel Dekker, Inc., 2001.
22. Hwangjun Song, Jongwon Kim and C. C. Jay Kuo, "Real-time encoding frame rate control for H.263+ video over the Internet," Signal Processing: Image Communication, Vol.15, Nos 1-2, pp.127-148, Sept 1999.
23. ITU-T, Video codec Test model, near-term, version 8 (TMN8), H.263 AdHoc Group, Portland, June 1997.
24. T. Chiang and Y. –Q. Zhang, "A new rate control scheme using quadratic rate distortion model," IEEE Trans. on Circuits and Systems for Video Technology, Vol. 7, pp. 246-250, Sept 1997.

Harmonic Block Windows Scheduling Through Harmonic Windows Scheduling

Yi Sun and Tsunehiko Kameda*

School of Computing Science, Simon Fraser University,
Burnaby, B.C., Canada V5A 1S6

Abstract. In *Harmonic windows scheduling* (HWS), a data file is divided into N pages and the pages are scheduled in c channels in such a way that each page i appears at least once in some channel in every window of size i. The optimal HWS problem aims to maximize N. Let κ be the largest integer satisfying $H_\kappa \leq c$, where H_n is the nth harmonic number. Then κ is an upper bound on N, if the HWS framework is used. Thus an optimal HWS schedule wastes "bandwidth" at least $c - H_\kappa$. *Harmonic block windows scheduling* (HBWS) generalizes HWS by grouping b consecutive pages into a superpage. Let N be the total number of pages scheduled. The ratio N/b is directly proportional to the maximum initial waiting time in Media-on-Demand applications. We propose a method that starts with a HWS schedule and modifies it to generate a HBWS schedule that achieves a higher ratio N/b. For up to five channels, we demonstrate that we can always achieve $N/b > \kappa$. We also prove that as we increase b, N/b approaches the theoretical upper bound.

1 Introduction

Recently, there has been much interest in the broadcast-based delivery of popular content in order to address the scalability issue [2,6,8,9,12,13]. As elaborated in these papers, when the demand for a video is high, it is more bandwidth-efficient to adopt broadcasting rather than the traditional client-server model.

Suppose that we divide a video into a sequence of fixed-size *pages*, $p_1, p_2, \ldots,$ p_N. We model a *channel* by a sequence of *slots*, such that a page of a video can be transmitted in each slot at the *display rate*. Note that the slot size is adjustable, so that if N is increased, then smaller slots are used. Recently, Bar-Noy et al.[1] formulated a combinatorial optimization problem, called the *optimal harmonic windows scheduling problem*, defined as follows: *Given c channels, find a schedule that contains the largest number of pages such that page p_i appears at least once in every i consecutive slots.* This problem is motivated by the video-on-demand (VoD) application of HWS as follows [1,9]. Let D be the total duration of the video and $d = D/N$ be the slot time. Suppose that for each i page p_i appears at least once in every i consecutive slots. If a user starts viewing a video starting

---

* This work was supported by a grant of the Natural Science and Engineering Research Council of Canada.

K.S. Candan and A. Celentano (Eds.): MIS 2005, LNCS 3665, pp. 190–206, 2005.
© Springer-Verlag Berlin Heidelberg 2005

only at a slot boundary, then he can view p_1 as it comes in. By the time he has finished viewing p_1, either p_2 has already appeared or is about to begin in some channel. In any case, he can view it either from the buffer (in the former case) or directly from the channel (in the latter case). Similarly, he can view all subsequent pages without interruption. Thus the maximum initial waiting time for a viewer is given by $d = D/N$, and, clearly, this waiting time is minimized if N is maximized.

For example, if $c = 3$, nine pages can be scheduled on the three channels, by repeatedly transmitting p_1 on the first channel, the sequence $\langle p_2, p_4, p_2, p_8, p_2, p_4, p_2, p_9 \rangle$ on the second channel, and the sequence $\langle p_3, p_5, p_6, p_3, p_5, p_7 \rangle$ on the third channel. It is still not known if 10 pages can be scheduled on three channels. Table 1 shows our current knowledge about the maximum numbers of pages that can be scheduled on c channels for several small values of c that are relevant to practical VoD broadcasting [1,2,3,5]. The upper bounds are obtained from the maximum κ such that $H_\kappa \leq c$. The values in the "Greedy" row of the table are attained by the heuristic algorithms given in [1,15].

Table 1. The number of pages that can be scheduled on c channels

No. of channels (c)	1	2	3	4	5	6
Upper bound	1	3	10	30	82	226
Best known	1	3	9	28	77	211
Greedy	1	3	9	25	73	201

In this paper, we adopt a generalization of HWS, called the *harmonic block windows scheduling* (*HBWS*), introduced in [14]. We first partition the time slots in each channel into *blocks*, each consisting of b consecutive slots, where b is an integer parameter. A *block window* of size w consists of w consecutive blocks. The pages of a video are also partitioned from the beginning into *superpages*, each containing b consecutive pages. Let $P_1, P_2, \ldots,$ be the successive superpages comprising a video. It is shown in [14] that the video can be displayed continuously starting at any block boundary, if the following two conditions are satisfied:[1] (1) for all i, each page of superpage P_i appears at least once in every block window of size i (not necessarily on the same channel), and (2) if a page of P_i appears exactly once in every block window of size i, then the page appears within a certain distance from the beginning of a block, as specified in the first definition given in Sect. 3.1.

Clearly HWS is a special case of HBWS where $b = 1$. In the VoD application of HBWS, we assume that a user can view a video starting only at a block boundary, and we want to reduce the initial waiting time. The maximum initial waiting time is given by $bd = bD/N$, where D is the total duration of the video and $d = D/N$ is the slot time. We thus adopt N/b as our performance metric to be maximized in this paper.

---

[1] In [14], a superpage is called a page set, and a page is called a fragment.

The remainder of the paper is organized as follows. In Sect. 2, we review some basic concepts and tools of scheduling. In Sect. 3, we briefly review our framework, HBWS, and present an algorithm called *BOOSTER* that takes a HWS schedule as an input and generates a HBWS schedule. Sect. 4 presents a detailed discussion of an example. The section also contains the results of many simulation runs. We observe that the ratio N/b approaches the upper bound with increasing b. Finally, in Sect. 5 we summarize our contributions and mention possible future work.

2   Preliminaries

2.1   Schedule for a Single Channel

A *channel* consists of a semi-infinite sequence of *slots*, numbered 0, 1, ... Let $\mathcal{T} = \{0, 1, \ldots\}$ denote the set of the slots in a channel, and let $\mathcal{P}$ denote a finite set of *pages*. A schedule (for a single channel) is a mapping $\sigma : \mathcal{T} \to \mathcal{P}$. If $\sigma(t) = p$, we say that page p is *scheduled* in slot t or that t is *allocated* to p. In general, a page is scheduled in many time slots. We often represent a schedule by the sequence of pages,

$$\sigma = \langle \sigma(0), \sigma(1), \sigma(2), \ldots, \rangle.$$

Schedule σ is said to be *cyclic* if for all $t \geq 0$ $\sigma(t) = \sigma(t + s)$ holds for some constant s, which is called a *cycle* of σ. In this case, σ is an infinite concatenation of $\langle \sigma(0), \sigma(1), \ldots, \sigma(s-1) \rangle$. Let S be a sequence of slots that are equally spaced, consisting of every $\pi(S)^{th}$ slot. If S consists of slots t, where $t \equiv O(S)$ (mod $\pi(S)$) for $0 \leq O(S) < \pi(S)$), then we say that S is periodic with *period* $\pi(S)$ and *offset* $O(S)$. We sometimes use the term *frequency* (or *bandwidth*) of a slot sequence to mean the reciprocal of its period, i.e., $1/\pi_i$. The *effective frequency* (or *effective bandwidth*) of a set of periodic slot sequences $\{S_1, S_2, \ldots, S_k\}$ is the sum of their frequencies, i.e., $\sum_{j=1}^{k} 1/\pi(S_j)$. A sequence of w consecutive slots is called a *window* of size w.

2.2   Tree Representation of a Schedule

Bar-Noy et al. [1] introduced the concept of a *round robin tree*, which is useful for representing cyclic schedules. For node v of a tree, let $deg(v)$ denote the number of child nodes of v.

Definition 1. [2] *A round robin (RR) tree T is a rooted tree such that $deg(v) \geq 2$ for each non-leaf node v, and two functions, the* period $\pi_T(v)$ *and the* offset $o_T(v)$,[2] *are defined for each node v as follows:*

- $\pi_T(root) = 1$. *For a non-root node v,*

$$\pi_T(v) = \pi_T(\text{Par}(v)) \times deg(\text{Par}(v)), \tag{1}$$

where $\text{Par}(v)$ *denotes the parent node of v.*

---

[2] Should not be confused with the offset of a slot sequence, $O(S)$, introduced earlier.

— $o_T(root) = 0$. *For a non-root node v,*

$$o_T(v) = o_T(\text{Par}(v)) + \ell(v)\pi_T(\text{Par}(v)), \tag{2}$$

where $\ell(v)$ $(\, 0 \le \ell(v) \le deg(v) \,)$ is the number of left siblings of v.

□

Thus for a node v, $\pi_T(v)$ can be computed as the product of the degrees of all its ancestor nodes. Let $\mathcal{L}_T$ denote the set of all leaves of RR tree T. We now label each leaf in $\mathcal{L}_T$ by a page to represent a schedule. An RR tree represents a schedule by the following rule:

RR rule

1. Initially the root gets a "turn".
2. When a non-leaf node gets a turn, it passes the turn to its "next" child node. The leftmost child node gets a turn first and the order "next" means the next sibling to the right, wrapping around back to the leftmost child node.
3. When a leaf gets a turn, its associated page is scheduled and the turn goes back to the root. □

A schedule represented by an RR tree is called an *RR schedule*.

For each leaf v in Fig. 1, we indicate its period and offset in the form $\pi_T(v)^{(o_T(v))}$. Applying the above RR rule, it is seen that the tree T in Fig. 1 represents the schedule

$$\langle p_4, p_6, p_5, p_7, p_4, p_8, p_5, p_6, p_4, p_7, p_5, p_8, \cdots \rangle.$$

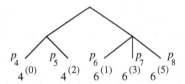

Fig. 1. A tree representation of a schedule

Theorem 1. *[1,5] Suppose the leaves of an RR tree T are labeled by pages. Then in the schedule represented by T, page p_i appears with effective frequency at least $1/i$ if and only if a set of leaves $\{L_1, L_2, \ldots, L_h\}$ are labeled by page p_i such that $1/i \le 1/\pi_T(L_1) + \cdots + 1/\pi_T(L_h)$ holds.* □

3 Harmonic Block Windows Scheduling

3.1 Brief Review of HBWS

From now on, we assume that there are c (≥ 2) channels. The slots on each channel are partitioned into consecutive blocks of b slots each, such that block boundaries are synchronized among all the channels. A schedule allocates the time slots to pages for each channel. We use the term schedule to mean either a page sequence for one channel or a collection of c page sequences for c channels, depending on the context. A sequence (or c sequences) of w consecutive blocks forms (or form) a *block window* of size w. If a page appears exactly once in every block window of size i in a schedule, then the page is said to have *block period i* and *block frequency* $1/i$.

For $i = 1, 2, \ldots$, let us designate the b pages in the ith superpage P_i of a video as follows:

$$P_i = \{p_{i,1}, p_{i,2}, \ldots, p_{i,b}\} \tag{3}$$

If the total number of pages N is not a multiple of b, the last superpage will contain only $(N \bmod b)$ pages. Therefore, there are $\lfloor N/b \rfloor$ "full" superpages and at most one "partial" superpage.

Definition 2. *Let $P_1, P_2, \ldots, P_n$ be superpages, such that P_i ($1 \leq i \leq n - 1$) contains b pages numbered as in (3) and P_n may contain fewer than b pages. A schedule σ is said to be* feasible *if for all $i = 1, 2, \ldots, n$ and for any $p_{ij} \in P_i$ one of the following holds:*

(a) Page p_{ij} has block period $< i$ in σ.

(b) Page p_{ij} has block period i in σ and it appears within j slots from a block boundary. □

It is proved in [14] that all the pages of a feasible schedule can be displayed continuously if display and downloading start at a block boundary. Condition (b) of Definition 2 often leads to conflicting requirements for pages in P_i for different i. In such a case, some initial pages of P_i must be *promoted* to be scheduled with block period $(i-1)$, so that the more relaxed Condition (a) applies to them. We can now define our problem precisely as follows:

Definition 3. [14] *The* Optimal HBWS Problem *is the problem of finding a feasible schedule that maximizes N/b, where N is the total number of scheduled pages in the given number (c) of channels and b is the block size.* □

Given a feasible schedule σ, let Q_i $(1 \leq i \leq n)$ denote the set of pages with block period i in σ. Clearly those pages consume bandwidth equal to $|Q_i|/ib$. Therefore, we must have

$$\frac{|Q_1|}{b} + \frac{|Q_2|}{2b} + \cdots + \frac{|Q_n|}{nb} \leq c. \tag{4}$$

Let $\Delta_i = Q_{i-1} \cap P_i$, i.e., the set of pages promoted from P_i. Then we have $Q_i = (P_i - \Delta_i) \cup \Delta_{i+1}$. Let $|\Delta_i|$ denote the number of pages in Δ_i. Clearly, $p_{i,|\Delta_i|+1}$ is the first page in P_i that is not promoted and hence $Q_i = \{p_{i,|\Delta_i|+1}, p_{i,|\Delta_i|+2}, \ldots\}$. To satisfy condition (b) of Definition 2, the first page of Q_i, $p_{i,|\Delta_i|+1}$, must appear within the first $(|\Delta_i| + 1)$ slots from the beginning of a block.

Theorem 2. [14] *Let κ be the largest integer satisfying $H_\kappa \leq c$. Then N/b can be bounded as follows:*

$$N/b \leq \frac{\kappa}{1-(c-H_\kappa)} = \kappa + \frac{\kappa(c-H_\kappa)}{1-(c-H_\kappa)} \tag{5}$$

$\square$

Note that for $c \geq 2$, we have $0 < c - H_\kappa < 1$, hence the above bound is larger than κ (which is an upper bound for HWS [1]). In Sect. 4, we demonstrate schedules for which N/b exceeds the upper bound κ for HWS. (5) is a tight bound that can be approached asymptotically [14].

3.2 Feasibility Condition

Suppose there is a set of c RR trees whose leaves are labeled by a total of n pages, such that each tree represents a schedule on a channel. We assume that for each $1 \leq i \leq n$, m_i (≥ 1) leaves with the *same* period π_i are labeled by page i and $1/i \leq m_i/\pi_i$ holds. We call m_i the *multiplicity*. For example, we have $m_7 = 3$ in Fig. 3. Such a forest can be used to represent a HWS schedule for n pages on c channels [1]. We call each tree in the forest a *base tree*.

We now use the RR rule described in Sect. 2 with the following modification: For $j = 0, 1, \ldots, i-1$, we define *coset j* of superpage P_i by $P_i^j = \{p_{ik} \in P_i \mid k = (j \bmod i) + 1\}$. Thus P_i has i cosets, and each coset contains either $n_i = \lceil b/i \rceil$ or $n_i - 1$ pages. We schedule the pages of P_i by spreading them among i consecutive blocks. For $k = 0, 1, \ldots$, we place all the pages of coset $P_i^{k \bmod i}$ in block k. In particular, superpage P_1 has just one coset P_1^0, and all its b pages appear in every block of one channel. We carry this out by using the base trees as follows: in constructing the schedule for block k, whenever a leaf of a base tree labeled by p_i gets a turn, schedule the next page from the pages of $P_i^{k \bmod i}$ one after another in any vacant slot on the corresponding channel. Since $1/i \leq m_i/\pi_i$, in block k of the constructed schedule for some k, there may be some unfilled slots. Each page $p_{i,j}$ will appear with block period equal to i in the above schedule. In other words, it satisfies condition (a) of Definition 2. Unfortunately, it may not satisfy condition (b). Therefore, we need to modify it to construct a feasible schedule.

Let $O_T(p_i)$ denote the offset of the leaf (if $m_i = 1$) of T to which page p_i is assigned in the original HWS schedule. (We assume there is only one such tree.) It can be computed using (2) and (1). If $m_i > 1$, $O_T(p_i)$ denotes the smallest among the m_i offsets of the leaves to which p_i is assigned.

Let us list the members of $P = \cup_{i=1}^n P_i$ as a sequence $p_{1,1}, \ldots, p_{1,b}, p_{2,1}, \ldots, p_{2,b}, \cdots, p_{n,1}, \ldots, p_{n,b}$. We now construct page sets $\{Q_i \mid i = 1, 2, \ldots, n-1\}$, taking pages from the above sequence, the leftmost first. For $i = 1, 2, \ldots, n-1$, the size of set Q_i is determined recursively as follows [14]:

$$|Q_i| = i \left\lceil b - \frac{\sum_{j=1}^{i-1} |Q_j| - O_T(p_{i+1})}{i} \right\rceil = i \left\lceil \frac{b - |\Delta_i| + O_T(p_{i+1})}{i} \right\rceil. \tag{6}$$

Set Q_n is computed by $Q_n = P - \cup_{j=1}^{n-1} Q_j$. Note that $|\Delta_i| = \cup_{j=1}^{i-1}|Q_j| - \cup_{j=1}^{i-1}|P_j| = \cup_{j=1}^{i-1}|Q_j| - (i-1)b$. Note also that the size of the promoted set $|\Delta_i|$ does not grow with b. This claim is obviously true for $i = 2$, since $|Q_1| = b + O_T(p_2)$ and $O_T(p_2)$ $(= |\Delta_2|)$ is independent of b. The above claim follows by induction, since we have $b - |\Delta_i| + O_T(p_{i+1}) \leq |Q_i| \leq b - |\Delta_i| + O_T(p_{i+1}) + i - 1$ from (6), and $O_T(p_{i+1})$ is independent of b. Based on this inequality, we can conclude that for all i, $|Q_i|/b$ approaches 1 as $b \to \infty$. We schedule the pages in $\{Q_i \mid 1 \leq i \leq n\}$ using Step 5(c) of algorithm BOOSTER in Sec. 3.3, and call the resulting sequence the *base schedule* for the given b.

Let us see if we can schedule more pages than those in the base schedule. If $1/i < m_i/\pi_i$ for some i, then we have *surplus* slots appearing with effective frequency $m_i/\pi_i - 1/i$ or effective period $1/(m_i/\pi_i - 1/i) = (im_i - \pi)/i\pi_i$. Thus, the surplus slots in the slot sequences represented by one or more of the m_i leaves can be freed to be allocated to other pages. We now examine an example to see how to take advantage of the usable surplus slots.

Example 1. Fig. 2(a) shows an RR tree that can be used to schedule two full superpages P_2, P_3. We use this tree as the base tree. (We schedule the b pages of P_1 on channel 1; Thus, channel 1 will have no surplus slots.) Each leaf in Fig. 2(a) represents slot frequency of $1/2$, which is exactly what the pages of superpage P_2 require but is more than necessary for the pages of P_3, which require slot frequency of $1/3$. Therefore, we split the right leaf into three leaves, each representing frequency $1/6$, as shown in Fig. 2(b). (For the general rule for generating the new tree T' from T, see below.) The three new leaves of T' represent three "subchannels", each consisting of every 6th slot. We allocate subchannel B to $P_3 - \Delta_3$, and the remaining two subchannels (C and D) to the promoted pages of $\Delta_3 = P_3 \cap Q_2$ and $\Delta_4 = P_4 \cap Q_3$. (See Table 2 in the next subsection.) □

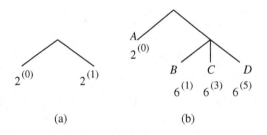

(a)   (b)

Fig. 2. RR trees for pages p_2 and p_3 (Leaf v is labeled by $\pi_T(v)^{(o_T(v))}$). (a) Base tree T; (b) T': The right leaf of (a) is split into three leaves

For the right leaf in the RR tree in Fig. 2(a), we have $1/3 < m_3/\pi_3$. In such a case, we introduce i child nodes to that leaf labeled by page p_i which has offset $O_T(p_i)$. The advantage of splitting a leaf into i leaves (when $m_i = 1$) is that each of the newly created leaves provides frequency equal to $1/i\pi_i$. Therefore,

π_i new leaves provide the exact frequency, i.e., $1/i$. We now want to schedule additional pages.

Lemma 1. *Suppose each page in page set Q_i, where $n + 1 \leq i \leq \kappa$, is scheduled with period $\leq i$, using the surplus slots represented by the leaves in $\mathcal{L}_i = \{L_{i_1}, \ldots, L_{i_h}\}$ of tree T', where T' denotes the tree resulting from expanding a leaf labeled by p_i satisfying $1/i < m_i/\pi_i$. Then we must have*

(a)

$$\frac{1}{i} \leq \frac{1}{\pi_{T'}(L_{i_1})} + \frac{1}{\pi_{T'}(L_{i_2})} + \ldots + \frac{1}{\pi_{T'}(L_{i_h})}, \tag{7}$$

(b) and, for any integer ℓ in the range $1 \leq \ell \leq b$:

$$\sum_{j=1}^{h} \max\left\{0, \left\lceil \frac{\ell - o_{T'}(L_{i_j})}{\pi_{T'}(L_{i_j})} \right\rceil\right\} \geq \left\lceil \frac{\ell - |\Delta_i|}{i} \right\rceil. \tag{8}$$

Proof. The need for condition (a) follows from Theorem 1. To prove the need for (8), consider the ℓth position in a block. Note that the number of slots within the first ℓ positions of a block that are in the slot sequence represented by leaf L_{i_j} is given by

$$\left\lceil \frac{\ell - o_{T'}(L_{i_j})}{\pi_{T'}(L_{i_j})} \right\rceil.$$

Since Q_i contains pages $p_{i,|\Delta_i|+1}, p_{i,|\Delta_i|+2}, \ldots$, in order to satisfy Condition (b) of Definition 2, they must occupy at least the number of slots given by the right hand side of (8) within the first ℓ positions of a block. Hence the inequality. $\square$

For the given block size b, the minimal number of promoted pages can be obtained as the minimum $|\Delta_i|$ that satisfies (8) for all ℓ in the range $1 \leq \ell \leq b$. Note that (8) is satisfied for all ℓ ($1 \leq \ell \leq b$) if and only it is satisfied for a subset of ℓ with $\ell - |\Delta_i| = 0 \mod i$.

For example, in Fig. 2(b), the three new leaves each have frequency $1/6$, so the pages of P_3 would need only two of the three new subchannels ($1/3 = (1/6)*2$).

Example 2. Table 2 shows an attempt to fit two full superpages P_2 and P_3 (of size $b = 12$ each) and a partial superpage P_4 (of size $6 < b$). Each group of four rows in the table shows the contents of one block. Four blocks are shown stacked up on top of each other in the table, but they should follow each other in time. Note, for example, that b ($= 12$) pages of P_2 are assigned to every other slot in subchannel A, so that they consume $1/2$ of the bandwidth.

Assume, for instance, that downloading and display started at the second block from the top of Table 2. It is easy to see that we can view the pages of P_1, P_2 and P_3 during the first three block periods, respectively. Consider now page $p_{4,3}$ (with an asterisk). It is needed in the third slot in the fourth block period after the download start time, but it won't be available until the 6th slot time. $\square$

Table 2. Tentative (non-feasible) schedule to illustrate the requirement just before page $p_{3,6}$ is to be displayed: $b = 12$, $i = 3$ and $x = 2$

RR Sequence	2	$6^{(1)}$	2	$6^{(3)}$	2	$6^{(5)}$	2	$6^{(1)}$	2	$6^{(3)}$	2	$6^{(5)}$
Subch 1 (A)	$p_{2,1}$		$p_{2,3}$		$p_{2,5}$		$p_{2,7}$		$p_{2,9}$		$p_{2,11}$	
Subch 2 (B)		$[p_{3,3}]$						$p_{3,9}$				
Subch 3 (C)				$p_{3,6}$						$p_{3,1}$		
Subch 4 (D)						$*p_{4,3}$						$p_{3,12}$
Subch 1 (A)	$p_{2,2}$		$p_{2,4}$		$p_{2,6}$		$p_{2,8}$		$p_{2,10}$		$p_{2,12}$	
Subch 2 (B)		$[p_{3,4}]$						$p_{3,10}$				
Subch 3 (C)				$p_{3,7}$						$p_{3,2}$		
Subch 4 (D)						$p_{4,4}$						$p_{4,1}$
Subch 1 (A)	$p_{2,1}$		$p_{2,3}$		$p_{2,5}$		$p_{2,7}$		$p_{2,9}$		$p_{2,11}$	
Subch 2 (B)		$[p_{3,5}]$						$p_{3,11}$				
Subch 3 (C)				$p_{3,8}$						$p_{3,1}$		
Subch 4 (D)						$p_{4,5}$						$p_{4,2}$
Subch 1 (A)	$p_{2,2}$		$p_{2,4}$		$p_{2,6}$		$p_{2,8}$		$p_{2,10}$		$p_{2,12}$	
Subch 2 (B)		$[p_{3,3}]$						$p_{3,9}$				
Subch 3 (C)				$p_{3,6}$						$p_{3,2}$		
Subch 4 (D)						$p_{4,6}$						$p_{3,12}$

Suppose $1/i < m_i/\pi_i$ and we create i new leaves as described just before the above lemma. We want to "deallocate" some of the i new leaves and assign the slots they represent to pages of page set(s) other than Q_i. Let x denote the minimum number such that the xth (from left) new leaf can be deallocated without violating the requirements for the pages of Q_i. The time (in terms of the number of slots from the beginning of the schedule) when the leftmost new leaf is about to get its "turn" is $t_1 = O_T(p_i)$ and the time just before the xth new leaf gets its turn is $t_2 = t_1 + (x - 1)\pi_i$. The interval $I_1 = [t_1 + 1, t_2]$ corresponds to the columns between the second and third double vertical lines in Table 2, if $x = 2$ and $i = 3$ (hence $t_1 = 1$ and $t_2 = 3$). The display of the first page of Q_i starts at $t_1 + 1$ or later. During the interval I_1, $(x - 1)\pi_i$ pages are displayed, while $(x - 1)im_i$ pages of Q_i become "displayable". Here, a page is "displayable" if each of its predecessors has been displayed or is in the buffer. Out of $(x-1)im_i$ pages of Q_i that become displayable, $(x-1)m_i$ become displayable in the current block in the interval I_1, while the remaining $(x - 1)(i - 1)m_i$ pages were placed in the buffer during the previous $i - 1$ blocks.

Therefore, the net increase in the number of pages (of Q_i) in the buffer during I_1 is given by $(x - 1)(im_i - \pi_i)$. For $i = 3$ and $x = 2$, for example, these are the three pages in square brackets in Table 2. We also define t_3 to be the time when the next subtree (if $m_i > 1$) assigned to page i is about to get its turn. We now consider the time interval $I_2 = [t_1 + 1, t_3]$ and compute the net increase in the number of buffered pages of Q_i during I_2. Let $\delta_i = \sum_{j=1}^{i-1} |Q_j| - (i-1)b - O_T(p_i) = |\Delta_i| - O_T(p_i)$. This is the number of pages in the buffer at time t_1, excluding those belonging to Q_i, which we count separately. The total number of pages in the buffer at time t_3 is represented by the left hand side of (9). Note that there is no increase in the number of pages of $|Q_i|$ in the interval $I_3 = [t_2 + 1, t_3]$. Therefore, the second term is $(x - 1)(im_i - \pi_i)$ that we computed above. The number on the left hand side of (9) must be sufficient to supply pages to be displayed until the next page of Q_i becomes available from the sequence represented by another of the m_i (≥ 2) leaves. This number is at most i, since T schedules page i with period at most i.

$$\delta_i + (x - 1)(im_i - \pi_i) \geq i \ (\pi_i \text{ if } m_i = 1). \tag{9}$$

The right hand side is π_i if $m_i = 1$, since the period of the split leaf is π_i ($< i$) if $m_i = 1$. Solving the above equation for the minimum integer x, we get

$$x = (1 - \delta(m_i, 1)) + \left\lceil \frac{i - \delta_i}{im_i - \pi_i} \right\rceil.$$

where $\delta(\ )$ is defined by: $\delta(a, b) = 1$ (resp. 0) if $a = b$ (resp. $a \neq b$). For the case $i = 3, m_3 = 1, \pi_3 = 2$ and $\delta_3 = 1$, we get $x = 2$ from the above formula. This means that the second subchannel, i.e., C can be considered as surplus, and pages $p_{3.6}, p_{3,7}, p_{3,8}$ can be scheduled in subchannel D instead. Then, $p_{4,3}$ can be scheduled on subchannel C. However, the user will still starve for $p_{4,3}$, unless it is promoted to Q_3. If this is done Q_3 can also contain $p_{4,4}$ and $p_{4,5}$ but $p_{4,6}$ doesn't fit anywhere. We thus have $|Q_2| = 14$, $|Q_3| = 15$ and $|Q_4| = 0$.[3]

In the general case, where $\alpha - 1$ of the new leaves have already been identified as representing surplus slot sequences, we have

$$\delta_i + (x - \alpha)(im_i - \pi_i) + (\alpha - 1)(i(m_i - 1) - \pi_i) \geq i \ (\pi_i \text{ if } m_i = 1). \tag{10}$$

Thus, the next surplus leaf x is determined as

$$x = (1 - \delta(m_i, 1)) + \left\lceil \frac{i\alpha - \delta_i}{im_i - \pi_i} \right\rceil. \tag{11}$$

3.3 Algorithm BOOSTER

Based on the theoretical development described so far, we now present our algorithm.

Input: c base trees, $T_1, T_2, \ldots, T_c$, and block size b.
Output: c sequences representing a HBWS schedule.

1. For $k = 1, 2, \ldots, c$, repeat steps 2 to 7, using base tree T_k.
2. Let $p_1, p_2, \ldots, p_n$ be the pages that appear as the labels of the leaves of T_k.

---

[3] These values also result from (4), (6) and the method used to prove Theorem 2 (not given in this paper but can be found in [14]), which introduces $Q_{\kappa+1}$. It turns out that if we choose $b > 12$ then we can have $|Q_4| > 0$. But in this paper, we use only page sets up to Q_κ, where κ is defined in Theorem 2.

3. Read the offsets, $\{O_{T_k}(p_i) \mid 1 \leq i \leq n\}$ from T_k, and construct $\{Q_i \mid 1 \leq i \leq n-1\}$, using (6).

4. Let Π denote the set of the periods of the surplus slot sequences given by

$$\Pi = \{i\pi_i/(im_i - \pi_i) \mid 1/i < m_i/\pi_i\}. \tag{12}$$

For each g in the range $1 \leq g \leq \kappa - n$, use the *simulated annealing* algorithm [16] to partition the periods in Π into g groups,[4] $\Pi_{n+1}, \cdots, \Pi_{n+g}$, such that $\Pi = \bigcup_{i=n+1}^{n+g} \Pi_i$ and $\sum_{\pi \in \Pi_i} 1/\pi \geq \frac{1}{n+i}$ for $1 \leq i \leq g$. Determine the maximum such g.[5]

5. Repeat the following two steps for each i satisfying $1/i < m_i/\pi_i$.

(a) Split one of the m_i leaves of T_k that is labeled by page p_i, with offset equal to $O_{T_k}(p_i)$, into i child nodes and call the resulting tree T_k'. Let $\delta_i = |\Delta_i| - O_{T_k}(p_i)$. Define α_{max} as the maximum integer α satisfying

$$(1 - \delta(m_i, 1)) + \left\lceil \frac{i\alpha - \delta_i}{im_i - \pi_i} \right\rceil \leq i,$$

where the right hand side (i) is the number of new child nodes (see (11)). For $\alpha = 1, 2, \ldots, \alpha_{max}$, compute the minimum offset of each surplus slot sequence by

$$O_{T_k'}(L_\alpha^i) = \pi_i(1 - \delta(m_i, 1)) + \max\left\{0, \left\lceil \frac{i\alpha - \delta_i}{im_i - \pi_i} \right\rceil\right\} \times \pi_i + O_{T_k}(p_i), \tag{13}$$

where L_α^i is the leaf of T_k' corresponding to the αth surplus slot sequence.

(b) Using (13) and Lemma 1, calculate the sizes of the promoted sets of pages $|\Delta_{n+1}|, |\Delta_{n+2}|, \ldots, |\Delta_{n+g}|$. Compute $|Q_n|, |Q_{n+1}|, \ldots, |Q_{n+g-1}|$ by (6), with $O_T(p_{i+1})$ replaced by $|\Delta_{i+1}|$. Compute $|Q_{n+g}|$ from[6]

$$|Q_{n+g}| = cb(n+g) - (n+g) \sum_{i=1}^{n+g-1} \frac{|Q_i|}{i}. \tag{14}$$

6. For $i = 1, 2, \ldots, n+g$, partition page set $Q_i = \{q_{i1}, q_{i,2}, \ldots\}$ into i cosets as follows: For $j = 0, 1, \ldots, i-1$, $Q_i^j = \{q_{ik} \in Q_i \mid k = (j \bmod i) + 1\}$.[7]

---

[4] We define the system energy to be the number of subsets that satisfy $\sum_{\pi \in \Pi_i} \pi \geq \frac{1}{n+i}$ for $1 \leq i \leq g$. The partition problem can be polynomially transformed to the problem of finding the optimal solution to forming surplus slot sequences, which makes the problem NP-complete.

[5] It turns out that for all the examples in Sect. 4, $n + g = \kappa$ (Kappa), i.e., the largest possible.

[6] This is obtained by making (4) an equality and replacing n in it by $n+g$. Since each $|Q_i|$ ($1 \leq i \leq n+g-1$) is an integer by (6), $|Q_{n+g}|$ is also an integer.

[7] Since there are i cosets, each coset contains $n_i = |Q_i|/i$ pages, which is an integer due to (6).

7. Traverse tree T_k and schedule pages in the first block of Channel k as follows: Whenever a leaf labeled by p_i gets a turn in T_k, schedule the next page of Q_i^0 one after another. Then reset the traversal of T_k and schedule pages of Q_i^1 in the second block, and so forth, until the pages of Q_i^{i-1} are placed in the ith block.[8]   □

We state the following easy lemma without proof.

Lemma 2. *The schedule obtained by BOOSTER is a cyclic schedule with period $LCM(2, \cdots, n+g)$, where LCM stands for "Least Common Multiple".*   □

Theorem 3. *For sufficiently large b, the performance metric N/b of BOOSTER is given by*

$$N/b = c(n+g) - \frac{1}{b} \sum_{i=1}^{n+g-1} \left(\frac{n+g}{i} - 1 \right) |Q_i|. \tag{15}$$

Proof. The total number of pages is $N = \sum_{i=1}^{n+g} |Q_i| = \sum_{i=1}^{n+g-1} |Q_i| + |Q_{n+g}|$. The theorem is proved by plugging (14) into this expression.   □

4   Scheduling Example and Simulation Results for BOOSTER

In this section, using N/b as a performance metric, we study the performance of BOOSTER for up to six channels, The results will reveal that N/b approaches the optimal value asymptotically as b is increased. We analyze the performance for different numbers of channels c, ranging from 2 to 6, which is probably enough for practical MoD applications.

Let $C_1, C_2, \ldots, C_c$ denote the c channels. We assume that the pages of P_1 are scheduled on C_1, and focus on the schedules for $C_2, C_3, \ldots$. As a non-trivial example, we shall give a detailed description for the case $c = 4$.

As the base trees we use the best RR trees discovered by Bar-Noy et al. [1] which are shown in Fig. 3. They represent a cyclic schedule that is denoted as $\langle 4, 28 \rangle$, indicating that four channels are used and 28 pages are scheduled. Throughout this section, we choose block size $b \le 1000$.

The base trees in Fig. 3 provide us with a feasible HBWS schedule for 28 superpages. Note that 28 falls short of the upper bound $\kappa = 30$ for HWS obtained from $H_\kappa \le 4$. We are interested in knowing if we can achieve $N/b > 28$ for some b. We try to schedule two extra superpages P_{29} and P_{30}, taking advantage of the surplus slot sequences listed in Table 3 below, which is obtained in Step 4 of the BOOSTER from the base trees of Fig. 3. Each column in the table represents $(im_i - \pi_i)$ surplus slot sequences.

---

[8] If $|Q_i| > b$, at least $|Q_i| - b$ pages of Q_i belong to Δ_{i+1}. Since the Condition (b) in Definition 2 does not apply to them, we can put them in surplus slots starting from the end of each block; the first extra page in block 1, the second extra page in block 2, etc. These surplus slots are available, since (4) holds.

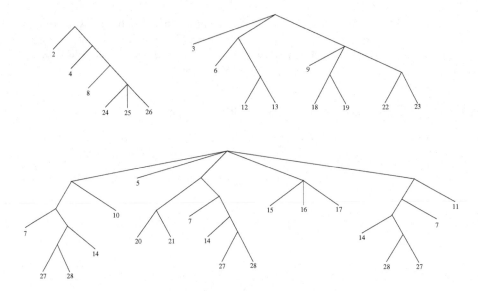

Fig. 3. Base tree for four channels [1]

Table 3. 27 $(=\sum_i [im_i - \pi_i]$; see the last row) surplus slot sequences in the RR trees of Fig. 3

i	11	16	22	23	7	13	14	17	19	21	25	26	27	28
π_i	10	15	18	18	20	12	40	15	18	20	24	24	80	80
Period $(i\pi_i)$	110	240	396	414	140	156	560	255	342	420	600	624	2160	2240
Offset	79	218	a	b	80	130	c	d	86	332	159	e	1290	f
m_i	1	1	1	1	3	1	3	1	1	1	1	1	3	3
$im_i - \pi_i$	1	1	4	5	1	1	2	2	1	1	1	2	1	4

The first row in Table 3 lists i, such that a leaf allocated to page i has surplus slots. The second row shows π_i for the leaf. The fourth row shows the offset for the surplus slot sequence. In this row, $a = \{44, 134, 242, 332\}$, $b = \{17, 125, 197, 287, 359\}$, $c = \{204, 484\}$, $d = \{103, 238\}$, $e = \{215, 527\}$, and $f = \{184, 744, 1304, 1860\}$. The fifth row shows how many leaves (of period π_i) are allocated to page i. The quantity $im_i - \pi_i$ shown in the last row indicates how many new leaves will represent surplus slot sequences, if the leaf is split into i leaves. The offset $O_T(p_i)$ is computed by (2), the page set sizes $|Q_i|$ $(1 \leq i \leq 27)$ are computed by (6), and they are listed in Table 4.

In order to compute the remaining $|Q_{28}|$ and $|Q_{29}|$, we first compute $|\Delta_{29}|$ and $|\Delta_{30}|$ and replace $O_T(p_{i+1})$ by $|\Delta_{i+1}|$ for $i = 28, 29$ in (6). We can finally compute $|Q_{30}|$ using (14). We used the simulated annealing algorithm first to group the periods of the surplus slot sequences in Table 3 into two subsets, Π_1 and Π_2, which will be allocated to page sets Q_{29} and Q_{30}, respectively. The results are indicated in Table 3: Let $\mathcal{S}_i$ denote the set of surplus slot sequences corresponding

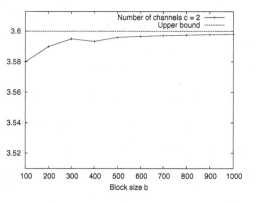
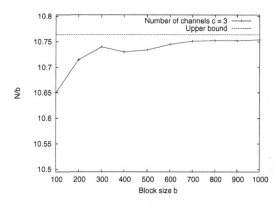

Fig. 4. Normalized number of pages N/b for $100 \leq b \leq 1000$; left graph: $c = 2$; right graph: $c = 3$

to the periods in Π_i. The eleven ($=1+1+4+5$) surplus slot sequences to the left of the double vertical lines in the middle of the table belong to S_1 and the rest to S_2.

We combine Lemma 1 with the minimum surplus sequence offset given by (13). Equation (8) in Lemma 1 gives rise to the following equation for the surplus slot sequences in S_1:

$$\max\left\{0, \left\lceil \frac{\ell - 79}{110} \right\rceil\right\} + \max\left\{0, \left\lceil \frac{\ell - 218)}{240} \right\rceil\right\} + \cdots + \max\left\{0, \left\lceil \frac{\ell - 359}{414} \right\rceil\right\} \quad (16)$$

$$\geq \left\lceil \frac{\ell - |\Delta_{29}|}{29} \right\rceil$$

The first term on the left hand side is for the first surplus slot sequence in Table 3. The denominator $110 = 10\pi_{10}$. Note that there are five terms with denominator equal to $414 = 23\pi_{23}$, because there are $23m_{23} - \pi_{23} = 5$ surplus slot sequences involved.

Similarly, we have the following equation for the surplus slot sequences in S_2:

$$\max\left\{0, \left\lceil \frac{\ell - 80}{140} \right\rceil\right\} + \max\left\{0, \left\lceil \frac{\ell - 130}{156} \right\rceil\right\} + \cdots + \max\left\{0, \left\lceil \frac{\ell - 1860}{2240} \right\rceil\right\} \quad (17)$$

$$\geq \left\lceil \frac{\ell - |\Delta_{30}|}{30} \right\rceil$$

Table 4. Offsets in the base trees and sizes of the computed page sets $\{Q_i\}$ for $c = 4$ and $b = 1000$. $O_T(p_{29})$ and $O_T(p_{30})$ don't exist, and the values (with an asterisk) shown in their places are $|\Delta_{29}|$ and $|\Delta_{30}|$, respectively.

i	$O_T(p_i)$	$|Q_i|$	i	$O_T(p_i)$	$|Q_i|$	i	$O_T(p_i)$	$|Q_i|$	i	$O_T(p_i)$	$|Q_i|$	i	$O_T(p_i)$	$|Q_i|$	i	$O_T(p_i)$	$|Q_i|$
1	0	1000	2	0	1000	3	0	1002	4	1	1000	5	1	1000	6	1	1002
7	0	1001	8	3	1000	9	2	1008	10	5	1000	11	9	1001	12	4	996
13	10	1001	14	4	994	15	3	1005	16	8	1008	17	13	1003	18	5	1008
19	14	998	20	2	1000	21	12	1008	22	8	1012	23	17	989	24	7	1008
25	15	1000	26	23	988	27	10	1026	28	24	1008	29	*43	1131	30	*173	900

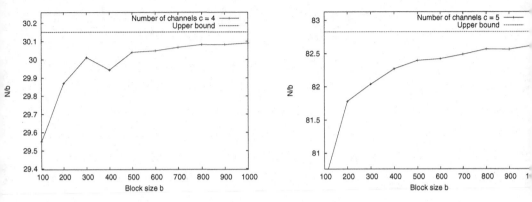

Fig. 5. Normalized number of pages N/b for $100 \leq b \leq 1000$; left graph: $c = 4$; right graph: $c = 5$

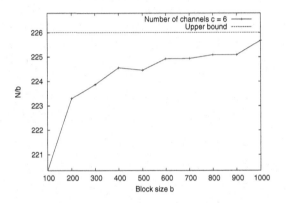

Fig. 6. Normalized number of pages N/b for $100 \leq b \leq 1000$. $c = 6$

The offsets $|\Delta_{29}| = 43$ and $|\Delta_{30}| = 173$ are determined as the minimum values that make (17) and (18), respectively, hold for all values of ℓ in the range $0 \leq \ell \leq b$. Note that the sizes of promoted sets $|\Delta_{29}|$ and $|\Delta_{30}|$ depend on b.

With the help of MATLAB, we examined the performance of the BOOSTER with respect to the block size b. Figs. 4, 5, and 6 plot our computation results for N/b as a function of b (horizontal axis) in the range $100 \leq b \leq 1000$. The horizontal line in each graph shows the upper bound given by Theorem 2. The vertical range in each graph is from 97.5% to 100% of the upper bound. It is seen that N/b approaches the upper bound as b grows and that how close the curve gets to the upper bound depends on the number of channels (c).

Table 5 lists the numbers of pages that can be scheduled in c channels. The "Upper bound (HBWS)" values are from Theorem 2. "BOOSTER" indicates the output results of BOOSTER for $b = 1000$. The others are as stated in the previous section. The two values in the "BOOSTER (modified)" row were obtained by introducing set $Q_{\kappa+1}$, Q_4 and Q_{11}, respectively, for the cases $c = 2$

Table 5. The number of pages that can be scheduled on c channels with block size $b = 1000$. The values with asterisk were computed by introducing $Q_{\kappa+1}$. (The method used cannot be explained due to lack of space.)

No. of channels (c)	1	2	3	4	5	6
Upper bound (HBWS)	1000	3600	10764	30151	82827	226009
BOOSTER	1000	3499	10701	30087	82619	225679
BOOSTER (modified)		*3598	*10754			
Upper bound (HWS)	1000	3000	10000	30000	82000	226000
Best known	1000	3000	9000	28000	77000	211000
Greedy	1000	3000	9000	25000	73000	201000
NPB	1000	3000	9000	26000	66000	172000

and $c = 3$. It is seen from Table 5 that, for all values $c \leq 5$, BOOSTER can schedule more pages than the upperbound for HWS. However, for $c = 6$, the number of pages scheduled by BOOSTER (225679) is slightly less than the HWS upperbound (226000) at least in the case $b = 1000$. This is due to the fact that the excess bandwidth $6 - H_{226} = 0.000039$ is extremely small.

5 Discussion and Conclusions

In this paper, we discussed a method of generating a good HBWS schedule starting from a known HWS schedule represented as a round-robin trees. The goodness is based on the performance metric N/b, where N is the total number of pages scheduled and b is the block size. This metric is equivalent to the number of pages in the context of HWS, and is directly related to the initial waiting time in MoD broadcasting. Our method generates a HBWS schedule whose performance is better than the original HWS schedule. In fact, we demonstrated many examples whose N/b exceeds the upper bound for HWS schedules. Different methods for the same purpose are reported in [10].

It will be interesting how the performance metric N/b of the resulting schedule is influenced by the base trees chosen.

Some methods for VoD multicasting could also be used for broadcasting. One such scheme, stream-patching (also called merging), was proposed in [7]. If patching is batched and done at regular intervals, then the method can be used for broadcasting. Bar-Noy et al. discuss optimal merging in [4], using such a model. It is reported in [11] that the server bandwidth requirement of such a scheme is exceeded by other known broadcasting schemes [8,17].

Acknowledgement

We thank the members of the Distributed Computing Laboratory, in the School of Computing Science at Simon Fraser University for stimulating discussions. Many thanks also due to Weihua Xiong for help on the program of Sect. 4. We thank Professor R.E. Ladner of the University of Washington for showing us the

$\langle c = 6, n = 207 \rangle$ schedule that he and his coworkers discovered. It was used in computing the data plotted in Fig. 6.

References

1. Bar-Noy, A., Ladner,R.E.: Windows scheduling problems for broadcast systems. Proc. 13th ACM-SIAM Symp. on Discrete Algorithms (2002) 433–442
2. Bar-Noy, A., Nisgav, A., Patt-Shamir, B.: Nearly optimal perfectly-periodic schedules. Proc. 20th ACM Symp. on Principle of Distributed Computing (2001) 107–116
3. Bar-Noy, A., Bhatia, R., Naor, J., Schieber, B.: Minimizing service and operation costs of periodic scheduling. Mathematics of Operations Research **27** (2002) 518–544
4. Bar-Noy, A., Gosh, J.,Ladner, R.E.: Off-line and on-line guaranteed start-up delay for media-on-demand with stream merging. Proc. 15th ACM Symp. Parallel Algorithms and Atchitectures. (2003) 164–173
5. Bar-Noy, A., Ladner, R.E., Tamir, T.: Scheduling techniques for media-on-demand. Proc. ACM-SIAM Symp. on Discrete Algorithms (2003) 791–800
6. Engebretsen, L., Sudan, M.: Harmonic broadcasting is optimal. Proc. 13th ACM-SIAM Symp. on Discrete Algorithms (2002)
7. Hua, K.A., Cai, Y., Sheu, S.: Patching: a multicast technique for true video-on-demand services. Proc. ACM Multimedia (1998) 191-200
8. Hu, A., Nikolaidis, I., Van Beek, P.: On the design of efficient video-on-demand broadcast schedules. Proc. 7th Int'l Symp. on Modeling, Analysis and Simulation of Computer and Telecommunication Systems (1999) 262–269
9. Juhn, L., Tseng, L.: Harmonic broadcasting protocols for video-ondemand service. IEEE Trans. on Broadcasting **43** (1997) 268–271
10. Lin, Z.: Near-Optimal Heuristic Solutions to Truncated Harmonic Windows Scheduling and Harmonic Group Windows Scheduling. M.Sc. Thesis. School of Computing Science. Simon Fraser University (2004)
11. Ma, F.: Comparison of broadcasting schemes and stream-merging schemes for video-on-demand. CMPT415 Course Project Report (2003)
12. Pâris, J.-F.: A simple low-bandwidth broadcasting protocol for video-ondemand. Proc. 8th Int'l Conf. on Computer Communications and Networks (1999) 118–123
13. Pâris, J.-F., Carter, S.W., Long, D.D.E.: A low-bandwidth broadcasting protocol for video-on-demand. Proc. 7th Int'l Conf. on Computer Communications and Networks (1998) 690–697
14. Sun, Y., Kameda, T.: Harmonic block windows scheduling for video-on-demand. School of Computing Science, Simon Fraser University. Tech. Rept. **2005-05** (2005) ftp://fas.sfu.ca/pub/cs/TR/2005/CMPT2005-05.pdf (Submitted for publication)
15. Tseng, Y.-C., Yang, M.-H., Chang, C.-H.: A recursive frequency-splitting scheme for broadcasting hot videos in VOD service. IEEE Trans. on Communications **50** (2002) 1348–1355
16. Van Laarhoven, P.J.M., Aarts, E.H.L.: Simulated Annealing: Theory and Applications. Kluwer Academic Publishers (1987)
17. Yan, E.M., Kameda, T.: An efficient VOD broadcasting scheme with user bandwidth limit. Proc. SPIE/ACM Conf. on Multimedia Computing and Networking Vol. **5019**(2003) 200–208

An Evaluation Method for Video Semantic Models[*]

Yu Wang, Lizhu Zhou, and Chunxiao Xing

wangyu02@mails.tsinghua.edu.cn, {dcszlz, xingcx}@tsinghua.edu.cn

Abstract. The development of video technology and video-related applications demands strong support in semantic data models. To meet such a requirement, many video semantic data models have been proposed. The semantic model plays a key role in providing query capability and other features for a video database. However, to our knowledge, the criteria for a good semantic model remain open at present. As a result, people lack the rules for evaluating an existing model and the guidelines for the design of a new data model when necessary. To address this issue, this paper proposes twenty one properties as the criteria for video semantic models, and gives the evaluation result of eleven existing rich semantic models according to these properties. It shows that these models mostly concentrate on basic expressive power and query capability, and fulfill users' primary requirements. But in some advanced features such as expressive power, acquisition and analysis of semantic information, and query capability etc., there are rooms for further enhancement. The paper concludes by indicating some research directions for video semantic models.

1 Introduction

The advances in video technology and the development of new applications in video related areas lead to an enormous growth in the volume of video data. To manage these data effectively, an appropriate video data model is needed since relational model and other traditional data models cannot fulfill the requirements for video data featured by complex structure and rich semantics. To catch these complex structure and rich semantics, video data are divided into three levels. The lowest level is the feature layer. It stores features such as color, texture, shape etc. for videos [1-3]. The mid-level is the spatio-temporal layer for data describing the spatio-temporal relations between video objects [4]. The highest level is the semantics layer for representing events. Various models have been proposed for these three levels.

The lowest level models use automatically extracted low-level features to represent the video. Apparently they are machine oriented and provide little semantic information to humans. The mid-level, for instance, in the salient object-based spatio-temporal models, semantics are represented by spatio-temporal relationships and are very limited.

The highest level semantic data models represent rich information that is perceived by human users in understanding the content of video. This information is human

---

[*] Supported by the National Natural Science Foundation of China under Grant No.60473078

K.S. Candan and A. Celentano (Eds.): MIS 2005, LNCS 3665, pp. 207–220, 2005.
© Springer-Verlag Berlin Heidelberg 2005

oriented and cannot be extracted automatically like the low level features. Among the three levels of data models, the high-level semantic data models are the most informative one and provide the most nature way for users to represent and query video data stored in computers. Such semantic model represents the content of videos by objects (including concrete objects and abstract concepts), events and relations between them. It supports queries in a language close to the one that a human uses to describe the content of video.

Since early 1990's when video semantic model was first introduced, it has experienced the development from annotation-based model to rich semantic model. The annotation-based model uses text annotated video data to represent video semantics. Its expressive power and query capability is limited. In contrast to annotation based model, rich semantic model is much powerful in these two aspects. The model can represent the real world objects appearing in the video, the abstract concepts such as events, or even those that do not appear but are implied in the video such as background knowledge. Queries like "give all the NBA games that player A and B played together over 30 minutes" can be answered by the query language of such models.

Although various rich semantic models have been proposed, however, no evaluation criteria have been presented to judge the power of a model in semantic representation and query language support. This observation motivates the writing of this paper. In this regard, the paper makes main contributions by

- A brief review of the evolution of video semantic models and classification of the models into two categories: annotation-based models and rich semantic models;
- A proposal of twenty one evaluation rules for rich semantic models covering expressive power, query capability, and support for facilitating semantics' acquirement; and
- The evaluation of eleven existing rich semantic video models and the analysis of the evaluation result. The conclusion is that current models have much room for further enhancement in representation of uncertainty, object history, domain-specific constraints, etc.

This paper is structured as follows. Section 2 is a review of existing semantic models. Section 3 gives a set of evaluation rules and the result of application of these rules to some typical existing models. Section 4 analyzes the evaluation results. Section 5 is the conclusion.

2 Review of Existing Models

The basic idea of annotation-based models is to put the content information on top of the video stream, instead of segmenting the video data into shots. Annotations may be predefined keywords, free text, or structured data. Each annotation is associated with a logical video segment. The relatively simple structure brings annotation-based models great flexibility, but also limits their expressive power and query support capability. Relations among semantic annotations are not specified; abstractions of videos that do not appear in the video can not be modeled due to the tight-couple between annotations and segment position; queries are barely supported in a structured language, except only using keywords or attributes.

OVID[5], VideoStar[6] and CCM[7-8], which were developed at early 1990's, all utilize the basic annotation method by adding an annotation layer on top of video data, and use attributes to describe semantics. In OVID[5], no schema is needed. Each video object is an independent object with its own attribute set. Description data can be shared by *"interval-inclusion based inheritance"*. VideoStar[6] is a type-strong model. Several Classes are predefined to model video structures and thematic indexing is supported by the class *Annotations*. CCM[7,8] represents a compromise between type-strong and type-weak data models. Objects in CCM are dynamically aggregated into *clusters*. Every cluster has its own attribute-set and method-set and can be modified at any time. A sub cluster may optionally inherit attributes/methods of its super clusters.

In late 1990's, new techniques were integrated into annotation-based models. VideoText[9] and WVTDB[10] used free text as annotations and use IR techniques to retrieve contents encoded in these free texts. The Strata-based approach proposed in [11] integrated video analysis techniques into data model. It segments video's contextual information into multiple layers or strata, each stratum describing the temporal occurrences of a simple concept. By performing video analysis, judiciously chosen strata can be extracted automatically. However, limited by the video analysis techniques at that time, semantics that could be extracted this way are very limited.

Rich semantic models have greater power in video representation and query support. They can represent real world entities, such as objects, events, and their relationships, that may be concrete objects, abstract concepts, or those implied by the video. They also provide more querying modes, such as browsing etc. As far as design is concerned, rich semantic models are usually layered, with the lowest layer corresponding to the raw video stream, and the highest layer representing semantic information. The representations of semantic information in these models are quite different in strategies. One strategy is to extend or utilize existing models; the other is to design a new model from scratch. The former one has the advantages of easy to learn and easy to perform transformation from legacy systems, but the base model may be inappropriate for modeling video data. The latter one leads to compact models since all model components are proposed for video, but it is difficult to learn and great effort is normally required in the transformation of existing systems.

Videx[16], Temporal OO Data Model[19], Extended ExIFO$_2$[23], Ahmet Ekin's model[26] and THVDM[27] take the "extending" strategy.

Videx[16] uses UML notions to represent the structure and semantics of video data in an object-oriented manner. Carlo Combi's Temporal OO Data Model[19] adopts and extends an existing temporal data model named GCH-OODM to consider multimedia data. All classes modeling objects having a temporal dimension inherit from the class *Temporal_Object*. A model that can deal with uncertain and imprecise properties is proposed in [23]. It is an extension of ExIFO$_2$ whose purpose is to handle complex objects along with their uncertain and imprecise properties. Ahmet Ekin's model[26] organizes the semantics of the video based on events. It is an extension of ER model with OO concepts. Entities in the model include Video Event and Video Object. The actor entity functions as Event-Object relations. THVDM[27] is an integrated model to handle both low-level feature and high-level semantics. Semantic information is described by using a model named ERR which is an ER extension with Rules.

VIMSYS[9],   AVIS[14,15],   VideoGraph[17,18],   CoPaV^2[20],   Semantic Associative Video Model[21,22], and BilVideo[24,25] take the "new model" strategy.

VIMSYS[9] is one of the earliest data models for the management of images and has influenced many succeeding data models. So although it is a model for images, we include it here. There are four levels in VIMSYS: image presentation level, image object level, domain object level and domain event level. Domain events are used to connect different domain objects with spatio-temporal relationship. Another earliest rich semantic video data model is AVIS[14]. It divides video into fixed-duration frame sequences and uses frame segment tree and a set of arrays to represent the structure of a video and objects, events, activities and their associations. In its later work[15], feature–subfeature relationships are extended to provides some support for reasoning with uncertainty. VideoGraph[17] and SemVideo[18] take the temporal relationships among semantic descriptions as model components and use them to infer implicit temporal information. In [20], a model named CoPaV^2 and a rule based query language is developed. Relations among objects are stated explicitly. No object type hierarchy is provided, so each object can be viewed as a unique type with its own attributes. Rules can be used to define new relations. Yong proposed a Semantic Associative Video Model[21,22], in which video's content is represented in three layers: scene layer, object layer and concept layer. Three data structures Scene Network, Semantic Object Net, and Hierarchical Concept Tree are used for these three layers respectively. BilVideo[24,25] is a video database management system which provides integrated support for spatio-temporal and semantic queries for video. Events, subevents and objects of interest form a hierarchy structure. Video consists of events and events consist of subevents. Objects are modeled in every level in the hierarchy.

3   Criteria and Evaluation of Rich Semantic Models

In Sections 2, we briefly described sixteen video semantic data models. However, to compare and better understand these models, this section defines comprehensive criteria for rich semantic models and evaluates the eleven rich semantic models using the criteria. Models in the evaluation result table are ordered chronologically.

These criteria are organized in rules and classified into three categories: the Expressive Power, the Acquisition of Semantic Information, and the Query Support Capability. These categories just fit in the three stages in developing video application, that is, the stage of schema definition, the stage of data creation of the schema, and the query on the established video database,

In the following sections, these criteria will be presented along with the evaluation results of the eleven models. For the evaluation of the models, it is important to have a precise and complete definition of the models. However, references of the existing models range from very formal and detailed to very vague. We tried our best to overcome this difficulty to make the evaluation objective.

3.1 Expressive Power

Expressive power is the basic component of data model concerned with what can be represented by the model. It forms the basis for query support. In this section, eleven rules E1, E2, E3 etc. are presented for evaluating the expressive power of a video semantic model. The result of this evaluation is given in Table 1 and Table 2 where columns from E1 to E11 indicate the evaluation result of every rule for the eleven models.

Table 1. Evaluation of Criteria E1-E4

Name	E1	E2	E3	E4
VIMSYS	Object, UDA	Event	No	Is_a(O)
AVIS	Object	Event, (UDA)	Yes	No
Videx	Object, UDA	Object, UDA	Yes	Is_a(O,E), temporal
VideoGraph	Internal Graph Node, UDA	Internal Graph Node, UDA	No	temporal
Temporal OO	Object, UDA	Object, UDA	Yes	Is_a(O,E) , temporal
CoPaV^2	Object, UDA	Object, UDA	No	No
Yong's	Concept/Semantic Object, UDA	Concept/Semantic Object, UDA	(Yes)	Is_a(O,E)
Extended ExIFO$_2$	Object, UDA	Event, UDA	Yes	Is_a(O,E)
BilVideo	Object, UDA	Event, UDA	Yes	Event-subEvent
Ahmet Ekin's	Object, UDA	Event	No	Is_a(O),Event-subEvent, causal, temporal
THVDM	Object, UDA	Event, UDA	Yes	Is_a(O,E), causal, temporal

E1 — Support for Object and User Defined Object Attributes. In the first part of the result of this criterion, the structure used to store objects are stated. From the table we can see that nearly all models use a specific structure Object to store object information, while two models VideoGraph and Yong's use slightly different structure. Besides object, additional attributes may be used to describe different aspects of objects related to the video by user defined attributes. This fact is indicated by the keyword UDA. The table tells us that except AVIS, all the other models support it.

E2 — Support for Event and User Defined Event Attributes. In the first part of the result of this criterion the structure used to store events are stated. From the result of this rule and the previous rule, it's apparent whether a model considers object and event equally. The difference between object and event is that objects usually have a longer life span and their attributes may take different values in different stages while events usually have a shorter life span and their attribute values do not change. Thus there are two strategies to treat them: equally or differently. With equal treatment, uniform structure can be used to model both objects and events, which reduces the complex of the model. On the other hand, although different treatment requires relatively more complex structure, it can provide more functionality regarding either objects or events. From the table we can see that in general, later models treat them differently while earlier models treat them equally, among which Videx and Temporal OO are extension of object-oriented models and inherit the idea that "Object is used to model everything". The same as objects, events also need user defined attributes to describe different aspects of them. The same keyword UDA is used as the output. The result show that nearly all models support user defined event attributes. In AVIS, event attributes can only be defined as roles, so the UDA is put in parentheses. In the description of VIMSYS, nothing is stated about event attributes. We infer that user defined attributes are not supported since events in VIMSYS are computed from image sequences or videos resulting from motion, spatial interactions, appearance, disappearance etc.

E3 — Distinguish Activity (event type) and Event. This rule examines whether activity and event are distinguished in a model. The relation between event and activity is like a relation between instance and class in an OO model. The advantage of distinguishing activity and event is that events can be managed by category and query about event category can be answered directly instead of scan all events. All models except VIMSYS, CoPaV[2], and Ahmet Ekin's model support this differentiation. In Yong's Semantic Associative Model, activities are nodes in the hierarchical concept tree while events are semantic objects in the semantic object net. However, how activity information is managed and how queries about activity are processed is not stated. So the evaluation output for this model is put in parentheses. In Videx, Temporal OO, Extended ExIFO[2], and THVDM, this feature is inherited from the base object-oriented model by means of class and instance.

E4 — Support for Special Relationships Between Objects or Events. This criterion evaluates to what extent a model supports special relationships between objects or events. These special relationships are not related to specific domain and the awareness of them can help understanding the video content and serving users more efficiently. These relationships are Is_a relationship between objects and events, event-subevent relationship, causal relationship, and temporal relationship. The result of this column tells if they are **explicitly** supported by each model.

By Is_a relationship, a hierarchical structure can be built for types of objects and events, which can help in many aspects: attributes can be inherited and reused; similarity between different types of objects or events can be measured; queries can be reformulated along the hierarchical structure, etc. Most models support Is_a relationship between object types, while fewer support that between event types. For Videx, Temporal Object-Oriented Data Model, extended ExIFO[2], Ahmet Ekin's model and THVDM, this feature is supported as class-subclass relationship as in OO model. Semantic Associative Video Model uses the hierarchical concept tree to describe Is_a relationship between concept classes.

Event-subevent relationship is used to detail an event by describing its components, called sub-events. This relationship is different from the Is_a relationship in that a sub-event is a part of an event, while a sub-class is a kind of an event. Two of these models, BilVideo, and Ahmet Ekin's model, have considered the event-subevent relationship.

Temporal relationship between events is also an essential aspect for describing video content. Totally five models support temporal relationship as shown in table 1. For BilVideo and CoPaV^2, although temporal relationships are not represented explicitly, they can be used in query definition by temporal comparison functions.

Causal relationships between events reveal an important aspect of the video. It helps to understand the semantics in the video and allows users to issue queries regarding the causal relationship. Even when queries do not include causal relationships directly, this kind of relationship can be explored to provide users with more information and answer queries more efficiently. Among these models, only two support causal relationship between events: Ahmet Ekin's model and THVDM.

Table 2. Evaluation of Criteria E5-E11

Name	E5	E6	E7	E8	E9	E10	E11
VIMSYS	No	(Yes)	No	No	No	Low,Mid	No
AVIS	Yes	No	No	No	No	No	No
Videx	No	Implicit	No	No	No	Low,Mid	Yes
VideoGraph	No	(Implicit)	SYS	No	Time	No	No
Carlo Combi's	No	Implicit	No	Yes	Time	No	Yes
CoPaV^2	No	(Explicit)	SYS	No	No	Low	No
Yong's	No	(Explicit)	No	No	No	Mid	No
Extended ExIFO$_2$	Yes	(Explicit)	No	No	Attribute, Class/object, Class/subclass	Low	Yes
BilVideo	Yes	No	No	No	No	Mid	No
Ahmet Ekin's	Yes	(Explicit)	No	No	No	Mid	No
THVDM	Yes	Explicit	No	No	No	Low,Mid	No

E5 — Objects' Roles. This rule evaluates whether roles of objects are supported for event participation. These roles should be modeled **explicitly** instead of as events' attributes since they identify the interactions between objects and events. In general, earlier models do not have this feature while later models have, except AVIS.

E6 — User Defined Relationships. Between Objects or Events. This criterion considers the modeling of user defined relationships between objects of events in a specific domain. The keyword "Explicit" and "Implicit" indicate whether relationships are modeled explicitly, or implicitly as attributes. Most models support user defined relationships between objects and events and the modeling method has experienced the evolution from implicit to explicit. VideoGraph uses the *c-link* to define relationships between objects (events) whose modeling power is limited by the no-circle-constraint; Semantic Associative Video Model and CoPaV^2 only support relationships between object instances, not object classes; Extended ExIFO$_2$, and Ahmet Ekin's model support only user defined relationships between objects, not events. To indicate these limitations, the results for these models are parenthesized. For VIMSYS, relationships between objects can be defined, however, how they are represented is not stated, so a Yes in parenthesis is provided as the output.

E7 — Constraint Representation. This rule evaluates the modeling power for constraints, including system constraints and user defined constraints. System constraints are used to constrain the model structures while user defined constraints are used to model domain-specific logics to ensure that information is correct and reasonable. This feature is poorly supported in all existing models. Only two of them provide support for system constraints. VideoGraph poses two constraints on the structure of the graph; CoPaV^2 uses constraints to associate a time interval to a temporal cohesion object. As far as domain-specific user-defined constraints are considered, no mechanism was mentioned in all these models.

E8 — Object History. This criterion evaluates whether object history is supported. In E2 we have stated that an object usually has a long life span and during its life span values of its attributes may vary. An important thing is that it must be known that all these different values are describing the same entity. That is, we need a history to record evolution of an object. However, in the reviewed models, only Temporal Object-Oriented Data Model has this ability. It uses the temporal functionalities provided by the temporal data model GCH-OODM to record history of objects of the type Observation.

E9 — Support for Uncertainty. This rule examines the modeling ability for uncertain information. The reason we need such a feature is that for video data, it is impossible or impractical to acquire complete semantic information, so information acquired may be very incomplete and uncertain. Besides, incomplete information may cause uncertainty in the results of queries. So, in order to provide as much information as possible to users, uncertainty needs to be considered inherently within the model. The result of this criterion is the kind of uncertainty supported in each model. Totally three models considered uncertainty to different extent. In VideoGraph and Temporal OO, only uncertainty in time representation is supported. The Extended ExIFO$_2$ supports three levels of uncertainty: attribute-level, class/object level, and class/subclass level.

E10 — Contain Low-Level or Mid-Level Information. This criterion considers the modeling ability for low-level and mid-level information. Although we concentrate on the semantic aspects of modeling, whether low-level or mid-level information is integrated is still an import aspect. One of the reasons is that although infrequent, queries about low or mid level information do exist. Another reason is that in the future, when semantics can be acquired automatically by video analysis, these algorithms can be integrated easily. The keyword "Low" and "Mid" indicate low-level information and mid-level information respectively. From the table we can see that most models support one or two of them.

E11 — Logical Video Segment Modeling. This criterion is to evaluate whether physical data independency is provided. This is necessary since one physical video file does not always represent a logical meaningful segment. However, from Table 2 we can see only Videx, Carlo Combi's Temporal OO Data Model , and Extended ExIFO$_2$ have this ability.

3.2 Acquisition of Semantic Information

A major issue concerned with video application is how to acquire data for the schema of selected models. We call it data acquisition problem. In traditional database like relational, data acquisition is not a big issue. But for video data model, data for objects, events, spatial or temporal relations etc. are related to the understanding of videos. A well designed video semantic model may provide support to facilitate the acquisition of semantic information. Criteria in this section are presented to examine this capability.

A1 — Encoding Domain Knowledge. This criterion evaluates whether domain knowledge can be integrated when defining a schema for a specific domain. Since for a specific application, videos in the database always have a uniform subject, so if domain knowledge can be encoded in the process of schema design, they can help a lot for semantic information acquisition, analysis and query evaluation. These domain knowledge may take various forms such as constraints about attribute values, video structures, temporal relationships, or aspects considered when design model components. Currently no model provides this capability.

To acquire semantic information, two steps should be taken: first an initial semantics set is got through video analysis or annotation, then inference should be performed to augment it and get an extended semantic information set.

A2 — Help the Acquirement of Initial Semantic Information. This criterion measures the ability of a model to facilitate the first step of acquiring semantic information from video. Initial semantic information may be acquired by video analysis or annotation. For annotation, users usually first form a logical video segment and then input semantics or select existing semantics and relate them to the logical video segment. If domain knowledge about the structure or subject of the video is known, hints may be given to help users to find a logical video segment or an existing semantics. This feature is also poorly supported.

A3 — Infer New Information from Existing Information. This criterion measures the ability of a model to facilitate the second step of acquiring semantic information from video. Due to the complexity of video content and different user views, enormous things are implied in the video. Annotating all these things is usually impossible or impractical. As the result, if new information can be inferred from existing information, users can get more information with the same workload which can also be viewed as the reduction of annotation workload. The output of this criterion is the kind of information that can be inferred. Three models support inference of information to different extent. In VideoGraph, non-key objects' temporal information can be obtained by considering temporal information of related key objects and temporal relationships between them. In CoPaV^2, new relations can be defined using existing relations, so the newly defined relation can be inferred given existing relations. In BilVideo, new spatial relations can be inferred based on known spatial relationships stored in a fact base.

A4 — Detect Logical Errors in Semantic Information. This criterion deals with the errors occur in the two steps of acquiring semantic information. Human annotator, video analysis algorithm, and inference algorithm are not absolutely correct and may cause logical errors in the semantic information acquired. For example, the first section of a match is labeled as the second section and the second one labeled as the first one. If rules can be defined to ensure that the first section should occur before the second one, this kind of mistakes can be detected and avoided. However, since no models provide the mechanism to define this kind of constraints, no capability of detecting errors this way is provided.

Table 3. Evaluation of Criteria A1-A4, Q1-Q2

Name	A1	A2	A3	A4	Q1	Q2
VIMSYS	No	No	No	No	S, IS	N.A.
AVIS	No	No	No	No	No	N.A.
Videx	No	No	No	No	S, T	N.A.
VideoGraph	No	No	Time	No	T	AND,OR,NOT IMPLY,EQ,UQ
Carlo Combi's	No	No	No	No	T	N.A.
CoPaV^2	No	No	Defined Relation	No	T	AND, IMPLY
Yong's	No	No	No	No	OS, SS,TL,B	N.A.
Extended ExIFO$_2$	No	No	No	No	S,TL,U	N.A.
BilVideo	No	No	Spatial relations	No	T, S	AND,OR,NOT
Ahmet Ekin's	No	No	No	No	T, B	N.A.
THVDM	No	No	No	No	S, T,A	AND,OR,NOT

3.3   Query Support Capability

The ultimate purpose of video database is to provide query service for users to find interested data conveniently and efficiently. Thus, query support capability is an important aspect subject to evaluation.

Q1 —Queries Supported. This criterion evaluates to what extent some special kinds of queries are support in each model. In Section 3.1, we put forward several criteria to evaluate the expressive power. Usually the information that can be represented can also be used to issue queries. So the ability evaluated in this criterion is about special kind of queries, including spatial(S), temporal(T), aggregate(A), uncertainty (U), query by object similarity(OS) and event similarity(ES), query by shot similarity(SS), and browsing(B). Spatial query is query about salient object, their spatial location(SL), and spatial relationships(SR). Temporal query refers to query about temporal location(TL) and temporal relation(TR). The aggregation query is like the GroupBy clause in SQL, which return information about a group of objects or events. Uncertainty query is query involving uncertainty in its definition or result. Browsing is an important and useful functionality, by which users can have an overview of the whole database or a specific video. The output of this criterion is the kinds of queries supported. From table 3 we can see that nearly all models support temporal query; spatial query is support by most models; query about object similarity and shot similarity is only supported in Yong's semantic association model; uncertainty query and aggregation query are supported by only one model, Extended ExIFO$_2$ and THVDM respectively; the browsing query mode is only provided in two models: Yong's model and Ahmet Ekin's model.

Q2 — Constructors for Query Condition. This criterion considers what constructors are provided in each model to construct query which decides how complex the query may be. Possible connectors maybe Boolean operators (including AND, OR, NOT), and logical constructors (including IMPLY, existential quantifier (EQ), and universal quantifier (UQ)). The result of this criterion is the constructors supported.

Q3 — Query Language. This criterion considers what kind of query language is provided. The form of the language decides how friendly it is, which may be declarative, procedural or graphical interface. When the effort taken by users to learn to use the query language is considered, the order of the three forms from easy to difficult is: graphical interface, declarative, and procedural. The output of this criterion is the form of the language provided in each model. Except AVIS, most models provide at least declarative language.

Q4 — Support for Query Evolution. This rule evaluates the ability of supporting query evolution. This is necessary since in video database sometimes user does not have a clear idea about what he wants to get. He may first randomly issue a query and browse the results, and refine the query when he sees something interesting. This requires that query can be issued over the result of previous queries. Among existing models, only VIMSYS has this ability.

Table 4. Evaluation of Criteria Q3-Q6

Name	Q3	Q4	Q5	Q6
VIMSYS	Graphical Interface	Yes	No	No
AVIS	Procedural	No	Relaxation	No
Videx	N.A.	No	No	No
VideoGraph	Declarative	No	No	No
Carlo Combi's	N.A.	No	No	No
CoPaV^2	Declarative	No	No	Defined Relation
Yong's	N.A.	No	No	No
Extended ExIFO$_2$	N.A.	No	No	No
BilVideo	Declarative	No	No	Spatial Relationship
Ahmet Ekin's	Graphical Interface	No	Relaxation	No
THVDM	Declarative	No	No	No

Q5 — Support for Query Reformulation. This rule considers whether query reformulation is supported. In video databases, due to the great incompleteness and uncertainty, if empty result occurs, the reason may be the imprecise in query definition or query evaluation. In this situation, it is expected that the model can be adaptive to provide something that may be useful for users, that is, relax the query and return a superset. In another situation, when too many results are returned, to make it more informative, the query condition should be strengthened to reduce the size of result set. Two models, AVIS and Ahmet Ekin's model, support query relaxation. In AVIS, features can be substituted by sub features to relax a query condition; in Ahmet

Ekin's model, partial matching of query condition can be performed. However, support for query strengthens is not mentioned in all existing models.

Q6 — Support Inference. This criterion evaluates whether inference can be made during the process of query evaluation. In CoPaV^2, rules are used to define new relations using existing relations. When evaluating queries, with the knowledge of existing relations, these newly defined relations can be inferred and evaluated. In BilVideo, spatial relationships can be inferred from the fact base. The output of this criterion is the information that can be inferred when evaluating a query.

4   Learning from Evolution Process

AVIS is the earliest rich semantic model for video. It has many notable advantages superior to earlier annotation-based models: clear separation of objects and events; managing events by category (activity); and using ROLE and PLAYERS to relate objects to events. This kind of generalization is very close to human's perception of the real world. AVIS also has some drawbacks, such as using fixed-duration frame sequences; no relationships between event and object except Participation; attributes are only available as events' roles; and only a procedural querying facility is provided.

In later models, some drawbacks of AVIS are mended. The most remarkable improvements are in expressive power and query ability. For expressive power, almost all later models support user defined attributes of objects and events; most models distinguish event and event class; support user defined relationships between objects and events implicitly or explicitly; and shots are used as video segments instead of fixed-duration frame sequences. For query ability, they are improved in allowing users to define more complex query conditions, and providing declarative query languages or graphical interfaces. Some new features are added, including support for special relationships (Is_a, temporal, causal, event-subevent), object history and uncertainty.

Although great improvements have been achieved, there are still important advanced features that are supported poorly or even not supported at all by existing models. For expressive power, causal relationship, event-subevent relationship, object history and uncertainty are supported only in a few models with a very limited extent and unfortunately no current model provides mechanisms for the representation of domain-specific user-defined constraints which is a significant part of a data model. Only a small fraction of models support logical video segment modeling. For query ability, support for inference in query evaluation, query evolution, and query relaxation are very limited. Query modes provided are not very powerful. The significant browsing mode is only supported by two models with a limited browsing granularity. Query by uncertainty, object similarity, event similarity or shot similarity and aggregation query service are provided by few models. When considering utilizing the model to help the process of semantic information acquisition, nearly nothing is provided by existing models. However, these aspects are all inevitable for a model to serve a specific domain.

Another overall consideration for a video semantic model is whether the model should be general or specialized. The fact is that nearly all existing models are general. However, the generality has limited the utilization of properties of videos in a specific domain, thus requirements concerned with these properties cannot be supported by these models. In the other extreme, specialized models may be well designed powerfully for a certain domain but cannot be used in other domains. As a result, we have to achieve a good balance between the generality and powerfulness for video semantic models.

5 Conclusion

To evaluate existing models and to make requirements for future models, we present twenty one rules for evaluating rich semantic models. They cover the whole process of video application development supported by a model. According to these criteria, eleven existing rich semantic models are evaluated. The evaluation result shows that most efforts are put on the basic expressive power and basic query ability. Some advanced features (such as support for uncertainty and object history in expressive power category, inference, and query evolution and query relaxation in query category) are poorly supported. Representation of domain-specific constraints and facilitation of acquisition of semantic information are seldom considered. Furthermore, to avoid repeated work when applying a model to different applications, the design of semantic model for a class of domains with common features is needed.

References

1. Aas, K.; Eikvil, L. A Survey on: Content-based Access to Image and Video Databases. Report 915, Norwegian Computing Center, March 1997.
2. Pekovic, M.; Jonker, W. An Overview of Data Models and Query Languages for Content-based Video Retrieval; proc of International Conference on Advances in Infrastructure for Electronic Business, Science, and Education on the Internet 2000
3. Bashir, F. I.; Khokhar, A. Video Content Modeling Techniques: An Overview; 2002
4. Spatiotemporal Data Modeling and Management:A Survey; 1999, http://www.itee.uq.edu.au/~zxf/_papers/STDBSurvey.pdf
5. Eitetsu Oomoto; Katsumi Tanaka. OVID: design and implementation of a video-object database system. IEEE TRANSACTIONS ON KNOWLEDGE AND DATA ENGINEERING 1993, pp. 629-643
6. 6. R. Hjelsvold and R. Midtstraum. (1994) Modeling and Querying Video Data. Proc. 1994 Intl. Conf. on Very Large Databases, pp. 686-694 Santiago. Chile.
7. Li, Q.; Lee, C.M. Dynamic object clustering for video database manipulation. In proceedings of IFIP 2.6 Working Conference Visual Database Systems (VDB-3), 1995
8. Qing Li A dynamic data model for a video database management system. ACM Computing Surveys 1995, 27, 602-606
9. H.T. Jiang, D. Montesi, and A. K. Elmagarmid (1997). VideoText database systems. In Proceedings of IEEE International Conference on Multimedia Computing and Systems, pp 344-351.
10. Haitao Jiang; Ahmed K. Elmagarmid. "WVTBD- A Semantic Content-Based Video Database System on the World Wide Web". IEEE Transactions on Knowledge and Data Engineering, 1998: 10(6), 947-966

11. Kankanhalli, M. S.; Chua, T.-S. Video modeling using strata-based annotations. IEEE Transactions on Multimedia 2000, 7, 68-74
12. Gupta, A.; Weymouth, T.; Jain, R. Semantic Queries with Pictures:The VIMSYS Model; VLDB 1991; pp 69-79
13. Data Model and Semantics in Visual Information Management Systems, http://www.cs.wisc.edu/~beechung/dlm_image_processing/image_processing/vimsys.html
14. S. Adali; K.S. Candan; K. Erol; V.S. Subrahmanian ; AVIS: An Advanced Video Information System, technical report, Presented at the First International Workshop on Multimedia Information Systems 1995
15. Adah, S.; S.Candan, K.; Chen, S.-s. The Advanced Video Information System: Data Structures and Query Processing. ACM Multimedia Systems 1996, 4, 172-186
16. Tusch, R.; Kosch, H.; Boszormenyi, L. VIDEX: An Integrated Generic Video Indexing Approach; ACM Multimedia, 2000; pp 448-451
17. Tran, D. A.; Hua, K. A.; Vu, K. VideoGraph:A Graphical Object-based Model for Representing and Querying Video Data; 2000; In Proc. of the 19th International Conference on Conceptual Modeling (ER2000), pp 383-396
18. D. A. Tran; K. A. Hua; K. Vu. Semantic reasoning based video database systems. In Proc. Of 11th International Conference on Databases and Expert Systems Applications, London, U.K, September 2000
19. Combi, C. Modeling temporal aspects of visual and textual objects in multimedia databases; International Workshop on Temporal Representation and Reasoning 2000; pp 59-86
20. Hacid, M.-S.; Decleir, C. A database approach for modeling and querying video data. IEEE Transactions on Knowledge and Data Engineering 2000, 12, 729-750
21. Yong, C.; De, X. Hierarchical semantic associative video model; In proc of IEEE International Conference on Neural Networks and Signal Processing, 2003; pp 1217-1220
22. Yong, C.; De, X. Content-based semantic associative video model; In proc of International Conference on Signal Processing, 2002; pp 727-730
23. Aygun, R. S.; Yazici, A. Modeling and Management of Fuzzy Information in Multimedia Database Applications; Technical Report, 2002, State University of New York, USA
24. Arslan, U. A Semantic Data Model and Query Language for Video Databases; Master thesis, 2002, Bilkent University
25. Donderler, M. E. Data Modeling And Querying For Video Databases; Phd thesis, 2002, Bilkent University
26. A. Ekin, Sports Video Processing for Description, Summarization, and Search (Chapter 2 Structural and Semantic Video Modeling), phd thesis, http://www.ece.rochester.edu/users/tekalp/ students/ekin_thesis.pdf , 2003
27. Yu Wang, Chunxiao Xing, Lizhu Zhou, THVDM: A Data Model for Video Management in Digital Library, proceedings of the 6th International Conference of Asian Digital Libraries, 2003; pp. 178-192

Author Index

Lecture Notes in Computer Science

For information about Vols. 1–3571

please contact your bookseller or Springer

Vol. 3623: M. Liśkiewicz, R. Reischuk (Eds.), Fundamentals of Computation Theory. XV, 576 pages. 2005.

Vol. 3621: V. Shoup (Ed.), Advances in Cryptology – CRYPTO 2005. XI, 568 pages. 2005.

Vol. 3620: H. Muñoz-Avila, F. Ricci (Eds.), Case-Based Reasoning Research and Development. XV, 654 pages. 2005. (Subseries LNAI).

Vol. 3619: X. Lu, W. Zhao (Eds.), Networking and Mobile Computing. XXIV, 1299 pages. 2005.

Vol. 3618: J. Jedrzejowicz, A. Szepietowski (Eds.), Mathematical Foundations of Computer Science 2005. XVI, 814 pages. 2005.

Vol. 3617: F. Roli, S. Vitulano (Eds.), Image Analysis and Processing – ICIAP 2005. XXIV, 1219 pages. 2005.

Vol. 3615: B. Ludäscher, L. Raschid (Eds.), Data Integration in the Life Sciences. XII, 344 pages. 2005. (Subseries LNBI).

Vol. 3614: L. Wang, Y. Jin (Eds.), Fuzzy Systems and Knowledge Discovery, Part II. XLI, 1314 pages. 2005. (Subseries LNAI).

Vol. 3613: L. Wang, Y. Jin (Eds.), Fuzzy Systems and Knowledge Discovery, Part I. XLI, 1334 pages. 2005. (Subseries LNAI).

Vol. 3612: L. Wang, K. Chen, Y. S. Ong (Eds.), Advances in Natural Computation, Part III. LXI, 1326 pages. 2005.

Vol. 3611: L. Wang, K. Chen, Y. S. Ong (Eds.), Advances in Natural Computation, Part II. LXI, 1292 pages. 2005.

Vol. 3610: L. Wang, K. Chen, Y. S. Ong (Eds.), Advances in Natural Computation, Part I. LXI, 1302 pages. 2005.

Vol. 3608: F. Dehne, A. López-Ortiz, J.-R. Sack (Eds.), Algorithms and Data Structures. XIV, 446 pages. 2005.

Vol. 3607: J.-D. Zucker, L. Saitta (Eds.), Abstraction, Reformulation and Approximation. XII, 376 pages. 2005. (Subseries LNAI).

Vol. 3606: V. Malyshkin (Ed.), Parallel Computing Technologies. XII, 470 pages. 2005.

Vol. 3604: R. Martin, H. Bez, M. Sabin (Eds.), Mathematics of Surfaces XI. IX, 473 pages. 2005.

Vol. 3603: J. Hurd, T. Melham (Eds.), Theorem Proving in Higher Order Logics. IX, 409 pages. 2005.

Vol. 3602: R. Eigenmann, Z. Li, S.P. Midkiff (Eds.), Languages and Compilers for High Performance Computing. IX, 486 pages. 2005.

Vol. 3599: U. Aßmann, M. Aksit, A. Rensink (Eds.), Model Driven Architecture. X, 235 pages. 2005.

Vol. 3598: H. Murakami, H. Nakashima, H. Tokuda, M. Yasumura, Ubiquitous Computing Systems. XIII, 275 pages. 2005.

Vol. 3597: S. Shimojo, S. Ichii, T.W. Ling, K.-H. Song (Eds.), Web and Communication Technologies and Internet-Related Social Issues - HSI 2005. XIX, 368 pages. 2005.

Vol. 3596: F. Dau, M.-L. Mugnier, G. Stumme (Eds.), Conceptual Structures: Common Semantics for Sharing Knowledge. XI, 467 pages. 2005. (Subseries LNAI).

Vol. 3595: L. Wang (Ed.), Computing and Combinatorics. XVI, 995 pages. 2005.

Vol. 3594: J.C. Setubal, S. Verjovski-Almeida (Eds.), Advances in Bioinformatics and Computational Biology. XIV, 258 pages. 2005. (Subseries LNBI).

Vol. 3593: V. Mařík, R. W. Brennan, M. Pěchouček (Eds.), Holonic and Multi-Agent Systems for Manufacturing. XI, 269 pages. 2005. (Subseries LNAI).

Vol. 3592: S. Katsikas, J. Lopez, G. Pernul (Eds.), Trust, Privacy and Security in Digital Business. XII, 332 pages. 2005.

Vol. 3591: M.A. Wimmer, R. Traunmüller, Å. Grönlund, K.V. Andersen (Eds.), Electronic Government. XIII, 317 pages. 2005.

Vol. 3590: K. Bauknecht, B. Pröll, H. Werthner (Eds.), E-Commerce and Web Technologies. XIV, 380 pages. 2005.

Vol. 3589: A M. Tjoa, J. Trujillo (Eds.), Data Warehousing and Knowledge Discovery. XVI, 538 pages. 2005.

Vol. 3588: K.V. Andersen, J. Debenham, R. Wagner (Eds.), Database and Expert Systems Applications. XX, 955 pages. 2005.

Vol. 3587: P. Perner, A. Imiya (Eds.), Machine Learning and Data Mining in Pattern Recognition. XVII, 695 pages. 2005. (Subseries LNAI).

Vol. 3586: A.P. Black (Ed.), ECOOP 2005 - Object-Oriented Programming. XVII, 631 pages. 2005.

Vol. 3584: X. Li, S. Wang, Z.Y. Dong (Eds.), Advanced Data Mining and Applications. XIX, 835 pages. 2005. (Subseries LNAI).

Vol. 3583: R.W. H. Lau, Q. Li, R. Cheung, W. Liu (Eds.), Advances in Web-Based Learning – ICWL 2005. XIV, 420 pages. 2005.

Vol. 3582: J. Fitzgerald, I.J. Hayes, A. Tarlecki (Eds.), FM 2005: Formal Methods. XIV, 558 pages. 2005.

Vol. 3581: S. Miksch, J. Hunter, E. Keravnou (Eds.), Artificial Intelligence in Medicine. XVII, 547 pages. 2005. (Subseries LNAI).

Vol. 3580: L. Caires, G.F. Italiano, L. Monteiro, C. Palamidessi, M. Yung (Eds.), Automata, Languages and Programming. XXV, 1477 pages. 2005.

Vol. 3579: D. Lowe, M. Gaedke (Eds.), Web Engineering. XXII, 633 pages. 2005.

Vol. 3578: M. Gallagher, J. Hogan, F. Maire (Eds.), Intelligent Data Engineering and Automated Learning - IDEAL 2005. XVI, 599 pages. 2005.

Vol. 3577: R. Falcone, S. Barber, J. Sabater-Mir, M.P. Singh (Eds.), Trusting Agents for Trusting Electronic Societies. VIII, 235 pages. 2005. (Subseries LNAI).

Vol. 3576: K. Etessami, S.K. Rajamani (Eds.), Computer Aided Verification. XV, 564 pages. 2005.

Vol. 3575: S. Wermter, G. Palm, M. Elshaw (Eds.), Biomimetic Neural Learning for Intelligent Robots. IX, 383 pages. 2005. (Subseries LNAI).

Vol. 3574: C. Boyd, J.M. González Nieto (Eds.), Information Security and Privacy. XIII, 586 pages. 2005.

Vol. 3573: S. Etalle (Ed.), Logic Based Program Synthesis and Transformation. VIII, 279 pages. 2005.

Vol. 3572: C. De Felice, A. Restivo (Eds.), Developments in Language Theory. XI, 409 pages. 2005.